THE BRANCH

THE BRANCH

A History of the
Metropolitan Police
Special Branch
1883–1983

Rupert Allason

SECKER & WARBURG
LONDON

First published in England 1983 by
Martin Secker & Warburg Limited
54 Poland Street, London W1V 3DF

British Library Cataloguing in Publication Data
Allason, Rupert
   The Branch.
   1. Metropolitan Police. *Special Branch*—History
   I. Title
   363.2'09421   HV8198.4
   ISBN: 0-436-01165-4

Printed in Great Britain by Richard Clay (The Chaucer Press) Ltd,
Bungay, Suffolk

CONTENTS

ACKNOWLEDGMENTS

This book could not have been written without the patient help of the staff at the British Library, Colindale, the Public Records Office, Kew, and the assistance and advice of several Branch officers who prefer to remain anonymous. I am also indebted to my secretary, Joy Whyte, and my researcher, Camilla van Gerbig.

ABBREVIATIONS

AAG	Assistant Adjutant General
AC	Assistant Commissioner
CID	Criminal Investigation Department
CPGB	Communist Party of Great Britain
DAC	Deputy Assistant Commissioner
DMI	Director of Military Intelligence
DNI	Director of Naval Intelligence
DORA	Defence Of The Realm Act
DC	Detective Constable
DCI	Detective Chief Inspector
DCS	Detective Chief Superintendent
DI	Detective Inspector
DS	Detective Sergeant
FBI	Federal Bureau of Investigation
GPO	General Post Office
IRA	Irish Republican Army
KGB	Soviet Intelligence Service
MI5	British Security Service
MI6	British Secret Intelligence Service
MO5	Military Operations 5, Later MI5
NID	Naval Intelligence Department
PUS	Permanent Under-Secretary
RCMP	Royal Canadian Mounted Police
RIC	Royal Irish Constabulary
RUC	Royal Ulster Constabulary

LIST OF ILLUSTRATIONS

The photographs numbered 1, 2, 3, 11, 12, 18 and 19 are from the BBC Hulton Picture Library

HEADS OF SPECIAL BRANCH

John Littlechild	1883–1903
Patrick Quinn	1903–1918
James McBrien	1918–1929
Edward Parker	1929–1936
Albert Canning	1936–1946
Leonard Burt	1946–1958
Evan Jones	1958–1966
Ferguson Smith	1966–1972
Victor Gilbert	1972–1977
Robert Bryan	1977–1981
Colin Hewett	1981–

COMMISSIONERS OF POLICE

Sir Edmund Henderson	1869–1886
Sir Charles Warren	1886–1888
James Monro	1888–1890
Sir Edward Bradford	1890–1903
Sir Edward Henry	1903–1918
Sir Nevil Macready	1918–1920
Sir William Horwood	1920–1928
Lord Byng	1928–1931
Lord Trenchard	1931–1935
Sir Philip Game	1935–1945
Sir Harold Scott	1945–1953
Sir John Nott-Bower	1953–1958
Sir Joseph Simpson	1958–1968
Sir John Waldron	1968–1972
Sir Robert Mark	1972–1977
Sir David McNee	1977–1982
Sir Kenneth Newman	1982–

FOREWORD
by
Leonard J. Burt
CVO CBE

Commander of the
Special Branch 1946–1958

I first joined the Metropolitan Police on 17 July 1912 as a raw recruit from Totton in Hampshire. I had never visited London before and I had little idea of what a young constable's lot in London was like. In the next forty-six years I was to experience the full range of challenges offered by the force. I served in the East End, the West End, the Murder Squad, the Drug and Vice Squad, and then finally the Branch.

When I was transferred to the Branch it was led by Albert Canning, a remarkable man who had been in the Branch since its very earliest days. He continued to command the Branch until his retirement in 1946, when I was appointed to succeed him.

As this book describes, a major part of the Branch's work concerns the safety of the State and this demands close liaison with the Security Service, MI5. In September 1940 I was invited, together with a handful of my CID colleagues, to join this secret organisation for the duration of the war. This enabled me to participate in counter-espionage operations both as a policeman and an officer commissioned into the Intelligence Corps. It was a thoroughly rewarding experience for it also enabled me to see MI5 from the inside. It certainly helped me to get to grips with the complexities of some of the postwar spy cases.

It is sometimes said that the only lesson that history teaches us is that no one learns from history. Reading about some of the Branch's earliest cases is a grim reminder of the realities of police work today. Irish bomb outrages and political extremists were the preoccupations of the Special Branch of the last century much as they are, I imagine, today. I hope this book will help to dispel some of the myths surrounding the Branch and remind the reader that so long as there are people to be protected and a democracy to be preserved, there will always be a need for the detectives of the Special Branch of the Metropolitan Police.

Leonard J. Burt

INTRODUCTION

Histories of the various British intelligence organisations abound, and so do books on the Metropolitan Police. How odd, then, that the Special Branch should have been in existence for a hundred years without someone having attempted to write an account of its activities. As Tony Bunyan pointed out in *The Political Police in Britain** "One of the problems in examining the Special Branch is that no history of it has yet been written. Passing references are made to it in books on the police, but little else." This book is intended to fill that gap.

The Branch, as it is referred to by the *cognoscenti*, does not seek the limelight. According to Leon Brittan MP, the Parliamentary Under-Secretary at the Home Office, who fielded questions concerning the Branch in the House of Commons in 1979, "We should face the fact that much of the work of the Special Branch precludes it from being conducted in the full glare of public scrutiny."

Why the secrecy? The answer, quite simply, is that the Branch itself is a favourite target of those who have most to fear from the Branch's surveillance. In 1885 the Fenians attempted to destroy the Special Irish Branch (as it then was) with a bomb left at Scotland Yard. In 1974 the Angry Brigade tried the same thing. In the intervening years Branch detectives were attacked by suffragettes, anarchists, spies, IRA fanatics, and nationalists of every persuasion.

The work of the Branch is concentrated in the field of assassination, terrorism, revolution, sabotage, subversion and espionage. Their brief is protection, surveillance, infiltration and intelligence-gathering. This might sound like the natural environment of a secret intelligence service, and so it is, but what makes the Branch unique in the world is that the individual officers are answerable to the Head of the Branch, and he in turn is accountable not to a politician or a faceless secret service bureaucrat, but to the Commissioner of the Metropolis. Branch detectives have no extra powers that distinguish them from other police officers. They are not, contrary to myth, the overt arm of MI5. If the Security Service want co-operation or information in a particular investigation they request it, not demand it. Furthermore, such requests have been declined when the Head of the Branch has considered it his duty to do so. MI5 may not be publicly

* Julian Freidmann, 1976.

accountable, but the Branch likes to think that its staff are. The fact that two recent Heads of the Branch have served in the Yard's Community Relations department is a reflection of this essential difference between the Branch and their more covert colleagues.

No history of the Branch would be complete unless access had been given to its enormous Registry. Naturally such a request is never likely to be granted, so I have had to be content to rely on the surprisingly large amount of relevant material in the Public Records Office and other sources available generally.

I have been generously helped by a number of former Branch officers, including two retired Heads of the Branch. Both pointed out that sometimes a Branch officer's success can be judged by the inverse proportion of the publicity he personally receives. Thus many very highly-rated detectives have completed their Branch careers without ever having given evidence in court or ever having come to the public's attention. In the CID an observer can use court appearances or convictions as a useful yardstick with which to judge a particular squad's performance. This measure fails when it is applied to the Branch as only a tiny proportion of their workload ends in court. So, within these limitations, the reader is invited to review one hundred years of what is arguably the most fascinating area of police activity in Britain.

Rupert Allason

CHAPTER I

The Fenian Bombers

If there was one incident that can be said to have led to what we now understand to be the Special Branch, it was the Home Secretary's decision in March 1883 to post Royal Irish Constabulary officers to guard government buildings in Whitehall.

On 15 March 1883 a device exploded outside the newspaper offices of *The Times,* and another detonated later the same evening outside the Local Government Office in Charles Street. The first did little damage, but the second blew out most of the windows in Parliament Street. The bombs caught the Metropolitan Police completely unawares. When the Commissioner of Police, Sir Edmund Henderson, had been appointed in January 1869 by Gladstone's Home Secretary, Henry Bruce (later Lord Aberdare), in succession to Sir Richard Mayne, there were just fifteen detectives at the Criminal Investigation Department. They wore plain clothes but had not undergone any special training. Away from the Metropolitan Police headquarters at Scotland Yard the situation was worse. Not one of the London Divisions could boast a single detective.

Henderson had spent thirteen years running a penal colony in Australia and had returned to the Home Office in London as Surveyor-General of Prisons, a job that he had held for six years. His first task as Commissioner of Police was completely to re-organise the internal structure of the Criminal Investigation Department, and he wasted no time. As a start he appointed nearly two hundred detectives and posted one hundred and eighty of them to individual police stations around the capital. The remaining twenty-seven were based at Scotland Yard, under the leadership of Superintendent Adolphus Williamson, four Chief Inspectors, and three Inspectors. This transformation was not entirely well received, for the Commissioner later noted in his first Report in 1869 that the detective system was "viewed with the greatest suspicion and jealousy by the majority of Englishmen and is, in fact, entirely foreign to the habits and feelings of the nation".

1

Accordingly, strict regulations were imposed on the detectives, such as the one which prohibited them from associating with criminals, but this did not prevent almost the entire department from collapse a few years later. The new elite force proved extremely corruptible, and in 1877 three of the CID's four Chief Inspectors were convicted of helping to run a betting fraud from France. A bogus newspaper entitled *Sport* was circulated in France, describing how "Mr Hugh Montgomery" had been blacklisted for winning too much money from English bookmakers. Readers were invited to help defeat the bookies by placing bets as Montgomery's nominees. In fact the recommended bookmaking firms were bogus, and as soon as a punter risked some of his own cash, as opposed to the impressive cheques from Mr Montgomery, the stake vanished, as did the bookie. In fact "Montgomery" was an alias used by a confidence trickster named Harry Benson who had already been discovered pretending to be the Comte de Montagu, the Mayor of Châteaudun, a town devastated by the Germans during the Franco-Prussian War. Shortly after the Lord Mayor of London had handed over a charitable grant of £1,000 to Benson, the impostor was unmasked.

One of the subscribers to the Montgomery bookmaking scheme was a certain Comtesse de Goncourt who believed she had won more than £30,000. She became suspicious when she was asked for a further £1,200 on top of her original stake, so as to "iron out certain formalities in England". The Comtesse became suspicious and called in a lawyer who eventually traced the fraudsmen to a country house near Shanklin, on the Isle of Wight. He therefore consulted Chief Inspector Nathaniel Druscovitch of Scotland Yard. The detective branch launched an investigation into Benson's gang, but did not realise that Benson had already bribed an Inspector Meiklejohn to warn him of any police activity. Meiklejohn ensured that the warrants obtained for the arrest of the gang only mentioned the aliases Benson had used in France, and when the investigation finally identified Benson as the central figure, Meiklejohn recommended that Chief Inspector Druscovitch and Chief Inspector Palmer should also be bribed.

It now seems certain that Superintendent Williamson had at least begun to suspect that his senior staff had been corrupted, for none seemed able to make the reasonably straightforward arrests of Benson and his gang. Druscovitch was sent to Rotterdam to extradite Benson, while one of his confederates, a con-man named William Kurr, was detained at the public house he owned in Islington. Meanwhile Williamson informed Commissioner Henderson of his suspicions, and the Treasury Solicitor was called in to examine Scotland Yard's investigation of Benson.

In April 1877 Benson and Kurr were sentenced to fifteen years imprisonment at the Old Bailey, and in an effort to reduce their sentence denounced Meiklejohn, Druscovitch and Palmer as fellow conspirators. The three detectives were promptly arrested, and were later charged with conspiracy to obstruct justice, together with Chief Inspector Clarke. After a trial lasting twenty days Meiklejohn, Druscovitch and Palmer were convicted. The jury acquitted Clarke, who was then aged sixty, on the grounds that he had been a fool rather than a criminal.

As a consequence of the scandal, and while the Old Bailey trial was still in progress, a Committee of Inquiry was appointed under the chairmanship of Sir Henry Ibbotson to review the CID's detective branch. The case had been a particularly galling defeat for the Commissioner because Chief Inspector Druscovitch had been one of the senior police officers specially recruited into the force to add some expertise to Scotland Yard.

The Home Office Departmental Commission spent a year dissecting the CID, and eventually recommended an entirely new structure for the force. In March 1878 the new proposals were adopted, and the rank of Assistant Commissioner introduced to head the Criminal Investigation Department. Ibbotson suggested that the Assistant Commissioner should be a lawyer rather than a professional police officer, and an ambitious young barrister, Howard Vincent, was selected for the post which was entitled Director of Criminal Investigations.

In fact Vincent had had his eye on the job from the moment that the Commission had begun its work, and had travelled to Paris to learn how the French organised their detectives. As soon as he took office in Scotland Yard he reshuffled the two hundred and fifty detectives under his command, promoting Williamson to the new rank of Chief Superintendent. Beneath him were three Chief Inspectors, twenty Inspectors and one hundred and fifty-nine Sergeants spread over sixty London Divisions.

It was this Detective Branch, still reeling from the 1877 corruption trial, that had to cope with an Irish bombing campaign in London. To say that Scotland Yard did not have the confidence of the public is an understatement. It did not even enjoy the confidence of most of the senior uniformed staff, for few could say how far the corruption had extended.

The Home Secretary, Sir Matthew White Ridley (later Lord Ridley) took a grave view of the wave of bombings even though there had been no loss of life and, no doubt bearing in mind the poor performance to date of Scotland Yard, requested the assistance of the Royal Irish Constabulary.

The Royal Irish Constabulary had unrivalled experience in combating the more extreme Irish nationalists, and in 1865 had managed to suppress an armed uprising led by James Stephens. Around 1858 Stephens had formed the Fenian organisation, so called after one of the Gaelic words for Irish people, Fene. The Fenians were dedicated to the cause of home rule for Ireland by means of revolution and were financed by American-Irish sympathisers. The movement had gained considerable public notoriety in 1882 for the murders, in Phoenix Park, Dublin, of Lord Frederick Cavendish, the Chief Secretary for Irish Affairs, and his Under-Secretary, Mr Burke. It was clear to everyone that the latest outrages in London were planned and executed by Irish extremists, and probably the Fenians, so the Home Secretary authorised a request for help to the Royal Irish Constabulary.

A detachment of these green-uniformed armed militia was brought to London and posted outside many of the important buildings in Whitehall. The Home Secretary, like the government, expected the worst, and rushed the Explosive Substances Act through Parliament. Sixteen years earlier, in December 1867, a Fenian bomb outside Clerkenwell Prison, in an attempt to free some Fenian prisoners, had killed four people and mutilated forty. The government had responded by enrolling fifty thousand volunteers as Special Constables. The Fenian responsible for placing and lighting the bomb, George Barrett, was arrested and sentenced to hang. (His execution, on 26 May 1868, was the last one in England to be held in public.)

When Vincent retired in 1884 he had built up the Detective Branch into a force of some six hundred officers, and had also taken a hand in drafting the new Metropolitan Police Act which created two posts carrying the rank of Assistant Commissioner: one for Civil Business, the other to lead the Criminal Investigation Department. The latter post went to James Monro, an Inspector-General of Police from Bengal who found himself responsible for dealing with the first of the Irish-American bomb incidents in the capital.

Shortly before his retirement Vincent had also recommended the creation of a specialist squad to track down the Fenian dynamiters, and Monro saw that his predecessor's idea was taken up. A Special Irish Branch was hastily formed, and Inspector John Littlechild was appointed to lead it, having been promoted to the rank of Chief Inspector. Littlechild himself was a Scot, and had been one of the few senior officers to emerge from the 1877 scandal with any credit, for Williamson had turned to him to make the arrest of William Kurr. At the time Littlechild had been a Detective

Sergeant, and he was one of the tiny number of officers that Williamson believed reliable. In the event Littlechild executed his instructions to the letter and arrested Kurr without confiding in any of his untrustworthy colleagues. By the end of the Commission's investigation, only he and Williamson were entirely free of suspicion of being corrupt. His Special Irish Branch was known to the rest of Scotland Yard as the Political Branch, but this epithet was quickly lost when it became clear that such a title was unacceptable to the public.

The idea of a political "secret" police was an entirely alien concept for Londoners, although two years earlier just such an organisation had been created with some success in Dublin, the brainchild of Colonel Henry Brackenbury, a former British Military Attaché in Paris who was then serving in Dublin with the civilian rank of Under-Secretary. In June 1882 a public meeting of the Land League in Bermondsey had been warned of a "vast secret detective organisation" headquartered at Dublin Castle which would "extend its ramifications all over the three kingdoms".

As well as being inaccurate in respect of the Branch being based in Dublin, this report was also a trifle premature. However, Littlechild did select detectives with Irish backgrounds to form his squad, and chose Detective Sergeant John Sweeney as his deputy. One of the first recruits was Sergeant Patrick Quinn, from County Mayo, who was later achieved the distinction of being the first police officer to be knighted.

The public were not to discover the identities of the London bombers for some years but, as we shall see, the Branch were particularly well-informed about the activities of the Fenian Brotherhood because they had an invaluable source right at the heart of the movement. On just a few occasions the Branch took what must have been calculated risks to neutralise the bombers, and one such incident took place in Birmingham in May 1883.

On 27 March 1883 a group of eight dynamiters arrived in Liverpool aboard the Cunard liner *Parthia*. Led by a Dr Gallaher and his brother Bernard, the six other Irishmen were named Dowd, O'Connor, Norman, Henry Wilson, John Curtin, and a chemist, Alfred Whitehead.

They quickly established a bomb factory in Jedrane Street, Birmingham, which was kept under close observation by the Birmingham police. On one occasion a detective disguised as a painter was able to enter the building and draw up a plan for a police raid. When this took place all but two of the Fenians were arrested. The remaining two surrendered to Littlechild at their lodgings in Nelson Square, Blackfriars, before they could plant a single bomb. Norman gave evidence for the Crown at the subsequent trial in May, and each of the defendants was sentenced to life imprisonment. Observers believed that Norman had been responsible for tipping off the police but in fact the Branch's source had alerted the authorities long before the *Parthia* had docked.

On 30 October 1883 two further bombs went off in the London underground system, one on the line between Charing Cross and Westminster, the other at Praed Street Station where some sixty people were injured. On 27 February the following year an explosive device went off in a cloakroom at Victoria Station, but on this occasion the owner of the suitcase in which the bomb had been concealed was traced to a hotel in Great Portland Street. There he was identified as an Irish-American named John Daley, and he was subsequently arrested at Birkenhead on Good Friday by Superintendent John Humphrey, head of the Royal Irish Constabulary detachment in Liverpool, and Sergeant Canning, who found three more bombs in his luggage.

On 28 February two similar bombs were recovered from Charing Cross and Paddington Stations and successfully defused. Both consisted of dynamite linked to a timing mechanism of American manufacture. Evidently the timers had failed to work. On 1 March a third device was found at Ludgate Hill Station and made safe.

Daley's arrest at Birkenhead was no lucky break for the police. It was, in fact, the culmination of a long surveillance operation which had begun the previous October. Daley was well-known in extremist circles in Dublin and had frequently been questioned by the police, once in connection with the murder of a policeman. Soon after that incident, in 1867, Daley had fled to New York, and had not been spotted until the previous autumn when an informant identified Daley living in the Sparkbrook district of Birmingham and using the alias "John Denman".

At that time there was no evidence to link Daley to any crime so he was simply kept under observation by Inspectors Stroud and Black of the Birmingham police. At first the police had rented rooms in Grafton Street directly opposite those occupied by Daley, but as the operation progressed Stroud arranged to meet the suspect and eventually moved into the same house. They became firm friends, although Daley never realised Stroud was a detective.

Once Daley had been caught with explosives it only remained to round up his principal accomplice, James Egan, who was also his landlord. A search of Egan's home revealed a number of incriminating Fenian documents, which the Crown argued were treasonable, and both men were sentenced at Warwick Assizes in May to long terms of imprisonment. Daley received life whilst Egan was sentenced to twenty years.

The cases of Daly and Egan were to be very significant for the Branch. They effectively outlawed possession of Fenian literature and established the idea of infiltrating detectives into the ranks of suspect organisations. Stroud had achieved a remarkable success, and eliminated two dangerous bombers. It was shortly after the arrests of Daley and Egan that the British public learned officially of the Branch's formation. On 24 March 1884 *The Times* reported:

> It is stated that the authorities have within the last few days summoned to London a large number of detectives from the south of Ireland for the purpose of assisting in watching and detecting the supposed dynamite conspirators.

While Daley and Egan were awaiting trial, on 30 May 1884, a constable spotted a suspicious-looking object whilst on patrol in Trafalgar Square. Closer examination revealed sixteen sticks of dynamite tied to the foot of Nelson's Column. The fuse was removed before an explosion could take place, but another bomb went off that same evening in a public convenience beside Scotland Yard. Only minutes beforehand Detective Inspector Sweeney and Sergeant Robson had been writing their report on the Trafalgar Square incident in an office directly behind the public convenience. The bomb wrecked The Rising Sun public house next door to Scotland Yard and started a small fire in the Special Irish Branch offices (See Plate No. 2). Two further bombs also went off: one outside the Junior Carlton Club and the other at the home of Sir Watkin Williams-Wynn in St James's Square.

The bombings continued until the end of January 1885 when two men, Cunningham and Burton, were arrested. During that month they had caused an explosion near Gower Street Underground Station, blown up the crypt of the House of Commons and left a bomb in the White Tower of the Tower of London, injuring in all some sixteen visitors. Both were sentenced to life imprisonment. Two other conspirators, John Fleming and a former Captain in the United States Army named Mackay Lomasney, were believed to have been killed in December whilst trying to place their dynamite on a buttress under the south-west end of London Bridge. The bomb had gone off prematurely, destroying all trace of the two men and their boat, but hardly damaging the bridge.

Between March 1883 and February 1885 there was a total of thirteen bombings in London, but the campaign ended as suddenly as it had begun. The new Branch was sufficiently confident of its victory to order the removal of the Royal Irish Constabulary detachments posted to the ports. Their withdrawal was completed by 1886.

The end of the Fenian bombing campaign in 1885 did not, as some might have expected, mark the closure of the Special Irish Branch. Instead the word Irish was dropped from its title and the Branch continued under the leadership of Inspector John Littlechild.

During the course of Sir Edmund Henderson's tenure at the Yard the Metropolitan Police strength grew from 8,500 to 13,804, but a substantial number of that total, some 1,100, were permanently engaged on fixed-point guard duties on government buildings in the centre of the capital. In addition the contingent of the Royal Irish Constabulary stood, rifles at the ready, at strategic intersections of Whitehall. This long-term commitment of manpower enabled the CID to retain the increasingly specialised services of the Special Branch, and provided a useful source of detectives suitable to act as bodyguards to potential victims of assassination.

The Metropolitan Police had, in fact, been providing this service for a number of years, possibly since the reign of George III, whose life was once saved by a Bow Street Runner named Townsend. The runner happened to be passing when the King rushed out of his carriage at St James's Palace. A madman suddenly stepped forward out of a crowd of onlookers and advanced on the King with a knife in one hand and a petition in the other. Townsend wrestled the man to the ground and disarmed him with such speed that the King ordered that in future two Runners should be attached to the Court.

The first two such Runners were MacKenna and Sayers. On the formation of the Branch, John Sweeney and Patrick Quinn acted as Queen Victoria's bodyguards.

One of the disadvantages suffered by the police at the beginning of the Fenian attacks was the complete lack of any advance warning, and the absence of a network of informers. Littlechild decided to remedy this by detaching Inspector Maurice Moser on a permanent surveillance of the Fenians.

Moser began in Paris, where a senior Clan-na-gael Fenian,* James Stephens, had been directing operations, having travelled from his base in New York to do so. Moser kept constant watch on Stephens, who had previously escaped from Bridewell Prison, and

* The Clan-na-gael was a particularly ruthless off-shoot of the Fenian Brotherhood, thought to have been formed in America in 1870.

was able to tip off Littlechild when two Fenians, Mooney and Coleman, attempted to plant a bomb near the Mansion House in the City of London. The plot was foiled but the two Irishmen made a successful escape and returned to France where there was little chance of obtaining their extradition. Mooney was traced to a small hotel in Paris, where he was living under the name of Gourbois, and when Moser reported this to Scotland Yard it was decided to give Mooney a harsh warning never to cross the Channel again. Williamson, Littlechild and Meredith, all from the Yard, set off from London, accompanied by Inspector Hancock of the City Police and Inspector Caminada of the Manchester Police. Moser lured Mooney into the street outside his hotel, where he was surrounded by the six police officers who proceeded to deliver him a verbal warning.

Unhappily for the police officers, the French authorities had observed this confrontation and all six were arrested at the Gare du Nord on their way home. Williamson, who spoke fluent French, was eventually able to extricate himself and his party after prolonged negotiations, and Moser remained in Paris to continue his watch on Stephens and his accomplices. None ever returned to England. The French evidently remained somewhat sensitive about the Special Branch operating on its territory for some years later Detective Sergeant Radcliffe underwent a similar experience and was detained in Paris for some hours before his credentials could be checked and his release secured.

The situaton at home, however, remained tense, and in February 1886 the Police Commissioner's resignation was accepted by the Home Secretary, Hugh Childers, after the police had failed to prevent two outbreaks of rioting in London's West End, following political gatherings. General Sir Charles Warren, a Royal Engineers officer then serving in East Africa, was appointed in Henderson's place. Warren proved to be a disastrous choice, for he challenged the right of anyone, including the Home Secretary, to give him either advice or orders. His own Assistant Commissioner, James Monro resigned in protest in August 1888, but was then hastily recalled in December to take over from Warren when the latter himself resigned.

Monro's unexpected return to the Yard might have been expected to herald further important developments within the CID, especially since he had been responsible for nurturing the Branch through its early days, but this was not to be. As Commissioner, Monro made himself unpopular with the government by pressing for a larger CID strength and continually warned of the dangers presented by the foreign extremists. In June 1890, after less than eighteen months in office, Monro resigned, apparently believing that the new Home Secretary, Henry Matthews (later Lord Llandaff), intended to replace him with his private secretary, Mr Ruggles-Brise. In the event a one-armed Indian Army officer, Colonel Sir Edward Bradford, was appointed Commissioner and the important vacancy of Assistant Commissioner filled by Monro's nominee, Charles Howard.

Bradford had wide political experience and, at the time of his appointment, was heading an intelligence department in the India Office. He was a tough officer, having lost his arm in a struggle with a tiger whilst hunting in India. By the end of Bradford's tenure the Fenian threat had been removed, but it was while he was in office that details became known of just how the police had been able to identify so many of the leading members of the organisation.

The principal informant in the Fenian ranks was an Englishman named Thomas Beach, born in Colchester in September 1841. Being something of an adventurer, Beach travelled to America and, under the *nom-de-guerre* Henri Le Caron, fought in the Civil War with the 8th Pennsylvanian Reserve. During the course of his military service he came into contact with an Irish nationalist named John O'Neill who took him for a Frenchman. O'Neill confided in Beach that his American Branch of the Fenian Brotherhood intended to organise an "invasion" of Canada from Buffalo, in New York State. Beach was horrified, and wrote to his father in Colchester giving details of the attack. Beach's father promptly warned his MP, John Rebow, who passed on the information to the Home Secretary. The attack, which duly took place in June 1866, was repulsed, with the loss of some sixty Fenians and a handful of Canadian infantry, but it served to establish Beach as an important source for the British government within the Irish Republican movement. Thereafter Beach communicated with the Governor-General of Canada, Lord Monck, and his Chief Commissioner of Police, Judge J. G. M'Micken. For the next twenty-two years Beach sent detailed reports to Canada describing future Fenian operations. His information led to the interception of several Fenians in England, including John Daly and James Egan. Beach's tip-offs also resulted in the discovery of the Jubilee Plot, and the arrest of two further bombers from America, Thomas Callan and Michael Harkins.

Callan and Harkins arrived at Liverpool on the *City Of Chester* on 21 June 1887 and took lodgings in London under false names. Once established in the capital the two Irish Americans made contact with an existing Fenian cell, consisting of Joseph Melville and Joseph Cohen. However, unbeknown to the two newcomers,

Melville had long been kept under surveillance by the Branch, following a tip-off from Beach. They were both regarded as potentially dangerous political activists although to date there had never been any evidence against them of a criminal nature. The surveillance continued throughout September, until Melville suddenly disappeared. His vanishing act was followed a month later by Cohen's, and the Branch decided to question Harkins before he too left the country.

On 19 October Quinn called on Harkins at his lodgings in Alfred Street, Islington, and questioned him about his contacts with Cohen. Harkins admitted having met Cohen, whom he called "Joseph Brown" and explained that he had tried unsuccessfully to get Brown admitted to hospital, as he was apparently very ill. He volunteered the information that Mr Brown lived at 42 Lambeth Road, and he agreed to accompany Quinn to the address. When they got there they discovered Cohen's corpse. He had evidently died the previous day. Among his belongings they found a loaded Smith & Wesson and a quantity of ammunition.

Meanwhile Harkins' room was being searched by Detective Sergeant Walsh, who discovered a revolver and a suitcase that smelled of dynamite. Quinn challenged Harkins about the second revolver, which was also a Smith & Wesson and Harkins admitted possessing it. He also agreed to lead the Branch to Callan. Quinn accepted the offer and released Harkins who then called on Callan's address in Falmouth Street. Callan, however, had moved on, and for the next week Harkins and the Branch toured the East End trying to find the elusive Irishman. Each evening Harkins returned to his room in Alfred Street where he was guarded by five Branch detectives.

Meanwhile Callan had taken a room in a boarding house in Baxter Street and was busy disposing of his hoard of dynamite. At first he tried flushing it down a WC, but this blocked the drains. The landlady complained about the blockage and made Callan pay for workmen to clear the offending material which was then placed in a dustbin. But this was not to be the end of the matter. A neighbour decided to use the damp, clay-like dynamite to cover the floor of his pigeon loft, and put it in an oven to dry out. The resulting explosion escaped the attention of the police, but on 19 November Callan was arrested shortly after cashing one of Melville's cheques at the Bank of England. The Bank staff, who had been alerted by the Branch, called the City Police and Detective Sergeant Downes was quickly on the scene. He arrested Callan and escorted him to Littlechild's office at Scotland Yard.

While Littlechild interrogated Callan, Patrick Quinn and

Sergeant Patrick M'Intyre searched 24 Baxter Road. There the landlady, Mrs Bright, recounted the story of the blocked WC and Mr Johns, the neighbour, explained how his oven had exploded. Inspector Quinn then instructed his sergeant to gather up the remaining dynamite (of which there was nearly twenty pounds' worth) and deliver it to the Chief Inspector of Explosives at the Home Office, Colonel Vivian Majendie. The two policemen also found a loaded revolver among Callan's effects. It was the same type as those owned by Cohen and Harkins.

Having successfully detained Callan, Quinn broke the news to Harkins and charged him with offences under the new Explosive Substances Act. The case against Callan and Harkins was now complete, although Melville appeared to have slipped through the net. When Beach was asked about Melville he revealed that Melville had returned to New York via France and had taken up residence on Fifth Avenue under the name Joseph Moroney. Accordingly a police constable who had once seen Melville, Harkins and Callan together (at the House of Commons) was sent to New York to identify "Moroney". Constable Oram did indeed spot Melville and even trailed him to a restaurant. His mission completed, Oram returned to London and gave evidence linking Melville to Callan and Harkins at their trial.

The trial opened at the Old Bailey on 1 February 1888 and lasted three days. The jury deliberated for just twenty minutes and then convicted both defendants. They were each sentenced to fifteen years imprisonment by Mr Justice Hawkins (later Lord Brampton). The trial was concluded by the foreman commending Littlechild for his "great tact and ability in the case".

Beach's extraordinary role in penetrating the Fenian Brotherhood remained a closely guarded secret for a further year, until February 1889, when he publicly denounced the Fenian dynamiters and described their American backgrounds. In 1893 Beach described his experiences in *25 Years In The Secret Service* (Heineman).

No sooner had the Branch eliminated the Fenian threat with Beach's help than another group of political extremists began.

Early in January 1892 Inspector William Melville, assisted by Inspector Black of the Birmingham police, scored a considerable success with the help of an informant by raiding a bomb factory in Walsall and arresting a group of Anarchists. The case had begun with routine surveillance on a political extremist, Joseph Deakin, who was suspected of casting bombs for some Anarchists who frequented the Autonomy Club in Windmill Street. The Club was a regular meeting-place for the Anarchists so, not surprisingly, it had also become the haunt of Branch detectives. Deakin was arrested by Melville and Sweeney moments after he had left the Club on 6 January, and was found to be carrying a quantity of chloroform. Two days later Frederick Charles, William Ditchfield and Victor Cailes were arrested in Walsall. The last to be arrested was Jean Battola, an Italian shoemaker, who was intercepted in Great Titchfield Street on 13 January. All five were tried at Stafford Assizes, and the Court heard how Ditchfield had manufactured bombs for his fellow-conspirators. At one stage the Counsel for the Defence cross-examined Melville about how he had gained entry into the Autonomy Club and who had been paid for information. Melville declined to answer and the defence made a formal application to compel the witness to answer. The judge, Mr Justice Hawkins, rejected the application after hearing the Attorney General's objections.

Quinn, Melville and Sweeney gave evidence at the trial, and eventually the Anarchists altered their defence to a claim that although they were indeed making bombs, the bombs were intended for use against the Czar in Russia. This argument failed to impress the jury who convicted Charles, Cailes and Battola. They were sentenced to ten years imprisonment while Deakin got five years (after a recommendation for mercy). Two others, who had been arrested in London, were acquitted for lack of evidence.

The Branch had long been aware of the dangers presented by foreign exile organisations, although they could not know of the internecine struggles taking place within some of the overseas communities in London. Occasionally, however, there were unmistakable signs. In 1883 the body of an agent of the Czar's secret police, the Okhrana, was found in Strutton Ground, directly opposite the modern location of New Scotland Yard. Documents found in his pockets showed that he was an *agent provocateur* sent from St Petersburg to identify Russian Nihilists. Other European police forces reported similar assassinations, but it was not until 1914, as we shall see, that attempts were made to institutionalise communications between police authorities. It should be remembered that in these early days there was not even a commonly recognised system of personal identification, such as the classification of fingerprints, which was itself only cautiously introduced by Galton in late 1894 as a successor to the French Bertillon method.

Quite apart from the foreign extremists, Scotland Yard had their hands full monitoring the home-grown variety. In April 1892 the Branch seized several copies of *The Commonweal*, an Anarchist newsletter. In that Branch operation an activist named David

Nicoll was arrested for sedition and incitement to murder the Home Secretary, Henry Matthews, Mr Justice Hawkins (who had sentenced the Walsall Anarchists), and Inspector Melville himself.

The offending article, signed by Nicoll, first appeared in the newsletter on 9 April, copies of which were bought by two Branch detectives, Francis Powell and Edwin Gray. The following day Sweeney attended a public meeting held by Nicoll in Hyde Park and took shorthand notes of his speech. It was highly inflammatory and was enough for Littlechild to apply for a warrant for Nicoll's arrest. On 19 April Nicoll was arrested by Inspector William M'Lynchy, and on the same day Littlechild arrested *The Commonweal*'s printer, Charles Mowbray. When he read him the warrant Mowbray led him to the rotting corpse of his wife... who had died more than five months earlier.

Nicoll and Mowbray stood trial in May 1892 for incitement to murder, and Nicoll was found guilty and sentenced to eighteen months hard labour by the Lord Chief Justice. Mowbray was acquitted and discharged.

The Nihilists and Anarchists were taken rather more seriously than perhaps they are today, but at the time of Nicoll's conviction Nihilists had successfully assassinated President Carnot of France and exploded bombs in several European capitals. The French authorities had responded to the Anarchist threat by publishing a dossier containing no less than five hundred photographs of wanted Anarchists, and it was the circulation of this album that led to the arrest of Joseph Meunier by Melville in London in May for blowing up a Paris restaurant in April 1892. After a successful extradition Meunier was sentenced to twenty years' imprisonment.

By 1893 the Branch were confident that most of Nicoll's confederates had gone into hiding, but nevertheless maintained a vigilant watch for the few thought to be still in England. In March of that year a French tailor, Martial Bourdin, attempted to demolish the Royal Observatory at Greenwich, but only succeeded in blowing off his own arm. He died on the way to hospital, but not before William Melville had learned from him the address of his fellow conspirators. The Branch promptly concentrated their efforts on a hairdressing salon in Bennett Street, Soho, which was apparently used as an alternative meeting-place to the Autonomy Club. All the regular visitors to the salon were followed home by a team consisting of Sergeants Kane, Maguire and Flood, and by chance one notorious Anarchist, George Charpentier, was caught red-handed whilst indulging in a little burglary on his way home. Charpentier appeared before Sir Peter Edlin at Clerkenwell

Sessions in March 1894 and was sentenced to six months hard labour for possession of house-breaking implements.

The Charpentier case was quickly followed by that of Francesco Polti and Giuseppe Farana. The Branch's attention had been drawn to the two Italians after the manager of Cohen's Iron-foundry, Mr Thomas Smith, reported an order for some bomb casing. John Sweeney instructed the manager to allow Polti to collect the offending article, and the eighteen-year-old Anarchist was arrested by Sweeney and Riley as he alighted from an omnibus with the parcel under his arm. Soon afterwards Quinn arrested Farana at his lodgings in the East End and confronted the Italian with his plan to blow up the Stock Exchange. At their trial at the Old Bailey in May Polti pleaded not guilty and was sentenced to ten years' imprisonment by Mr Justice Hawkins. Farana pleaded guilty and, being considerably older than Polti, received twenty years.

This case marked a temporary respite in political violence, with only two further serious incidents during Queen Victoria's reign. Late in May of the same year a Branch raid on an Anarchist commune in Park Walk, Chelsea, resulted in the arrest of a group of extremists led by Fritz Brall. The basement of their house contained a coin-counterfeiting laboratory as well as a bomb factory, and on 3 July Brall was sentenced to a long term of imprisonment by Mr Justice Grantham. In another, similar case, Rolla Richards was sentenced to seven years for blowing up post offices in South London. Some four years later, in April 1897, another bomb went off on an underground train, killing one passenger, but no one was ever arrested for the offence.

Littlechild continued to head the Branch until 1903, by which time several administrative changes had taken place at the Yard. In May 1901 the CID Assistant Commissioner, Sir Robert Anderson, retired and was succeeded by Edward Henry who had previously held senior police posts in Bengal and Johannesburg.

Littlechild's departure from the Yard was a considerable milestone in the history of the Branch. He had supervised its transformation from the Special Irish Branch to what was commonly referred to as the Political Branch. He had also established what was, in effect, Britain's first domestic intelligence organisation.

CHAPTER II

The End of an Era

The success of the Special Branch against the
Fenians, the Anarchists and the Nihilists proved it
was too valuable to be disbanded. At the beginning of
this century it was decided to maintain it on a
permanent footing, and its scope was expanded to
include all matters of national security, not confining
its activities solely to the Metropolitan Police District.

Sir Ronald Howe in *The Story of Scotland Yard* (Arthur
Barker, 1965)

On John Littlechild's retirement in 1903 his deputy, Patrick
Quinn, was promoted by the outgoing Commissioner, Sir Edward
Bradford, and Sir Melville Macnaghten appointed Assistant
Commissioner for the CID.

The Branch inherited by Superintendent Quinn had a strength
of fifteen, including John Macarthy, John McBrian, William
Melville and Dan Maclaughlin. The takeover marked an important point in the development of the Branch. Its reputation had
been greatly enhanced by the speed with which the Fenian
bombers had been identified, traced and arrested. Similarly, in the
field of personal protection, their reputation had grown. No less
than three unsuccessful attempts had been made by madmen to
assassinate Queen Victoria. None had succeeded, and although this
was not strictly due to the Branch, they nevertheless reaped some
advantage. It was by now an established tradition that the Branch
provide the monarch's family with bodyguards, and with the
increase in assassination attempts in Europe the Branch were also
called on to protect visiting dignitaries. In one incident, when the
Czar and Czarina were staying at Osborne House, on the Isle of
Wight, John Sweeney prevented the kidnapping of the Czarevitch,
Alexis. Sweeney was escorting the Czarevitch and his tutor on a
visit to Southsea when he spotted two suspicious men trailing them.
The detective signalled to his two assistants, who were keeping
watch from a discreet distance, and had both suspects detained.

They were Russian Nihilists, and both were armed with knives. It turned out that they had committed a number of offences in England so they were deported back to Odessa where, no doubt, they were met by representatives of the Okhrana.

Certainly the threat of assassination was real enough: King Humbert of Italy had been assassinated in 1900; the following year President McKinley became the third American President to be killed in office * and in 1903 King Alexander of the Serbs and his wife, Queen Draga, were murdered. Consequently, John Macarthy accompanied the Prince and Princess of Wales to Vienna in April 1904 when they called on Emperor Franz Josef and paid their respects to him after the murder of his wife, the Empress Elizabeth. She had been stabbed by an Italian Anarchist in Lausanne some six years earlier. When the Archduke Franz Ferdinand visited England later that year Macarthy and George Riley acted as his bodyguards, and the Branch representatives were reinforced at the wedding of Princess Ena and King Alphonso in Madrid by a detachment from the 16th Lancers. Their presence, however, failed to prevent an Anarchist throwing a bomb at the carriage carrying the King and Queen of Spain away from the church after their marriage. Though the bomb exploded close to the royal couple, they escaped unharmed, but the blast killed a Spanish bodyguard and several horses. The Anarchist was subsequently hunted by Macarthy and his French counterpart, Xavier Paoli, the Commissaire Spécial Attaché à la Direction de la Sûreté Générale. The perpetrator was eventually shot dead by two Spanish Civil Guards. (The incident was the second lucky escape for the Spanish King who had previously been attacked whilst travelling in a carriage in Paris with the French President, M. Joubert. Two gunmen in the Rue de Rivoli had stepped forward to fire their weapons but were promptly cut down by the cavalry escort.)

The roles played by the Branch as protectors did not go unrecognised, and a number of foreign monarchs expressed their thanks by decorating individual Branch officers. Thus King Albert of the Belgians conferred an award on his 'shadow' in London, Charles Frost, and George Riley received a medal from King George of Greece.† Virtually all the Branch officers undertook royal protection duties at one time or another, but it was after the death of Queen Victoria in 1901 that overseas visits became a regular occurrence. Edward VII, for example, frequently travelled abroad, especially to Russia to see the Czar and the Kaiser, and he was

* Lincoln was shot in 1865, Garfield in 1881.
† King George was later murdered in Salonica in 1913.

invariably accompanied by John Sweeney and George Riley. On
only one occasion, near Brussels in 1909, did anyone attempt to
assassinate him. A young Belgian revolutionary named Spido fired
two shots at the train in which the King was travelling, but little
harm was done. Spido was arrested and the King sent the Belgian
government a plea for clemency on his behalf.

The succession of Edward VII ended an era, and heralded new
developments, in both the social and scientific fields. Improved
systems of identification classification were experimented with at
the Yard and greater emphasis was placed on the retention and
collation of comprehensive criminal records. The twentieth century
would bring revolution, and again revolutionise the Metropolitan
Police's approach to law enforcement, personal protection and the
gathering of intelligence. Within the decade the Committee of
Imperial Defence were to authorise the introduction of a Secret
Service Bureau (which, in spite of the title of Thomas Beach's book,
did not formally exist until 1909) and establish a covert arm to
liaise with the Branch.

The Branch did not have to wait long to see the signs of the new
age. In 1905 a newly recruited Detective Constable, Herbert Fitch,
who spoke German, Russian and French, was given the task of
monitoring a particularly active group of revolutionary exiles from
Russia who met regularly and booked private rooms in the name of
the "Foreign Barbers of London". On one occasion Fitch hid in a
cupboard in an Islington public house while a speaker named
Vladimir Uljanov harangued a gathering of some twenty comrades. Uljanov later became more widely known under his *nom-de-
guerre* of Lenin. At another meeting, which Fitch attended dressed
as a waiter, Uljanov shared a platform with a Jew, named Leib
Bronstein, who adopted the *nom-de-guerre,* "Lev Trotsky". Fitch was
also present (in disguise) at a revolutionary meeting in Great
Portland Street, at which Lenin and Trotsky proposed a motion
calling for a general strike in Russia. The motion was adopted by
twenty-one votes to seven, and later that year the strike took place,
accompanied by mutinies on two Russian Naval vessels and in
several army units, and by the fall of the Czar's government. For his
part in the Branch's surveillance operation Fitch was promoted to
Detective-Sergeant.

Fitch was quickly recognised as an expert on the various Russian
political extremists resident in London and was always consulted
by the CID whenever an incident involving Russian revolutionaries
took place within the Metropolitan Police district. In May 1907 he
attended several of Maxim Gorky's meetings, and in the same
month was called in to investigate the apparent suicide of Marie

Derval in Pimlico. He established that Miss Derval had married a well-known revolutionary, Tscherkesov, but had been deserted by him. In revenge she had betrayed several of his fellow-conspirators to the Okhrana in St Petersburg, and had then tried to shoot her former lover in Paris. No doubt Tscherkesov had been anxious to eliminate Derval himself, but she had saved him the trouble and blown her brains out in despair.

In January 1909 the Branch were called in to another, similar case. A young robber in Tottenham tried unsuccessfully to steal a factory payroll and then shot a youth who had intervened. The robber shot himself when he was eventually cornered. He died in hospital later the same evening, but his identification as one Paul Hefeld caused a sensation... and a manhunt for his accomplice who had shot more than a dozen of his pursuers and killed a police officer, PC Tyler, who had been on point duty in the vicinity.

Hefeld had in fact been on the run from the French police since May 1907 when he and three fellow Anarchists had tried to assassinate the French President. The bomb had gone off prematurely, killing Peter Lapidus, but Hefeld and Lapidus's brother Jacob had escaped in the ensuing confusion.

The Branch's search for Hefeld's accomplice led them to a cottage in Walthamstow, where Detective Sergeant Fitch called for the surrender of the occupant, believed to be Jacob Lapidus. Rather than give up, Lapidus shot himself.

Another assassin who tried to shoot himself was Madan Lal Dhingra who had pumped six bullets into Sir William Wyllie, ADC to the Secretary of State for India, and into Dr Cawas Lalcaca, at the Imperial Institute in South Kensington. Dhingra and his empty revolver were seized by onlookers, and the assassin later explained that he had killed Sir William by mistake, for he had intended to shoot the Secretary of State himself, Lord Curzon. Dhingra was subsequently tried for murder and hanged.

One of the largest security operations ever conducted by the Branch took place for the funeral of Edward VII in May 1910. No less than forty-eight European Royals walked in the procession, flanked by Quinn and Superintendents Macarthy, Spencer and Woodhall. The funeral passed without serious incident, although the Branch were prepared for the worst.

It was in December the following year that the Branch were once again called in to deal with what was believed to be the work of some Russian revolutionaries. A gang of burglars were surprised in a police trap whilst attempting to force their way into a Houndsditch jeweller's shop. The burglars drew guns and in the unequal battle that followed three City of London police officers

were shot dead and two others badly wounded. All the raiders
escaped but the ensuing investigation led the police to a known
Italian Anarchist named Enrico Malatesta, the purchaser of a
canister of acetylene gas found abandoned by the gang. The
ringleader was believed to be a mysterious Lett named Pieter
Piatkow and a reward was offered for information leading to his
arrest. Piatkow, who had occasionally worked as a scenery painter
in an Anarchist club in Jubilee Street, was quickly dubbed Peter
the Painter, and (probably falsely) represented as a master
criminal.

The day after the massacre the police raided the Stepney home of
another well-known Lett and Anarchist, Levi Gardstein, but he
shot himself before he could be arrested. However, his Russian
companion, Nina Vassileva, was successfully detained.

The police made no further progress in the case until a Branch
informant betrayed the hiding place of Fritz Svaars and Joseph
Vogel, two men thought to have been involved in the Houndsditch
murders. On 3 January 1911 a combined force of police and
soldiers surrounded 100 Sidney Street, less than a mile from the site
of the first murders. Also in attendance were the new Home
Secretary, Winston Churchill, the Commissioner of the City Police,
Sir William Nott-Bower, the CID Assistant Commissioner, Sir
Melville Macnaghten, and Superintendent Quinn. The gun battle
that followed lasted for six hours and soon became known as the
Sidney Street Siege. The two occupants of the building, Svaars and
Vogel, were both killed, the former from the effects of the fire that
raged through the house, the latter by a bullet through the head.
Seven other members of the gang were eventually traced but none
was convicted of the original murders at Houndsditch.

The only known associate of the gang who failed to escape
punishment was Enrico Malatesta, who was deported back to Italy.
The alleged ringleader, Piatkow, disappeared completely and was
never seen again. Even Nina Vassileva, who was convicted on a
conspiracy charge, was later released after a successful appeal.

Because in its early years the Branch was Britain's only official
security organisation a number of roles fell to it which were
subsequently taken on by other departments of government.

The Branch's security responsibilities fell into two categories: the
protection of the Metropolitan Police District from foreign political
extremists and the more general business of guarding the realm
from espionage. The Branch was created, as we have seen, to fulfil
the former role, with the Fenian menace specifically in the
Commissioner's mind, but even before the bombing campaign had

reached its climax the Branch had been called in to deal with a new threat.

On 30 May 1878, some five years before the Branch had formally come into existence, the *Globe* newspaper had seriously embarrassed Disraeli by disclosing details of a secret agreement between Great Britain and Russia. A few days later the Foreign Secretary, Lord Salisbury, had been questioned about the *Globe*'s report, and had denounced it as "wholly unauthentic". The *Globe* responded to the denial by publishing all eleven clauses of the still secret Anglo-Russian Treaty on their front page. The text was entirely accurate, and the Foreign Office realised that one of their own employees had been the source. The Foreign Secretary had therefore consulted Sir Howard Vincent and initiated what was arguably Britain's first modern investigation into the leakage of secrets.

Vincent's men identified the *Globe*'s source without too much difficulty. The editor of the *Morning Advertiser* had produced a letter from a Foreign Office clerk confirming the authenticity of the *Globe*'s original report, and examination of the man's bank account revealed a recent payment of forty guineas from the paper.

The culprit was a linguist named Charles Marvin, and he was arrested on 26 June 1878. The following day he was charged with the theft of a government document, but the defence claimed that whilst Marvin admitted being the *Globe*'s informant, he had simply memorised the document, word for word, and had not stolen it as theft is defined by the Larceny Acts. The presiding magistrate at Bow Street, Mr Vaughan, accepted the defence's interpretation and dismissed the case. The prosecution's collapse was a defeat for the Treasury Counsel, Sir Harry Poland, and it was a watershed for the law. Marvin had relied on his memory and had not even broken any Foreign Office regulations, for there was nothing to prevent Foreign Office officials from working for Fleet Street as well.

The consequence of Marvin's acquittal was the introduction of the original Official Secrets Bill in 1888, soon after Lord Salisbury had succeeded Disraeli as Prime Minister. The Bill was quickly on the Statute Book, and thereafter it fell on the Branch to investigate possible breaches and prosecute future offences.

Within six years of the passing of the Official Secrets Act the Attorney-General, Sir Richard Webster, attempted to tighten up its provisions on the grounds that some cases had failed in the courts because of the difficulty involved in obtaining evidence of espionage and proving an illegal motive. Just such a case had taken place in April 1899 when a former Royal Engineers Quartermaster, Edward Holden, had been accused of attempting to procure details of the fortifications of Gibraltar from a Lance Corporal who had

been stationed there. Holden had apparently been acting on behalf
of a mysterious third party based in Paris, but the prosecution had
been unable to prove that Holden had intended to pass the
information on to a foreign government, as the Act stipulated.
Holden was reluctantly given the relatively light sentence of twelve
months imprisonment by the Lord Chief Justice, Lord Coleridge,
who commented on the Act's impotence.

In fact, very few prosecutions were brought under the 1889
Official Secrets Act, the Branch's efforts being necessarily concentrated, as we have seen, on offenders against the Explosive
Substances legislation. The Branch had naturally been preoccupied
by the activities of the bombers, first the Fenians and then the
Anarchists, and had deliberately recruited police officers with a
knowledge of foreign languages. This inevitably led to the Branch
acquiring a certain expertise in dealing with the many exile groups
in London, particularly those within the Russian and German
Jewish communities in the East End. By the turn of the century the
Branch had gathered more information concerning London's
foreign residents than any other government department, and were
frequently called on to advise on Whitehall's policy towards them.

Until November 1899 the Branch was the sole official organisation dealing with security matters. However, in that month the
War Office decided to take a renewed interest in the "miscellaneous
subjects" of a secret service nature which the Boer War was
creating. Responsibility for secret service work had previously been
left to one officer, the Assistant Adjutant-General (AAG) at the
War Office, who worked under the Director of Military Intelligence. To describe his duties as secret service is perhaps misleading,
since he did not employ a single agent. Instead he distributed a
small quantity of Foreign Office cash to individuals who volunteered information. The outbreak of the South African War meant
an increase in such activities and a reserve officer, Major Forster,
was recruited to assist the AAG. Then, in December 1899, a new
section, known simply as "H", was created under Major (Sir) James
Edmonds. He brought in two further assistants, Lieutenant Colonel
H. Walker and Captain H. E. Kent RE. H's principal role was that
of cable censorship. By liaising with the Post Office H obtained
copies of all the cable traffic passing between London and Cape
Town, Durban, Zanzibar and Aden. This monitoring operation
was quickly spotted by the Germans in East Africa and, following
protests from Berlin, H was obliged to relax its restrictions and
allow certain foreign government codes to be transmitted freely.

As well as its cable censorship role, H maintained a watch on the
ordinary letter traffic and from time to time obtained a Home

Office warrant to intercept the mail of any suspect foreigners. This it did with the help of the Branch which provided detectives to keep suspects under surveillance. Scotland Yard received dozens of letters denouncing South African spies, and each case had to be investigated by Branch personnel, but invariably such information turned out to be without foundation.

Within a few months of the war, and by agreement with the Foreign Office, Section H took over all secret service operations, such as there were, and Major Edmonds travelled to the Cape to examine local security arrangements. In his absence Lieutenant Colonel James was appointed head of H. At the same time Colonel Walker founded a separate unit to issue the military permits required before landing in the Colony. This was effectively the first time that a British intelligence organisation had been granted control over civilian travel movements.

By the end of the Boer War section H and the Branch had gained a wealth of experience in dealing with security matters, and James' successor, Colonel J. F. Davies, prepared a large paper on the subject as a guide to others. The document included chapters on such diverse subjects as wireless telegraphy, cable censorship, control of the press, ciphers, dossiers on suspects, accounts, shipment of war stores and secret service organisation.

In 1904 the War Office underwent a reorganisation and, as an economy, the AAG's section H was placed in the charge of the War Office library and the post of DMI abolished. Two years later, when Colonel Davies was transferred elsewhere, the post of Deputy Director was also abolished although Major George Cockerill (later Tory MP for Reigate) was appointed to the section.

On 1 January 1908 Colonel Edmonds took over from Cockerill and concentrated on the apparently growing problem of foreign espionage. As well as drafting new amendments for the Official Secrets Act he began preparing contingency plans for the creation of a modern secret service. His work included drawing up a list of personnel with suitable qualifications for intelligence duties and developing assessments of the menace of Britain's large population of aliens.

It had been Gladstone's administration in 1885 that had first tried to monitor the growth of London's overseas residents by introducing an Aliens Registration Bill but it had been decisively rejected by Parliament. It was not until early in 1909 that the Committee of Imperial Defence invited the Police Commissioner, Sir Edward Henry, to serve on a special sub-committee to formulate policy on the subject for the Cabinet. Prior to that date the Branch had been able to supply the Home Office with estimates of the numbers of foreigners living in the capital, but there were no accurate statistics kept by statute.

The first meeting of the Sub-Committee on the Treatment of Aliens was held on 7 July 1910 and was chaired by the Home Secretary, Mr Herbert Gladstone. The others in attendance were Lord Haldane (War Minister), (Sir) Reginald McKenna (First Lord of the Admiralty), Major-General Sir Spencer Ewart (Director of Military Operations), Sidney Buxton (Postmaster-General), Sir George Murray (PUS at the Treasury), Sir Charles Hardinge (PUS at the Foreign Office), Brigadier-General Sir Archibald Murray (Director of Military Training), the Secretary of the Committee of Imperial Defence, Rear-Admiral Sir Charles Ottley, and Lord Esher, a former MP and Secretary for Works and Public Buildings.

The Committee's first task was to examine a paper prepared by Colonel Edmonds, and it was this document which was to be the basis of Britain's modern secret services.

Edmonds had been introduced to intelligence work during the Russo-Japanese War when he had monitored the hostilities for the Committee of Imperial Defence's Far Eastern section. In October 1906 Major-General Sir Spencer Ewart, the Director of Military Operations and Intelligence, transferred him to MO5, a newly formed security intelligence section which had inherited most of the Section H records and some of its responsibilities. MO5 was staffed by a retired Branch detective, John Macarthy, and Major William Adam who was elected to Parliament as MP for Woolwich in 1910.

The thrust of Edmonds' argument was that Britain had failed to recognise the threat from Germany. He claimed that a number of his German friends, now living in England, had been approached by German Embassy officials and asked to supply reports on such matters as movements of warships and work in dockyards. Edmonds said that he himself had recognised a German artillery Captain, whom he had been introduced to in Metz, working as the headwaiter at the Burlington Hotel, Dover. The man, who had been in the habit of taking lengthy walks along the coast, had apparently fled soon after Edmonds had challenged him.

Edmonds was particularly friendly with William Le Queux, the popular thriller writer who specialised in producing hair-raising tales of espionage. One of his many successes was a novel entitled *Spies of the Kaiser*. Largely thanks to Le Queux's efforts Scotland Yard, the government and the War Office were inundated with letters denouncing the activities of suspicious foreigners in ports and dockyard towns. Many of the cases were collated by Edmonds who produced a map of the British Isles marked with the location of every identified German agent. The map was reported to have had a remarkable effect on the Sub-Committee. Not everyone, however, took the German threat very seriously. On one occasion, Edmonds later recalled, a German officer wrote to his English girlfriend urging her to leave Bournemouth immediately as the south coast was about to be invaded. Edmonds was sent the letter by the patriotic lady, and showed it to the Chief of the Imperial General Staff, Sir William Nicholson. Nicholson thought the incident highly amusing and suggested that "it was a case for the Director of Public Morals". He was by no means the only person to underestimate the threat. In 1906 a joint War Office and Admiralty committee had reviewed the Official Secrets Act and asked Lord Desart, then Director of Public Prosecutions, whether the police might be granted a search warrant on the basis of a "moral certainty" that a suspect was a spy. Lord Desart replied that such a request would have to be refused.

The Sub-Committee listened attentively whilst Edmonds presented his paper, and were suitably appalled to learn that although there were comprehensive plans to defend each of the Colonies and the naval coaling stations, there was no overall defence scheme for the British Isles. Edmonds emphasised the dangers of the Anarchist bombers and urged the creation of an Empire Security Service. His plan was approved by the Sub-Committee and the Cabinet, and his former assistant in the Far East Section of the Committee of Imperial Defence, Major Vernon Kell, was appointed to head the Home Section of the new Secret Service Bureau.

The Bureau was initially divided into two semi-independent departments, the Home Section and the Foreign Section. Both were obliged to work with little financial or logistical support, although Kell made a point of building a strong friendship with the Branch's Commander, Patrick Quinn. Quinn was an Irishman from County Mayo, and Kell too had strong Irish connections. His wife, Constance Scott, whom he had married in April 1900, was the daughter of the White Star Line's manager in Cork.

The first major case of foreign espionage on which Quinn and Kell collaborated was that of Siegfried Helm who was caught mapping fortifications at Portsmouth in the summer of 1910. Helm admitted being a regular officer in the German Army and was convicted at his trial at Winchester in November 1910. However, the judge, Mr Eldon Bankes, freed Helm on the grounds that he had already spent quite enough time in custody already. In fact he had only been detained a month.

Helm's absurdly light sentence caused consternation in London where such blatant acts of espionage were regarded rather more seriously, and Asquith's Liberal government was again lobbied to have the Official Secrets Act tightened up. The previous attempt, made by the Lord Chancellor, Lord Loreburn, had failed in June 1908. A new Bill was accordingly introduced into the House of Lords on 17 July 1911 and received the approval of the Commons just over a month later, on 18 August. The speed of its passage through both Houses of Parliament remains a record. Indeed, the Act itself remains largely unchanged on the Statute Book today.

However, before the new Act received the Royal Assent a second German suspect came to the attention of the Branch. He was Oberleutnant Max Schultz, a 15th Hussars officer who was gathering naval intelligence in Plymouth while posing as a journalist representing the *German News Agency*. Schultz had been particularly interested to discover how quickly British seamen could be recalled from leave, and how long it might take the Mediterranean and Far East Fleets to return to home waters. His inquisitiveness was reported to the police in Plymouth by Samuel Duff, a local solicitor of his acquaintance, and early in the summer Herbert Fitch travelled down from Scotland Yard to investigate.

Fitch interviewed the solicitor and then arranged for him to attend further meetings with Schultz. At a second meeting, held aboard Schultz's houseboat on the River Yealm, the German offered Duff a salary of £50 per month for "interesting news items concerning the British army or navy". Once Schultz's guilt had been established the Branch obtained a warrant to read his mail, and a letter addressed to a certain "Monsieur Pierre Thissen" of Ostend was intercepted. The reply, which was postmarked Rotterdam, congratulated Schultz on gaining a recruit and warned him to beware of "the damned English Police". The solicitor drew up a formal contract of employment for Schultz to sign, and then began supplying him with bogus intelligence. Duff continued in his role as double agent until late in July, when Fitch judged that enough incriminating evidence had been obtained. Schultz was arrested and appeared before Plymouth magistrates on 19 August 1911 charged with breaches of the 1889 Official Secrets Act. He was tried at Exeter Assizes and sentenced to twenty-one months' imprisonment.

As well as changing the law, MO5 took a number of other precautions to improve Britain's security awareness. A new, relatively simple cypher, known as the Double Playfair, was introduced for field communications and liaison officers were sent to Japan to learn their counter-espionage skills. Intelligence classes were instituted for the benefit of junior officers to teach them basic security procedures, such as the routine burning of discarded signals and the secure handling of carbon copies. At one such lecture, conducted at a university lecture theatre in Liverpool, the German Consul was found sitting in the auditorium. Henceforth the identities of those in the audience were checked.

The Germans were increasingly being recognised as Britain's most probable opponent, and tension between the two countries was heightened during the summer of 1911 by the Franco-German dispute over Agadir. The Foreign Secretary, Sir Edward Grey, publicly warned Germany that Britain would take France's side if hostilities resulted and war fever gripped the country.

It was in this anti-German atmosphere that Germany tried to conduct its intelligence operations, and soon after Schultz's conviction the Branch were called in to investigate yet another case of espionage, this time in Portsmouth.

The case had begun when a retired naval rating named William Salter had placed an advertisement in a local paper offering his services as an enquiry agent. One of the replies came from a Captain Hugh Grant who suggested that a German coal magnate named Peterssen would pay well for information concerning British warships. Grant claimed that Peterssen had heard rumours of a coal strike in England and wished to supply the navy with coal the moment the strike began. Salter promptly reported his conversation to the Admiral Superintendent of Portsmouth who, in turn, handed the case to the Branch. Herbert Fitch was assigned the case, having covered himself with glory at Exeter, and interviewed Salter. Salter agreed to take on the role of a double agent and after a second rendezvous Captain Grant was followed back to a lodging house in Southsea.

Fitch made a covert search of Captain Grant's rooms while he was out one afternoon and found a number of incriminating letters in a cypher, as well as a loaded automatic. He was arrested, and subsequently identified as Heinrich Grosse, a German merchant navy officer who had once served a ten year sentence for forgery in Singapore. He claimed that a second forgery charge in Hamburg had been dropped on condition he spied against England. He was tried at Winchester Assizes the following February and sentenced to three years imprisonment. *

No sooner had Grosse been convicted than another case of German espionage came to light. An Edinburgh landlady denounced one of her lodgers, a Dr Armgaard Graves, as a spy and

---

* He was released from prison in April 1914, but was interned as an enemy alien the following August. He subsequently died in an internment camp.

the local police launched an investigation. The man claimed to be a
Dutch subject and indignantly called on the Chief Constable,
Roderick Ross, when he discovered that detectives had searched his
rooms. Ross denied his men had done any such thing, and Graves
moved on to Glasgow.

In fact the Edinburgh detectives had failed to find anything
suspicious about Graves, and it was not until the Branch were
called in on an apparently unconnected case that any progress was
made. It seems that Graves communicated with his employers in
Germany via a covert post office in London. Here his instructions
were readdressed and sent on to him as "James Stafford, c/o the
GPO, Glasgow." As additional protection the Germans had printed
several business envelopes marked with the name and address of
Burroughes, Wellcome, the chemical manufactuers. One such
letter, containing a set of instructions typed in German and five
ten-pound notes, went astray and was returned to the Burroughes,
Wellcome head office in Snow Hill, London. There the forged
stationery was quickly spotted and the matter placed in the hands
of the Yard.

On 14 April 1912 Dr Graves was arrested at the Central Station
Hotel in Glasgow by Detective Inspector Trench and charged with
espionage. A search of his hotel room revealed a wealth of
incriminating notes which, in the main, related to a new fourteen
inch naval gun then under construction at the Glasgow munitions
firm of William Beardmore. His trial began the following July, and
he was found guilty of Official Secrets Act offences. The Lord Chief
Justice of Scotland sentenced him to eighteen months' imprisonment.*

All these cases of German espionage served to highlight the
inadequacies of Britain's defences, for none of the spies had been
caught by routine detective work or successful counter-measures.
The arrest of each was entirely due to the prompt action taken by
ordinary members of the public. If three such cases had accidently
come to light, how many other agents were at work undetected?
This dilemma was one of the motivating factors behind the
compilation of the War Book, a series of general orders to be issued
in the event of an outbreak of hostilities with Germany. The
Branch calculated that there were some 50,000 Germans living in
England and one of the government's first tasks should be to
prevent them from returning to the fatherland to join up. Similarly,

---

* Graves did not complete his sentence. He accepted what was, undeniably, an ill-
judged offer from MO5 to work for them against the Germans, and was secretly
released from Barlinnie Prison in December 1912. By the following June Graves
was in New York publicising his deception of the British Secret Service.

a substantial tonnage of German shipping was invariably loading or unloading in British ports, and again the Cabinet were advised to seize these valuable assets at the earliest moment. The Branch reported that without a War Book of orders which could be executed instantly the police would have no authority to hold enemy ships. Indeed, if they attempted to sail, the police would not be legally able to request assistance from the military.

The War Book also provided instructions for dealing with aliens. The Branch, together with the Aliens Department of the Home Office, estimated there were probably 250,000 foreigners resident in England at any one time, but there was still no accurate method of arriving at an exact figure. The 1905 Aliens Act had not allowed for compulsory registration so the Branch had been obliged to set up an unofficial register of aliens known to be living near naval establishments.

The Branch's greatest coup took place soon after the funeral at Windsor of King Edward VII in May 1910. Superintendents Quinn and Spencer were anyway planning to conduct a major security operation for the procession, but one of their principal objectives was to provide a senior member of the Kaiser's entourage with round-the-clock surveillance. The officer concerned, Captain von Rebeur-Paschwitz, was suspected of being an intelligence officer and the Branch were anxious to record any contacts he might make while in England. Inspectors Drury and Seal were assigned to this job, and once the funeral was over they trailed the German back to London. The Branch men followed their quarry all over the capital, and at one point nearly lost him. After a heavy dinner at the Café Royal he retired to his hotel, only to slip out through a back door a short time later. The German took a cab to the Caledonian Road and then, well after midnight, spent more than an hour in a barber's shop. Drury and Seal telephoned the Yard and were soon joined by Superintendent Quinn. All three kept watch on the barber's shop and then followed the German back to his hotel, where he remained for the rest of the night.

The following day the Branch established that 402A Caledonian Road was rented to a German named Karl Gustav Ernst. A warrant was obtained to intercept his mail, and for the following three years every letter posted to and from the barber's shop was discreetly copied, with the name of every addressee entered on a Suspects Index. As we shall see, this remarkable operation was to pay high dividends, for Ernst was acting as a covert post office, servicing the communications of several German networks.

CHAPTER III

The German Networks

The wartime counter-espionage work of the Special
Branch remains in the obscurity which, for the same
reasons, shrouds the similar machinations of Military
Intelligence. In general the Official Secrets Act blocks
the curiosity of the historian – and no doubt rightly.

Douglas G Browne in *The Rise of Scotland Yard*
(Harrap, 1956)

Responsibility for monitoring German intelligence-gathering operations in England during the pre-war period was spread between
three quite separate organisations: the Branch, the GPO and Kell's
embryonic Security Service.

For the first twelve months the Home Department of the Secret
Service Bureau was staffed by Kell and one assistant from the Boy
Scout Movement, Stanley Strong. Eventually he obtained permission from the War Office to employ two retired Branch officers,
Superintendents William Melville and John Macarthy. Melville
had retired from the Branch in November 1903, having completed
thirty-two years in the Metropolitan Police, and there were few
officers with his encyclopaedic knowledge of espionage and
subversion. He had been responsible, as we have seen, for rounding
up the Walsall Anarchists in 1887 and had arrested several of the
Fenian bombers. His duties had included guarding Queen Victoria
and, up until the time of his resignation, he had been the King's
principal bodyguard. He had also performed similar services for the
Kaiser and the President of France when they had visited England.
No one was better qualified to advise Kell on counter-intelligence
and counter-espionage.

Although the Branch had initiated the surveillance on Ernst it
was left largely to Kell and Melville to co-ordinate the operation.
For example, it was Kell who explained the situation to the GPO
Chief, Sir Alexander King, and arranged for Ernst's mail to be
intercepted and photographed. This operation, sanctioned by

warrant from the Home Secretary, Winston Churchill, yielded instant success. Ernst and his assistant, Wilhelm Kronauer, had redirected letters to both Grosse in Portsmouth and Graves in Glasgow. In order to protect this important source no evidence was offered at either's trial concerning the mail intercepts, and in each case the convictions had been obtained on testimony from ordinary witnesses. Thus the Caledonian Road branch of the German Secret Service came increasingly under the control of the Security Service. Every day Ernst's post would be delivered to the GPO headquarters and carefully opened. The contents were copied by a team of photographers, and then the letters were returned into the regular post. The specially trained clerks who carried out this delicate operation were Edgar Bourne, Frederick Booth, John Duncan and Alfred Brodie. The letters were all written in German, and the copies were translated by DI John Briggs at the Yard. Gradually Kell and Melville developed an idea of the extent of the German espionage system in England and were able to request Quinn to assign Branch detectives to investigate individual cases. They also built up a card index of people communicating with Ernst, and it was this weapon which was to prove so effective at the outbreak of war.

In June 1912 the Ernst "post office" betrayed the identity of a Royal Naval Warrant Officer named George Parrott. Parrott was in charge of the Navy's rifle range at Sheerness and was an expert on naval ordnance, having served on *HMS Agamemnon* as a Gunnery Officer, and had been involved in the design and building of the ship's guns on the Clyde. On 11 July Parrott applied for leave and sent a telegram to one "Richard Dinger" in Berlin announcing his intended arrival. Two days later Parrott was tailed from Sheerness by DI Herbert Gray. The two men shared a second class railway compartment to Sittingbourne, where Parrott changed for Dover. On arrival he walked around the town and then bought a steamer ticket to Ostend. When he approached the pier Gray identified himself and questioned Parrott about his journey to the Continent. At first Parrott claimed to be a civilian, but when Gray challenged him Parrott reluctantly admitted that he was indeed a Royal Naval officer. He justified his subterfuge by concocting a story about having a mistress in Ostend. Gray searched both him and his bag, and in the absence of any incriminating evidence Gray allowed Parrott to catch his boat across the Channel, but Melville was in pursuit.

Melville kept his quarry under observation during the two hours that Parrott remained in Belgium and watched while he had an illicit rendezvous with an unknown man in the Gare Maritime. The two remained in conversation for more than an hour, and then

Parrott returned to England. The following day, when he turned up for work at Sheerness Dockyard, Parrott was questioned about his trip abroad. He claimed he had met a mistress. An official Naval Board of Enquiry followed, and Parrott was dismissed for failing to obtain permission to travel overseas.

The case, however, did not end there. Parrott moved to Juer Street, Battersea, in London and was soon engaging in further correspondence with Berlin via Ernst. He was apparently receiving mail in the name of "Mr G. Couch" at a tobacconist's in the King's Road, Chelsea. In addition to this a German language teacher in Sheerness, named Karl Hentschel, volunteered further details about Parrott's activities. The German, who had lived in England since 1909, claimed that he and his wife had been Parrott's accomplices, and that they had since suffered a cut in their pay from Berlin. Hentschel agreed to make a detailed statement to the Branch in exchange for a formal immunity from prosecution. Terms were agreed, and on 16 November two Branch officers, Detective Inspectors Riley and Parker, delivered a letter addressed to Mr Couch at the tobacconist's at 136 King's Road. Then they waited for Parrott to collect his mail and when he arrived they arrested him and took him to Chelsea police station. The next day Parrott was invited to open the envelope, which bore an East End postmark; inside was a five pound note and an intelligence questionnaire signed by "Richard".

A search of his bank account showed at least fourteen previous payments, all made with sterling notes that had been in circulation in Germany.

Parrott was charged with offences under the Official Secrets Act and was sent for trial at the Old Bailey in January 1913. He was found guilty and sentenced to four years imprisonment by Mr Justice Darling. The fact that Parrott had been arrested by George Riley was particularly ironical, for the GPO letter interception unit had copied a letter sent by Parrott to Ernst just four days before his arrest. In it he said:

> I have sent you last Sunday's paper. From what I can see of the case Hentschel will go over to the British Secret Service just as the doctor from Glasgow has done. It has also occurred to me that Hentschel's wife's maiden name was Miss Riley, and that one of Scotland Yard's Special Service inspectors, who had the case in hand, is also called Riley.

Hentschel was never called on as a witness, but he was clearly a marked man as far as the Germans were concerned so Kell financed a new life for him in Australia. Unfortunately life in New South

Wales failed to come up to Hentschel's expectations and he returned to England in October 1913. Kell declined to help Hentschel further so the German carried out a threat to make a new confession to the police. His first try, in Chatham, was rebuffed, but on the second attempt, in the City of London, Hentschel's statement was taken seriously and he was charged with offences under the Official Secrets Act. As soon as his case appeared before the Chief Magistrate in Bow Street Hentschel proclaimed his immunity from prosecution, and the Director of Public Prosecutions, Mr Archibald Bodkin, considerably embarrassed, withdrew the charges and had Hentschel dismissed. Nothing further was heard of Hentschel and he escaped internment during the war, so no doubt Kell's department decided to subsidise his continued silence.

Between the time of Parrott's dismissal from the Navy in August 1912 and his trial the following January, a further case of German espionage came to light. On this occasion the Ernst post office was not responsible for providing the first leads. The case began on 15 October when a hairdresser in Portsea, Levi Rosenthal, was approached by a man calling himself William Klare and asked if he could obtain a document concerned with submarines from Portsmouth Dockyard. Rosenthal said he could, and entered into negotiations with Klare. However, Rosenthal had no intention of betraying the country of his adoption and reported the matter to his neighbour, Councillor Edward Privett, who promptly informed Inspector Savage of the Dockyard Police.

At this stage there was little evidence against Klare so it was agreed that a third individual, Charles Bishop, should be introduced to the spy. Bishop was the senior clerk in the Paymaster-in-Chief's office and it was to be his task to establish Klare's intentions. Between October 1912 and the following February Bishop and Rosenthal met with Klare on several occasions and agreed a fee for smuggling a particular book out of the Dockyard, the annual Torpedo Report.

The negotiations continued, under Savage's surveillance, until 19 February when Klare announced that he had finally received the go-ahead from Berlin to purchase the Report. He showed the letter, briefly, to Rosenthal, who noticed it bore a London postmark, before throwing it on a fire. Later that same day Bishop delivered the Report to Rosenthal's shop and handed it over to Klare. As soon as Klare left the building with it he was arrested by Inspector Savage.

It was subsequently discovered that Klare was really Wilhelm Klauer, who had first come to London from Germany in 1902, as a

kitchen porter. He had married an English prostitute and had lived
off her income, although he occasionally masqueraded as a dentist
and had even put up a plate on the door of his lodgings. In fact he
had attracted less than half a dozen patients, of whom the majority
had been sailors. Klauer's trial opened at the Hampshire Assizes on
26 June 1913 before Mr Justice Ridley, and, having heard all the
evidence, the jury took just three minutes to convict him. He was
sentenced to five years imprisonment, and the Court burst into
applause.

There was a strong probability that Klauer's letter, spotted by
Rosenthal, had been redirected by Ernst in London, but it did not
appear among those intercepted by Kell. It may, of course, have
been one of the many which undoubtedly slipped through the net.

In any event, the Branch were not entirely occupied by counter-
espionage duties during the two years leading up to the Great War.
The Suffragette Movement had grown so militant that a number of
Cabinet ministers demanded Branch bodyguards. On one memo-
rable occasion Detective Sergeants Andrews and Woodhall fought
a male sympathiser in Gatti's Restaurant in the Strand who,
wielding a whip, was intent on leaving a permanent mark on Lloyd
George. In another incident DS Tom Nalty protected Winston
Churchill from a woman armed with a similar weapon who had
turned on the Home Secretary in a railway carriage.

In June 1913 Sir Melville Macnaghten retired after ten years as
Assistant Commissioner (Crime), and his place was taken by Basil
Thomson, then Inspector of Prisons and Secretary to the Prison
Commissioners. Thomson had been educated at Eton and New
College, Oxford, and had enjoyed what can only be described as a
remarkably varied life. He had been Governor of Northampton,
Cardiff, Dartmoor and Wormwoods Scrubs Prisons and, during a
ten year period in the Colonial Service, had served in Fiji and
British New Guinea, as well as having acted as Prime Minister of
Tonga. He had also been called to the Bar in 1896 and had written
a number of entertaining books and plays. In 1909 he had come to
the attention of Winston Churchill when he had been appointed to
help assist Sir Evelyn Ruggles-Brise in organising the Central
Association for the Aid of Discharged Convicts, one of Churchill's
brainchilds. On top of all that he had earned a silver medal for a
life-saving exploit in the South Seas.

Following an internal reorganisation at Scotland Yard in 1909,
the job of Assistant Commissioner (C) gave Thomson responsibility
for serious crime, naturalisation, the Convict Supervision Office
and the Branch. The moment Thomson took over Macnaghten's
office it was clear that the operation of the Branch was going to be

his prime interest. In many respects the Branch were completely unable to cope with the many duties they had inherited. Large numbers of their manpower were devoted to personal protection assignments, while the still unofficial Register of Aliens had reached a record 28,380, of whom 11,100 were Austro-Hungarian or German subjects. In addition, Kell was himself desperately short staffed and relied on the Branch's resources for keeping the Ernst network under a reasonable degree of surveillance, and for maintaining an up-to-date Suspects Index.

Quinn and Kell probably wasted little time in briefing Thomson, and one can be certain that he was fully aware of the continuing operation centring on Ernst by 22 February 1914 when DI Hester arrested Mrs Maud Gould at Charing Cross Station.

The case had begun when the new landlord of the Queen Charlotte public house in Rochester, Mr George Benyon, found some papers belonging to the previous landlord. In December 1913 Benyon gave them to the property broker who had arranged the sale of the pub, Claude Rogers. Rogers examined the documents and, instead of passing them to the vendor, gave them to the police. There were two portfolios of Admiralty maps, a rental agreement for a house in Wandsworth, and a book of handwritten correspondence. Among them was the copy of a letter dated 8 October 1903. It read:

Referring to the interview you kindly granted to me yesterday, for which I thank you, I take the liberty of giving a brief outline of my past. Born in Germany in 1854, I came to England in 1858, and visited the Savoy School until 1868, when I was sent to Germany to complete my education. In 1870 the war with France broke out and I joined the Army and remained there until 1882, having received an iron cross and a captaincy. I then engaged myself to some engineers, and in 1888 went to America for two years. Returning in 1900 I took out patents for sky signs, swinging letters, and reflectors and got on well until the County Council condemned sky signs. This crippled me.

I then had an unexpected offer to go in the Secret Service, for which I was well paid. I visited nearly the whole of Europe , and owing to several narrow escapes nearly losing my life I entered commercial life... If you will employ me I can satisfy you that the cost of organisation would be thoroughly studied by me. My reason for leaving Stockholm was the deplorable state of the department. Trusting you will favour me with an early reply, and apologising for obtruding, your humble servant,
F.A. GOULD SCHROEDER.

Quinn and Kell already had a German named Adolph Schroeder on the Ernst Suspects Index, but this was the first clue that Schroeder was in fact the real name of the Queen Charlotte's previous landlord, "Frederick Gould". Schroeder and his wife had since moved to Wandsworth, in South London, and he had become a cigar merchant. Other letters recovered from the pub clearly identified Schroeder as a badly paid spy working for a man he referred to simply as "St". There could be little doubt that "St" was Gustav Steinhauer, a senior member of the Kaiser's intelligence staff who headed the Berlin end of the Ernst network. Under various guises Steinauer had directed Graves, Grosse, Parrott and probably several others.

The Branch placed a permanent watch on Schroeder's new address in Merton Road, Wandsworth, and Kell had his mail intercepted. On 9 February 1914 Schroeder received a telegram from Brussels offering him £30 from someone signing himself Schmidt. Several telegrams followed negotiating the price of whatever Schroeder had on sale, and this was followed by Schroeder's wife purchasing a second class return ticket to Ostend. DI Hester followed her into a railway carriage at Charing Cross and then arrested her. As she stood up DS Ernest Passmore spotted three envelopes fall from her travelling rug. He recovered them and then accompanied Mrs Schroeder and DI Hester to Bow Street. On the way Mrs Schroeder tore up some paper and tried to throw the pieces out of the window. These too were retrieved and later produced in evidence.

Once Mrs Schroeder was locked up safely at Bow Street Hester and Passmore raided 340 Merton Road and arrested her husband. The house was thoroughly searched and a number of incriminating documents were found. Schroeder's desk contained a six page intelligence questionnaire listing thirty-six queries concerning Royal Naval warships, and various other naval and military records. When the three envelopes carried by Mrs Schroeder were opened they revealed an Admiralty chart of Spithead and Bergen, a gunnery book and the engine room plan of a cruiser which was marked "Restricted".

Schroeder and his wife were both charged with offences under the Official Secrets Act and the Branch was represented at the committal proceedings by it's Head, Patrick Quinn. The trial at the Old Bailey opened on 3 April 1914 before Mr Justice Atkin. Schroeder, still answering to the name Frederick Gould, pleaded guilty and received six years imprisonment. Mrs Schroeder pleaded not guilty and no evidence was presented against her by the Attorney-General. The Judge therefore directed the jury to acquit her. As Sir John Simon later explained, the Branch had never been able to establish that Maud Schroeder had the slightest knowledge of what the envelopes contained, and her innocence of the offence had been stoutly defended by her husband.

The Schroeders' case was not, however, to be the last dealt with before the outbreak of war in the following August. At the beginning of the Whitsun weekend an electrician employed in Portsmouth Dockyard, Samuel Maddicks, boasted to a dockyard official that he was a German spy. The matter was duly reported to the Branch, and the following Monday Chief Inspector Sewell and DI William Hayman challenged Maddicks near the Forton oil storage depot. Maddicks again admitted he was a German spy and claimed he was due to meet "a foreign agent" in Ostend shortly. He was promptly arrested and his home in Bryerly Road, Fratton, searched. There the detectives found enough correspondence with someone in Potsdam to convince them that Maddicks had indeed been a spy. Nevertheless, when he appeared before a police court in June it was decided that the defendant was of unsound mind.

These events on the eve of war might have been expected to result in a substantial increase in the size of the Branch, but this was not to be the case. The authorised strength of the Branch in 1914 was one Superintendent, one Chief Inspector, ten Inspectors, forty-five Sergeants and fifty-six Constables, making a total of 114 officers in all. Of this number thirty- four were employed in Section "C" (Ports); five were attached to the Aliens Registry; twelve were locating suspects up and down the country; ten were protecting royalty and the Cabinet; five were investigating cases of sabotage for the Admiralty; four were searching passengers and their baggage at Victoria Station. When all the other miscellaneous duties had been taken into account there were only sixteen officers left to deal with day-to-day incidents. The Branch was so overburdened with work that Quinn feared that some of his men might suffer breakdowns. As we shall see, Quinn's requests for extra staff were denied by the Home Office.

CHAPTER IV

The Great War

> Before the outbreak of the war the Metropolitan
> Police had for some years, in co-operation with the
> secret service department of which I am speaking,
> been actively combating espionage. The work was
> taken up by a special branch of the CID; skilled
> officers were employed; foreign agents were traced
> and marked down; and there were several successful
> prosecutions even at that time.
>
> The Lord Chancellor, Lord Haldane, addressing
> Parliament on 25 November 1914.

When the war did finally break out in August 1914 the Home
Office and the Branch were well prepared. The contingency plan
prepared by Kell and Quinn had been constantly up-dated
throughout the summer and Sir Edward Troup, the PUS at the
Home Office had a new draft Bill to replace the unsatisfactory 1905
Act. The Bill was introduced in the House of Commons on 5
August and by seven o'clock had received the Royal Assent.
Combined with the Defence of the Realm Act (DORA), which was
given the Royal Assent on 8 August, the two Statutes gave the
Branch extensive powers to arrest, detain and deport undesirable
aliens. Within an hour of the Aliens Restriction Act coming into
force the Home Secretary, Mr Reginald McKenna, had signed the
necessary Orders in Council invoking the new powers.

Immigration facilities were limited to fifteen named ports and
three airports. The Aliens Restriction Act also legitimised the
Central Register of Aliens and placed a duty on every alien to lodge
his name and address with the local police. The Branch itself had
already indexed 45,000 names. Within the month 9,000 Austrians
and Germans of military age (between seventeen and fifty-five) had
been interned. By the end of the war more than 35,000 civilians
would have experienced internment.

By the time the country was officially at war, at 11 pm on 5
August, the Branch had already taken Ernst into custody on an

Official Secrets Act charge. The previous evening Chief Inspector Alfred Ward had raided Ernst's shop in the Caledonian Road where several of Steinhauer's letters had been seized. None of these items, apparently, had impressed the magistrate at Bow Street, who had promptly discharged Ernst. The prisoner was therefore taken to Brixton Prison under the Aliens Restriction Act. Much to the Branch's embarrassment Ernst challenged the legality of his detention by sending a petition to the Home Secretary. In it he pointed out that he was in fact a British subject, born in Hoxton, This was indeed true, and Ernst was released. He was, however, rearrested by Ward for communicating information to Steinhauer as soon as he stepped through the gates of the prison.

While Ward was emptying Ernst's premises of incriminating letters other Branch detectives were rounding up the rest of the network. Altogether twenty-one people were arrested on a charge of espionage in the first twenty-four hours of the war. Among them were Auguste Klunder, a German hairdresser of Commercial Street, London, Friedrich Diederich, then living at the Kenilworth Hotel, Great Russell Street, and Adolph Schneider, a German bookkeeper of West Dulwich. All, except Ernst, were eventually made the subjects of routine Home Office Exclusion Orders and interned. This device enabled the Branch to remove the suspects from circulation without having to amass the evidence required for an Official Secrets Act conviction.

Similar measures were taken against less serious cases which were inevitably reported to the Branch. Karl Hammer, a waiter at the Hyde Park Hotel in Knightsbridge was found to have a Winchester repeating rifle in his room, together with an atlas and a number of maps. The German Consul at Sunderland, Adolphus Ahless, was remanded to Durham Gaol on an Official Secrets Act charge, as was the Consul in the Hartlepools, Emil Peter, and in London Wilhelm Kronauer's widow, Marie Kronauer, was arrested by DS Cooper and charged with continuing her late husband's occupation.* Ten days after the declaration of war DS Cooper also arrested a gang of suspected spies, a German, a Hungarian and a Russian, but it turned out they had merely been stealing American Express travellers' cheques.

The public's growing awareness of German spies resulted in the Branch investigating dozens of cases, some of which were simply manifestations of anti-German hysteria. Karl Stubenvold, an Austrian employee of the Swan, Hunter shipyard, failed to get back

* It had been Kronauer who had sent Wilhelm Klauer the letter which had resulted in Klauer being arrested in February 1913, as described in the previous chapter.

to the Continent in time and was charged with illegal possession of his own drawings. At Sheerness Franz Losel, a German photographer, was arrested for resting his camera on the sea wall outside his house. No evidence was offered against him under the Official Secrets Act so he too was made the subject of an Exclusion Order. In Northern Ireland an alleged "German Cavalry officer", Paul Wentezel, was remanded in custody for obtaining and communicating plans and information useful to an enemy. Again, no evidence was subsequently produced in court. One man to find himself under arrest was Max Laurens, a music hall artiste and amateur inventor, who had volunteered his patented "inflammable aeroplane projectile" to the Admiralty. Instead of accepting the offer the Admiralty called in the Branch.

Among the inevitable mistaken arrests were those which fell into the category of sensible precautions. Heinrich Grosse, for example, the German spy arrested by Herbert Fitch in August 1911, was rearrested by DS Hendry on 7 August, just four months after his release from prison.

In spite of the many arrests no attempt was made to place any of the prisoners on trial until November. In the meantime, on 8 October, the Home Office issued a remarkable statement explaining the action that had been taken. It suggested that a Special Intelligence Department had been created by the Admiralty and the War Office to combat German espionage, and that prior to 4 August arrests had only been made when spies had taken steps "to convey plans or documents of importance from this country to Germany". As well as the six cases of espionage which were dealt with before the war (Helm, Grosse, Graves, Parrott, Klauer and the Schroeders) the Home Office announced that a further twenty identified spies had been arrested in August, and that a larger number ("upwards of 200") had been kept under regular observation. The statement then went on to point out that the DORA made espionage a military offence:

> Power is given both to the police and the military authorities to arrest without warrant any person whose behaviour is such as to give rise to suspicion, and any person so arrested by the police would be handed over to the military authorities for trial by Court-martial. Only in the event of the military authorities holding that there is no *prima facie* case of espionage or any other offence triable by military law is a prisoner handed back to the civil authorities to consider whether he should be charged with failing to register or any other offence under the Aliens Restriction Act.

In effect this transferred responsibility for prosecuting espionage cases from the civil authorities to the military. As a consequence the crime now became a capital offence; the maximum DORA sentence was life imprisonment.

In the opinion of the Home Office,

The Special Intelligence Department, supported by all the means which could be placed at its disposal by the Home Secretary, was able in three years, from 1911 to 1914, to discover the ramifications of the German Secret Service in England,

and as a result "the spy organisation which had been established before the war" had been smashed. This indeed turned out to be the case, as the German Intelligence Service quickly realised, so they resorted to other means.

So too, did Quinn and Kell. The joint operation to monitor Ernst's activities had been an unquestioned success, and his loss had no doubt severely reduced the Germans' ability to gather intelligence in England. Nevertheless it was widely believed that Steinhauer had been authorised by the Kaiser's War Office to use "enormous efforts and lavish expenditure of money" to rectify the situation. In retrospect the forces ranged against Berlin seem paltry. In the twelve months prior to the war the Branch's strength was one hundred and twelve men of all ranks. Their total budget was £19,325 8s 7d. The much vaunted "Special Intelligence Department" under Kell boasted a staff of fourteen.

By the time Ernst's trial began at the Old Bailey on 13 November 1914 the British tactics had radically changed. The Branch had more than doubled in size and Assistant Commissioner Thomson had negotiated the transfer of a number of senior Branch officers, led by James MacBrien, to the jurisdiction of the military. In effect this meant an amalgamation of Kell's department and the detectives who had worked on the prewar cases of German espionage. The Suspects Index was retained so as to keep a record of German "cover addresses" in neutral countries, although every one of the identified names had either been served with an Internment Order or had been observed to leave the country.

The key to the round-up of 4 August had, of course, been Ernst, and the GPO's covert interception programme. In the first weeks of the war the GPO's small interception staff were removed from their headquarters in Mount Pleasant and established, with much greater facilities and personnel in Salisbury House, an office block close to the Bank of England in the City. As we shall see, the Censorship Department was to provide the clues for the Branch which led to their capture of the first German spy to be executed in

England. However, in the meantime the postal censors were placed in the limelight by Ernst's trial.

There had been no attempt to hide Ernst's arrest, and Scotland Yard had made a routine announcement of it in time for it to appear in the national press on 6 August. By October, when Ernst made three appearances at Bow Street, the Germans could have had little doubt about the fact that all their correspondence via his hairdressing salon had been completely compromised.

The first charge against Ernst concerned an incident that had taken place in January 1912. At some date prior to that one of Ernst's confederates, a barber named Kruger, had successfully infiltrated his nephew into the Royal Navy. The nephew had taken the name Frederick Ireland and had joined *HMS Foxhound* as a stoker. Ernst had been instructed to write to Kruger's nephew, Ireland, for information, and as soon as he did this the Director of Naval Intelligence, Admiral Sir Alexander Bethell, had been informed. Ireland was removed from *HMS Foxhound* at Oslo and sent back to England where he was discharged.

The defendant was confronted in Court by copies of his letters to Steinhauer at various addresses in Germany. There were also letters which had been readdressed by Ernst to Gould when he was the licensee of The Queen Charlotte in Rochester. Among the correspondence, which ran to some two hundred separate items, were references to the arrests of Grosse, Graves, Klauer and Parrott.

After a trial lasting two days the jury convicted Ernst without even retiring to consider their verdict. He was sentenced to seven years imprisonment by Mr Justice Coleridge. Even before Ernst had been convicted there was evidence that the German intelligence organisations had taken measures to replace their lost networks.

The first case of attempted espionage revealed by the more intensive use of mail interception was relatively straightforward and harmless. The German Ambassador to London, Prince Lichnowsky, had been escorted by Branch detectives to Harwich early on the morning of 8 October 1914. There he and his staff caught a steamship that had been chartered for the occasion by the Admiralty. Once the Ambassador had left, all his mail was delivered straight to Mount Pleasant, and one of the first letters to arrive after his departure was an offer to supply details of the Mersey defences from a man in Liverpool who conveniently supplied his name and address. The Branch were called in and an eighteen-year-old porter living in Liverpool, Arthur Blackburn, was subsequently arrested on an Official Secrets Act charge. After a brief trial before Mr Justice Darling at Liverpool Assizes in October Blackburn was sentenced to two years' borstal.

Blackburn proved to be the first, somewhat trivial, catch made by the GPO and the Branch, but another more important case was already under way. The second case began on 6 September 1914 when an envelope posted in Liverpool was examined by John Featherstone, one of the postal censors. Inside was a second letter addressed to "Herr J. Stammer, Berlin W, Courbierrestrasse 8". The latter address had long since been registered on the Suspects Index as a cover for Steinhauer. The Branch were alerted, although there was little anyone could do until September 14, when a second letter to the same destination was intercepted.

The Letter Interception Unit then began a back-tracking operation to trace any further communications sent to a "postbox" in Stockholm. They discovered that on 30 August a telegram had been sent from Edinburgh General Post Office by someone signing themselves "Charles" The text read: "MUST CANCEL. JOHNSON VERY ILL. LOST FOUR DAYS. SHALL LEAVE SHORTLY. CHARLES."

The Post Office counter clerk, William Mills, had asked the sender to write his name on the reverse of the form, and when this was recovered it read: "Charles A. Inglis, North British Hotel". An Edinburgh detective was sent round to the hotel but by the time he had arrived Inglis had long gone. Nevertheless Inglis was identified by the hotel staff as an American tourist, aged between thirty and forty and clean-shaven. He had left a forwarding address of c/o the Cunard Company, Liverpool. From there DI John Levett established that Inglis had stayed one night at the London & North-Western Hotel in Liverpool on 28 September and then caught a steamer to Ireland.

On October 2 Inglis checked into the Great Southern Hotel in Killarney and was arrested there by Inspector Cheeseman of the Royal Irish Constabulary. Inglis was questioned at Killarney police barracks, where he protested that he was an American citizen, and was then escorted to London. It was during further interrogation at Wellington Barracks, Chelsea, that Inglis admitted his real name ...Carl Hans Lody.

Lody was a German subject and an officer of the German Naval Reserve. Before the war he had worked for the Hamburg-Amerika Line and had been married in New York. At the end of July 1914 Lody had volunteered his services to the War Office in Berlin. There he had been recruited as a spy and dispatched to Scotland on a neutral vessel, carrying an American passport removed from a tourist visiting Germany. All of this was admitted by Lody, although he refused to disclose the identity of the senior officer who had first interviewed him. In fact the Naval Intelligence Department, then headed by Admiral "Blinker" Hall, had provisionally named the man as Captain Tappken, the acting Head of German Naval Intelligence.

Lody was charged with "War Treason" in respect of the two letters he had posted from Edinburgh and was court-martialled at the Middlesex Guildhall before Major-General Lord Cheylesmore who sat with eight other senior officers. The evidence against Lody was overwhelming and in cross-examination he confirmed many of the details of his assignment. He was found guilty and sentenced to death. The execution was carried out in the miniature rifle range at the Tower of London on 6 November.

Almost as soon as the court-martial had pronounced its sentence the Branch were presented with another, more bizarre, case of German espionage. The case, which was to have considerable repercussions, centred on an American named Bridgman Taylor who had presented himself at the Foreign Office in London and demanded to see "the Chief of the British Secret Service". Taylor's story was extraordinary. He claimed to be an officer in the Mexican Army and was in a position to supply a mass of information about German military intentions, and in particular offered details of forthcoming Zeppelin air raids.

The Foreign Office official who initially interviewed Taylor was indeed a senior Secret Service officer who introduced himself as "Mr Campbell". In fact he was probably the Vice Chief of the Secret Intelligence Service, Major Cameron. However, instead of welcoming Taylor into the organisation he telephoned the Yard and had him arrested.

The Foreign Office referred Taylor to the Branch, and Basil Thomson interviewed him at the Yard on 4 November 1914. Thomson's hostile cross-examination of Taylor evidently took him completely by surprise, for within the hour Taylor had admitted that his real name was Horst von der Goltz, and that his American passport was a forgery. Von der Goltz had arrived at Tilbury on 4 November from Rotterdam on board the steamship *Batavia*. He had been allowed to land in spite of the fact that his American passport had been endorsed in Berlin only days beforehand, and he moved into Buecker's Hotel, Finsbury Square. Von der Goltz was formally arrested by Detective Sergeant McGrath for failing to register as an enemy alien and on 26 November was sentenced to six months imprisonment, to be followed by deportation back to the United States.

This might well have been the end of the matter but for an intelligence coup pulled off early in January the following year.

The coup centred on Franz von Papen, the German Military Attaché to Washington. Von Papen had long been suspected of master-minding the sabotage of Allied munitions in America. The President, Woodrow Wilson, was reluctant to fight a European war and the Germans were equally anxious to prevent vital war material from crossing the Atlantic. It was widely believed that one of von Papen's networks on the eastern seaboard had been responsible in May 1915 for alerting the U-boat fleet to the *Lusitania's* route and her cargo of military equipment.* In December 1915, after a series of botched sabotage operations and a successful propaganda campaign waged by Captain Sir Guy Gaunt, the British Naval Attaché in Washington, von Papen was declared *persona non grata* and ordered back to Berlin.

Von Papen's recall wrecked German plans for the execution of widespread sabotage operations in America and Canada, and at the same time gave the authorities in England the chance to make a detailed analysis of his efforts to date. This opportunity came about thanks to German insistence on keeping comprehensive financial records. When von Papen sailed for Germany, accompanied by the Naval Attaché who had also been expelled, he carried with him a complete financial statement dating back to the outbreak of the war when the Intelligence Service had entrusted him with large sums of cash earmarked for the recruitment of waterfront sabo-teurs. Naturally the Attaché was instructed to record every transaction so he could account for his considerable expenditure. The two Germans made the Atlantic crossing aboard the SS *Nordam,* and were afforded diplomatic immunity from internment when the vessel docked in Falmouth. As was customary von Papen had been granted a safe conduct to make his journey, but his immunity did not extend to his papers, at least according to the Branch detectives on the quay who seized them. Von Papen and his companion, Captain Boy-Ed, made furious protests, but to no avail. Among the more incriminating documents (which were later published in a government White Paper) was a cheque for two hundred dollars, in favour of a certain "Bridgman Taylor". Evidently von Papen had employed von der Goltz and an officer in the German Reserve named Werner Horn to blow up an important railway bridge in Canada in 1914. The bridge, which spanned the Welland Canal, was a vital link in the mobilisation of Empire troops in Canada. Its destruction would have delayed the departure

* In his 1952 memoirs Von Papen admitted signalling Berlin with the information but claimed it "had no direct connection" with the subsequent torpedo attack which sank the liner with terrible loss of civilian life.

of many thousands of troops destined for France. Horn had been intercepted before he could place his charges but it had proved impossible to establish that von Papen had been behind the plot. His meticulous financial records provided the necessary proof, and also served as damning evidence against van der Goltz, among many others.

Von der Goltz had routinely endorsed the reverse of von Papen's cheque and it was a fairly straightforward matter to compare his handwriting with the signature of Bridgman Taylor. On 30 January von der Goltz was escorted up to the Yard from Reading Gaol and confronted with the cheque by Basil Thomson. Also present were Vernon Kell (using the cover-name Carter), and Captain Hall, the DNI. Von der Goltz admitted his involvement with von Papen and on 2 February signed a long confession before Superintendent Quinn which identified several other saboteurs in Canada and the United States. His sworn statement was given extensive press coverage in the US and was also the subject of a government White Paper in April 1916. Thomson, delighted at his prisoner's apparent show of remorse, suggested that von der Goltz should be deported to the States immediately so he could testify publicly at the grand jury hearings of his former fellow conspirators. Von der Goltz seemed anxious to co-operate and was therefore granted an immunity from further criminal prosecution in England and was transferred to Lewes Prison pending his deportation. He later appeared as a witness at the trial of a German saboteur in America, that of Hans Tauscher, and von Papen's secretary, von Igel. As it turned out his evidence was inconclusive and resulted in only one conviction, that of an agent named Fritzen who received a mere eighteen month prison sentence.

The American authorities offered to return von der Goltz to England after he had given his evidence but Scotland Yard declined. As we shall see, the Branch already had quite enough German spies to deal with. Meanwhile von der Goltz busied himself with writing his memoirs which were published in New York in September 1917.*

* *My Adventures As A German Secret Agent*, McBride & Co.

CHAPTER V

The Espionage Offensive

> Also under the control of the Assistant Commissioner
> C is the Special Branch, whose functions briefly are to
> "keep an eye" on subversive elements, to protect
> members of the Royal Family or any other persons
> whose positions may make them possible objects of
> attack by lunatics or evilly disposed persons, to carry
> out enquiries in naturalization cases and, in war-time,
> to advise and assist in those obscure activities
> connected with national security about which wise
> men do not ask questions.
>
> H.M. Howgrave-Graham in *Light and Shade at Scotland
> Yard* (Murray, 1947)

The German espionage offensive against Britain was renewed in
the New Year of 1915 with the arrival of Anton Küpferle from New
York. He was a third class passenger aboard the White Star liner
Arabic which docked at Liverpool on 14 February. The ship had
completed a non-stop journey which had omitted the customary
stop at Queenstown in southern Ireland. This landfall had been
abandoned the previous November because of the increasing U-
boat activity in the western approaches, but if the *Arabic* had
stopped there it would have been met by the local White Star
manager, James Scott, who happened to be Vernon Kell's father-
in-law.

Within a day of arriving in Liverpool Küpferle had posted a
letter to a cover address in Holland which attracted the attention of
the censors. Written on the letterheading of "Küpferle & Co,
Importers of Woollens, De Kalb Avenue, Brooklyn" the text read:

> Just a few lines to let you know that I have arrived in Liverpool
> today and I am expecting to do business in London by tomorrow.
> I shall arrive in Rotterdam at the end of the week and I hope I
> have a little rest there until I am sailing off again after a few
> days. If I could fudge about till I will be done with my business

47

you could get me on the station but it will be very hard to tell. Expecting you are prepared for me, I remain, etc.

The censors handed the letter to Mrs Maud Smith, the Deputy Assistant Censor, who arranged for it to undergo some routine chemical tests. These were carried out by Mr Charles Mitchell, a chemist specialising in secret inks. When the letter was subjected to heat a separate message in German was revealed, written in between the lines of the original. The covert message detailed sightings of several Royal Naval vessels in the Irish Sea and disclosed that the author proposed to visit Dublin the following day. The Branch were quickly informed and a detective was available on 15 February to observe Küpferle board a ferry at Holyhead, bound for Ireland. Later that evening Küpferle booked into a Dublin hotel. He remained there for two nights, and then returned to England via Holyhead. Once again Küpferle's American passport was examined by a Branch detective who judged it to be genuine. Küpferle then travelled by train to London and registered at a hotel close to Euston Station. Meanwhile a second letter, posted by Küpferle in Dublin, was being examined by the censors. It provided further damning evidence so Detective Inspector Buckley and Sergeant McGrath were instructed to arrest the suspect. However, when they arrived at Evans's Hotel they discovered that Küpferle had left minutes earlier, and it was not until the following day that he was traced to the Wilton Hotel in Victoria. During the twenty-four hours he was missing Küpferle posted a third letter, enclosing a card from the Wilton Hotel. He was arrested at one o'clock on Thursday, 19 February, by DI Buckley. Amongst his luggage were found a bottle of a formalin-based disinfectant, a pen, and the remains of two lemons. It was later established that the secret ink used in his communications was a combination of lemon juice and formalin.

Küpferle maintained that he was a naturalised American citizen and denied being a German spy, but when he appeared at the Old Bailey on 14 May the prosecution had accumulated a good deal of evidence against him. The main evidence, of course, was the collection of letters intercepted by the censors, but the defendant was also confronted with another damaging item: a letter written by him in Brixton Prison which he intended to smuggle out to another German detainee who occupied an adjoining cell. In it he stated:

I believe Ypres and the neighbourhood have now fallen. If I could only see the day when the whole English trickery is exposed and her preparation and even alliance made known by the

Allies. English shame must be made known otherwise there will be no justice... Oh if only I could be at the front again for half an hour.

This letter made it perfectly clear that whatever Küpferle's claims, he was indeed a German national. This had a profound effect on the defendant who was also impressed by evidence given by the DNI, Captain Hall, who confirmed the damaging nature of Küpferle's secret messages. At the end of the day's session the defendant was driven back to Brixton, where, early the following morning, he committed suicide. He was found in his cell by a warder at 4.15 am, suspended from a ventilation grill by a white silk scarf. On a nearby slate he had written the following confession, addressed "To whom it may concern":

'My name is Küpferle, born at Sollingen in Baden. I am a soldier with rank I do not desire to mention in regard on my behalf lately. I can say that I have had a fair trial of the United Kingdom, but I am unable to stand the strain any longer, and take the law in my own hand. I have had many a battle and death is only a saviour for me. I would have preferred the death to be shot, but I do not wish to ascend the scaffold as a G and hope that the Almighty Architect of this Universe will lead me in the unknown land in the East. I am not dying as a spy but as a soldier. My fate I stood as a man, but I cannot be a liar and perjure myself. Kindly I shall remit to ask to notify my uncle, Ambros Droll, Sollingen in Baden, Germany, and all my estate shall belong to him. What I have done I have done for my country. I shall express my thanks, and may the Lord bless all yours.

On the reverse of the slate Küpferle had stated:

My age is 31 years and I am born June 11, 1883.

The letter "G" in the message was inside a masonic symbol (see Plate no. 4), indicating that Küpferle was a practising freemason. The entire text was read out to the Court later that day by the Attorney-General, Sir John Simon, who explained that Küpferle had stood on a thick book borrowed from the prison library to attach his scarf to the grill, and had then kicked it away. The Lord Chief Justice discharged the jury, and then set a date for the trial of two further German spies, Karl Muller and Peter Hahn.

The tight control over communications exercised by the British censors was responsible, once again, for bringing two further cases of German espionage to the Branch's attention. A letter posted to a

suspect cover address in Holland revealed secret writing. The text
of the message reported that "G" had recently travelled to
Newcastle, so the author was writing from "201" instead.

Censorship passed this information to the Branch, just as they
had in the cases of Lody and Küpferle, and enquiries were initiated
in Deptford. The local police explained that only one street, the
High Street, numbered beyond two hundred, and that 201 High
Street was owned by a baker named Peter Hahn who, in 1913, had
been declared a bankrupt. Despite his name, Hahn was a British
subject, born of a naturalised German father in Battersea. His
premises were searched by Branch detectives but no evidence was
found of espionage. Hahn denied knowledge of anyone calling
himself "G", but his neighbours remembered him being visited by a
tall Russian named Müller who lived near Russell Square,
Bloomsbury. The police there confirmed a Russian alien named
Muller registered with them, and apparently he had recently
moved to Newcastle. Müller was traced to his forwarding address in
Newcastle and arrested. He was fifty-eight years old, but was not a
Russian. He was in fact a Latvian, having been born in Libau.

Müller and Hahn were tried together at the Old Bailey and on 4
June 1915 were found guilty of espionage. Hahn was imprisoned
for seven years; Müller was sentenced to death, and was executed at
the Tower of London on 23 June. When Basil Thomson described
the case in 1922 (*Queer People,* Hodder & Stoughton), he suggested
that "the Germans did not hear of his death for some time, for
letters containing remittances continued to be received". This
would appear unlikely, given that *The Times* announced the
sentences in a brief statement on 5 June 1915.

In any event, the elimination of three spies in as many months
did little to dampen German enthusiasm for launching intelligence
operations. Between May and June 1915 no less than seven spies
were to be arrested by Branch detectives in England.

Credit for the first of these arrests, once again, was claimed by the
postal censors, but on this occasion there was an element of luck
involved. The letter which initiated the investigation had been
misdirected by postal sorters in Denmark, and instead of reaching
Berlin as intended, found its way to London. The letter was mailed
by a German American named Robert Rosenthal, who announced
his intention to spy in England under the cover of a patent gas-
lighter salesman. By the time the censors had passed the
information to the Branch, in May 1915, Rosenthal had virtually
completed his mission and was embarking on a ship at Newcastle
bound for Copenhagen. Rosenthal was detained before the ship
sailed and confronted with the incriminating letter. At first he

claimed that he was an employee of the American Relief Commission, but it later turned out that he was a former trainee baker who had been convicted of forgery before the war in Magdeburg.

Rosenthal was convicted of espionage and sentenced to death. He made two unsuccessful attempts at suicide and was hanged on 15 July 1915.

By August 1915 there were some one hundred and seventy postal censors working at Salisbury House, each averaging one hundred and twenty letters a day. In addition, nearly two thousand parcels had to be inspected for contraband. Every addressee was checked in the Suspects Index of known cover addresses in neutral countries, and it was comparison of this kind which led the Branch to Willem Roos in May 1915.

Roos was evidently a cigar salesman, for he submitted regular orders for Havana cigars to a Dutch firm of importers, Dierks & Company. In fact, according to the censors, he was one of two salesmen, for a man named Haicke Janssen was also doing a roaring trade in cigars with the same firm. Roos was eventually tracked down to the Three Nuns public house in Aldgate by Herbert Fitch, and arrested. His room was searched and, remarkably, no order books or cigar samples were to be found. Instead Fitch discovered several notes referring to naval towns visited by the Dutchman recently. It was later established that the notes were a code. "Hull, AGK" indicated *alter grosse kreuzer* (large old cruiser) while "KS" meant *kriegschiff* (battleship). A reference to "Coronas" signified a recent departure and "Rothschild" meant a recent arrival.

The arrest of Roos was quickly followed by the placing of a telegram order for cigars at a post office in Southampton. It contained the words "3,000 Cabanas AGK", meaning that the port contained three cruisers (which it did indeed), so Fitch travelled down to Southampton and arrested Janssen at his lodgings. Janssen denied knowing Roos but, when they were brought together at Scotland Yard, Roos acknowledged his fellow conspirator. Following this confrontation Roos feigned madness and tried to slash his wrists on the broken pane of a glass door in Cannon Row police station. When the Branch examined the belongings of both men it was discovered that they shared the same brand of cologne, which also doubled as a secret ink. Roos and Janssen were tried by court-martial in July 1915 at the Guildhall and sentenced to death. They were executed by firing squad on 30 July. Roos kept up his pretence of insanity until the last moment but Janssen made a complete confession and co-operated with MO5 and the Branch. In describing his background he claimed to have been decorated with a silver medal by the Board of Trade for taking part in the rescue of some five hundred passengers from the steamer *Volturno* in 1913. A check in the records confirmed that the claim was true.

While Fitch was engaged in tracing Roos and Janssen, other Branch detectives were on the trail of Lizzie Wertheim, a German woman separated from her naturalised British husband. Mrs Wertheim came to the Branch's attention after several naval officers based at Rosyth in Scotland had reported her inquisitiveness about the Grand Fleet. Mrs Wertheim was placed under discreet observation and followed back to London, where she met a young American in a Bloomsbury hotel. He was subsequently identified as Reginald Rowland, and was watched by Branch detectives.

The surveillance failed to turn up any incriminating evidence although the censors coincidentally spotted a letter in secret ink which contained information about *HMS Tiger*, then in Rosyth and due to sail to Scapa. A handwriting comparison indicated that Mrs Wertheim was the author of the letter, but before she could be arrested she had driven back to London. She was eventually arrested in Regent's Park Road and escorted to Scotland Yard for interrogation.

Meanwhile all letters posted by Rowland were being examined by the censors, and he appeared to be in the habit of sending copies of the London evening papers to various addresses abroad. Chemical tests on the pages revealed some writing in German in the stop-press spaces and this was enough to justify his arrest. Although Mrs Wertheim admitted nothing, Rowland's American passport betrayed him. It was a poor forgery and an interrogation by Basil Thomson yielded an admission of espionage. He stated that his real name was Georg Breeckow, a German subject who had lived in America since 1908. He claimed to have attended a German espionage school in Antwerp where he had been supplied with a secret ink disguised as hair tonic. A chemist confirmed that his hair tonic matched the secret ink found in the intercepted newspapers.

Mrs Wertheim and Breeckow were tried at the Old Bailey on 20 September 1915 and found guilty of espionage. Wertheim was sentenced to ten years imprisonment, but after serving five years at Aylesbury Gaol, died insane in 1920 in Broadmoor. Breeckow was sentenced to death and shot in the Tower of London on 26 October. Witnesses to the execution later suggested that Breeckow had appeared to succumb to a heart attack moments before the volley was fired.

While the cases of Mrs Wertheim and Georg Breeckow were being heard at the Old Bailey another spy trial was being conducted across the city at the Guildhall. Fernando Buschmann was a Brazilian who had been recruited into the German intelligence service before the war. Earlier in 1915 he had travelled to England as a commercial traveller but had run out of money. His first letter to Dierks & Co pleading for more funds was traced to his address in South Kensington, and he was arrested. He was executed at the Tower of London on 19 October 1915.

Fitch's next case was indeed a triumph of detection. The censors had intercepted a series of letters to a suspect cover address in Holland from a Joseph Marks in Gravesend. His correspondence centred on his stamp collection and he frequently referred to particular stamps which he either wished to acquire or exchange. A lengthy comparison between his lists and philatelist guides confirmed that several of the stamps mentioned simply did not exist. One, for example, was a French twenty centime stamp, unperforated and unwatermarked. No such stamp had ever been issued so Marks was called in for questioning. He explained that he was a Dutch tourist but when Fitch searched his rooms he found several incriminating notes, including the key to an elaborate code based on stamps. "Unused" meant arrived, "perforated" meant defended, "unwatermarked" meant submarines, etc. Instead of facing a court-martial Marks agreed to co-operate with Kell's department as a double agent and escaped with a five year prison sentence. While he served his sentence his Dutch contact was kept supplied with bogus military statistics. On his release in November 1919 he was escorted by Fitch to Dundee where he was deported back to Germany aboard the *SS Weimar*.

In spite of the obvious successes of the censors, the Germans continued to dispatch agents with the same cover-addresses and similar secret inks. Shortly after Buschmann's arrest, several postcards addressed to Rotterdam were intercepted in Edinburgh. They had been posted by a Uruguayan trader named Augusto Roggin. Roggin was traced to Luss, a tiny village on the banks of Loch Lomond, directly opposite the site of a torpedo testing range. Roggin was arrested without delay but he claimed to be entirely innocent of any espionage. He insisted that he had been buying agricultural machinery for his estate in South America, although during interrogation he made several slips about his alleged country of origin. Eventually he was confronted with his last postcard, mailed to a cover address in Norway, announcing a big horse purchase. Roggin was forced to admit that he had not bought a single animal since he had arrived at Tilbury at the end of May.

Roggin was court-martialled at the Guildhall in August and shot at the Tower of London on 17 September 1915.

Roggin had remained free in the United Kingdom for just eleven days, but even during those eleven days another German agent was traced by the censors. The trick of writing in the margins of newspapers had first been spotted in the Breeckow case, when the Branch had asked the censors to examine his outgoing mail. Further inspections of newspapers in the post led to a Swedish manager of a steamship company, Ernst Melin, who was posing as a Dutchman whose business had been ruined by U-boats. Melin was arrested at his lodgings in Hampstead, and he quickly admitted communicating with the Germans in a code based on a Baedeker Guide and a dictionary. He said he had been recruited before the war when he was short of money in Hamburg and claimed that he never intended to give away secrets. He merely wanted the Germans to keep him in funds. Melin was convicted at a court-martial on 20 August 1915. The death sentence was carried out on 18 September. It was by no means the last to take place in the Tower in 1915.

Even though the German Intelligence Service had suffered the loss of eleven agents in the first half of 1915 they continued to send replacements. Each was quickly identified by the postal censors and arrested by Branch detectives.

The first of the replacements to suffer this experience was Courtenay de Rysbach, a naturalised Briton of Austrian origins. He was a music hall actor, with a trick-cyclist act, appearing at a theatre in Glasgow when the postal censors alerted the Branch. They had intercepted a package containing two music scores addressed to someone in Zurich. The letter accompanying the songs was signed by "Jack Cummings" from the Palace Theatre, London. Examination of two of the scores, *On The Ladder of Love* and *On The Way To Dublin Town,* revealed a message written in secret ink between the bars of music. The case was given to the Branch, who quickly established that no "Jack Cummings" was known at the Palace Theatre. All the artistes who had appeared there were traced and de Rysbach was interviewed in Glasgow. This proved unsatisfactory, and he was brought down to London for detailed interrogation.

Apparently de Rysbach had been touring Germany when war broke out and he had been interned at the notorious Ruhleben Internment Camp with several hundred other British subjects. He claimed that in order to escape from the camp he had agreed to spy for the Germans, and on his release had made his way back to England via Switzerland, arriving at Folkestone on 27 June 1915. Ironically, on his return he had applied for a job in postal censorship. At his trial he argued that the secret message sent to Zurich had contained no useful information, and some of the jury at the Old Bailey evidently believed him because they were unable to reach a verdict. However, at a second trial in October 1915 he was found guilty and sentenced to life imprisonment.

De Rysbach was followed by a young Peruvian, Ludovico Hurwitz y Zender, who communicated with the German Intelligence Service through a cover address in Norway. During his brief career as a spy Hurwitz sent a series of cables to his "head office", a fish wholesaler in Oslo. He was interviewed by a Branch detective in Newcastle on 2 July but was unable to name a single person in either Glasgow or Edinburgh who might account for his large orders of sardines. His cables had been intercepted from both those cities. The Foreign Office then confirmed that the cover address was not that of any reputable merchant, and Zender was duly charged. He claimed the right to call character witnesses from Peru and his court martial was delayed until March the following year so they could appear for the defence. He was found guilty in spite of their testimony and was shot at the Tower of London on 11 April 1916. He was the last enemy agent in England to be executed during the Great War.

The next agent to arrive was Irving Ries, an American of German extraction who landed in Liverpool early in July 1915. The censors spotted him because of a letter containing English banknotes, and although it was not illegal to receive currency from abroad a routine enquiry was made by the Branch. He claimed to be a corn merchant and, unlike the other German agents, was able to produce a considerable amount of business correspondence to support his cover. The Branch accepted his story but sent his passport to the American Embassy for examination. Experts at the State Department denounced the document as a forgery and on 19 August Irving Ries was arrested at his hotel. He was court martialled on 4 October and executed on 27 October.

The last of the German agents to be arrested in the momentous year of 1915 was Albert Meyer, a German Jew who made a minor reputation for himself in the East End as a con-man. He had defrauded a number of landladies before he was finally arrested on a relatively minor charge. He claimed that he was about to receive funds from his parents who lived abroad, but the address he gave the police turned out to be a cover address high on the Suspects Index. Indeed, when a specimen of his handwriting was taken it matched several letters intercepted by the censors, each signed in a fictitious name. Meyer was tried by court martial on 5 November and executed on 2 December 1915.

All of the Branch's cases in 1915 were the result of close co-operation between the censors and, to a lesser degree, MO5, which updated the various Indices referred to by the censors. The key to the Branch's counter-espionage successes lay in the inability of the Germans to arrange a secure channel of communication with their agents. Each was obliged to use the GPO for transmitting messages, for all other means of communicating overseas was forbidden. It was even illegal for travellers to carry letters abroad for third parties. On 6 October 1916 a Belgian businessman was convicted under the Defence of the Realm regulations for allowing another person to take a letter back to Antwerp for him. A Branch detective at Tilbury had found the letter, together with about £120 in currency, on the courier. The letter was entirely innocent, and the businessman thoroughly respectable, but he was fined anyway. These port searches for both incoming and outgoing passengers proved a difficult obstacle for the Germans. The search procedure, carried out under the direction of MO5 Port Control Officers, also involved the completion of a financial questionnaire. This led the Germans to supply their agents with only the minimum of cash, which in turn required further funds to be transmitted through the regular mail. This fundamental weakness was exploited by MO5 who maintained a stable of controlled or "double" agents. Each time MO5 learned the location of a new cover address it was promptly added to the Suspects Index. It was then a relatively straightforward exercise for the censors to intercept all the letters posted to that address. By the end of 1915 there were 3,700 postal censors reading the mails at Carey Street, near the Strand, with smaller sub-offices in Liverpool (employing 1,700 censors), Folkestone, Gibraltar and Alexandria. In addition to this four British wireless interception stations (at Lowestoft, York, Murkle and Lerwick) monitored every signal broadcast by the German Foreign Office's transmitter at Nauen.

Very occasionally the system failed. In January 1915 a Belgian academic, Professor Emile Dupuis, was convicted of "communicating information gathered when an Examiner in the Censor of Neutral Countries' Mail office". In another, remarkable case, Julius Silber claimed to have spied in England completely undetected. He announced in 1931 in his book *Invisible Weapons* (published by Hutchinson & Co in England) that he had successfully penetrated the Postal Censorship Department between October 1914 and June 1919. Perhaps not surprisingly the Germans initially rejected the information he sent to addresses on the Suspects Index as being an obvious trap.

It seems the Germans eventually decided to test Silber's bonafides by dispatching an agent to make personal contact with him in London. The agent chosen for the mission was Eva de Bournonville, a Swede of French extraction who had been recruited whilst working as a typist for the German Military Attaché in Stockholm. However, instead of contacting Silber directly on her arrival in England in October 1915 she applied for a job in the Postal Censorship Department. She was turned down on the grounds that her referees were merely slight acquaintances. Shortly after her rejection the censors began intercepting letters containing secret writing. The letters were traced to a hotel in Upper Bedford Row but there was no means of identifying their author without employing a "barium meal". This exercise involved an MO5 officer checking into the hotel and telling the other guests prepared stories about military matters. This took place early in November 1915 and in due course one of the "indiscretions" appeared in an intercepted letter, in spite of a last-minute warning from Silber. The author was, of course, Eva de Bournonville who was arrested by Branch detectives on 15 November. A handwriting comparison confirmed her guilt and she was interrogated by Basil Thomson. Fortunately for Silber her subsequent confession omitted any mention of him. Thomson congratulated himself on concluding what he regarded as a successful case and Silber escaped undetected. Miss de Bournonville was tried at the Old Bailey on 12 January 1916 and sentenced to death by Mr Justice Darling. Her plea for clemency was granted by the King and her sentence was commuted to life imprisonment. She remained at Aylesbury Gaol until February 1922 when she was repatriated to Sweden.

Her arrest and conviction served further to undermine German confidence in Silber and, although he continued to forward naval and military information to Colonel Nicolai of the German Intelligence Service, apparently not much credence was attached to it.

The first weeks of 1916 saw the Branch preoccupied with a detailed analysis of the documents seized from Franz von Papen at Falmouth. They yielded a wealth of information concerning German espionage in North America and resulted in a number of previously unknown cover addresses being added to the Suspects Index. Meanwhile von Papen, who had completed his journey to Berlin on 6 January, was transferred to his regiment on the Western Front.

To date Britain's two major counter-espionage organisations, MO5 and the Branch, had dominated the intelligence battle in England. Unquestionably the successes they achieved prior to the New Year of 1916 can be attributed to the work of the post and cable censors who were by now fully established under the leadership of Colonel Arthur Churchill. They were, however, not entirely immune to the occasional lapse in security themselves, as has been seen in Silber's case, but early in 1916 a further, more embarrassing episode was unfolding.

Ignatius Lincoln, the son of a Hungarian rabbi named Trebitsch, had been born in 1880, in the small town of Paks, near Budapest. By a remarkable chain of adventures he was, by 1910, a naturalised British subject, a former Church of England curate (of Appledore in Kent) and the Liberal MP for Darlington. He was also a confidant of Lloyd George and an adviser of Seebohm Rowntree, the cocoa magnate. Two years later he was a bankrupt and had embarked on a career of espionage in the Balkans. Exactly who he worked for remains uncertain, but on 18 August 1914 he was back in London with a new position... that of Offical Censor at Mount Pleasant Post Office in the Hungarian and Rumanian Section. Lincoln only lasted a few weeks as censor before offering his (unspecified) services to the Home and Foreign Secretaries, who declined them, and to Winston Churchill, who also turned him down. Undeterred, Lincoln obtained an introduction to MO5 via a colleague in the Censorship Bureau, Colonel Bellamy. Lincoln was interviewed at the War Office by Vernon Kell, who wisely adopted the cover-name "Captain Kenny". Lincoln proposed a bizarre deception scheme to lure the German Grand Fleet into a trap, but the disadvantage of his plan was the requirement to disclose to him the current movements of the Royal Navy. Not surprisingly, the Admiralty vetoed the idea, whereupon Lincoln volunteered to act as a double agent against the Germans and pretend to offer them his services. "Captain Kenny" turned him down again so Lincoln apparently decided to go to work on his own. On 17 December 1914 Lincoln travelled to Rotterdam and wormed his way into the confidence of the German Consul there, Herr Gneist. Gneist evidently accepted Lincoln's tale of his determination to revenge himself for his bankruptcy by spying against his adopted country and recruited him into the German Intelligence Service.

Once Gneist had accepted him Lincoln sent a message reporting his success to "Captain Kenny" via the British Consulate in Rotterdam. On 2 January 1915 Lincoln returned to London equipped with a list of cover addresses and no less than three German codes. The following day he handed all of them over to MO5. This embarrassing turn of events left MO5 thoroughly confused, and Kell sought the help of Mansfield Cumming, the Chief of the Secret Intelligence Service, MI6. In the meantime a letter was sent to Gneist informing him that his latest recruit had fallen ill with pneumonia. Lincoln, however, was impatient to pursue his new role as double agent and pressed MO5 for action. After numerous brush-offs the ex-MP contacted various senior politicians, including Sir Henry Dalziel and Winston Churchill. In the face of further delays Lincoln actually presented himself at Churchill's office at the Admiralty and demanded to see him. The First Lord of the Admiralty said he was too busy to see his unwelcome visitor and sent him to the DNI, Captain Hall. In fact Hall had already been consulted about Lincoln's case and promised to see what progress had been made by the Security Service.

Nothing happened for a fortnight, but on 25 January Lincoln was summoned back to the Admiralty to receive a somewhat hostile interrogation from Hall and his Assistant DNI, Lord Herschell, who told him that his proclivity for espionage was both dangerous and unwelcome. Thoroughly alarmed by Hall's threats of impending arrest Lincoln decided to leave the country but before he could do so Hall ordered him to attend a second interrogation with Superintendent Quinn present. Lincoln survived the experience but the following day, on 20 January 1915, he was observed to board the *Philadelphia,* bound for New York.

Lincoln's enforced flight solved the problem of what to do with him, but any optimism about its duration was dashed on 23 May when Lincoln published "an authentic account of his work for the British Secret Service" in a New York newspaper, *The World.* These "disclosures" were followed by more the following week, and early the next month McBride & Company announced that Lincoln's forthcoming book would contain yet more "sensational revelations".

Lincoln was certainly in a good position to embarrass the British government as he had had dealings with virtually every intelligence organisation in the country and was on intimate terms with a number of senior Liberal politicians, including Lloyd George, who was then Chancellor of the Exchequer. As one might expect, it did not take long for a new solution to be found.

The ingenious method chosen to extract the government (*et al.*) from its predicament came in the form of affidavits sworn by two of Lincoln's former business associates. The first, made by a moneylender named Goldstein, centred on a financial guarantee used by Lincoln to secure a loan of £750. The document bore the signature of Seebohm Rowntree. The second affidavit, sworn by Rowntree, denounced the guarantee as a forgery. On the basis of this evidence a warrant was issued in London for Lincoln's arrest to answer a charge of forgery. As soon as the warrant had been issued the Foreign Office instructed the British Consul in New York to apply for the fugitive's arrest. On 4 August 1915 Deputy Marshal George R. Proctor detained Lincoln at his New York address and soon afterwards two Branch officers, Chief Inspector Ward and Detective Sergeant Cooper, arrived to escort the prisoner back to London. Although Lincoln's incarceration in a Brooklyn prison prevented him writing further newspaper stories it did give him time to fight the extradition proceedings, and it was more than six months before he finally appeared in the dock at the Old Bailey before Mr Justice Scrutton.

Lincoln's trial took place in July 1916, and he pleaded not guilty to two charges of forgery. His defence was weak, even though one of the prosecution witnesses, Mr Goldstein, admitted that the Admiralty had compensated him to the value of the forged guarantee. His attempts to call Winston Churchill, Sir Henry Dalziel, Captain Hall and "Captain Kenny of the War Office" all failed, and he was sentenced to three years imprisonment. He was never charged with espionage, in spite of the admission contained in his memoirs *Revelations Of An International Spy** that his motive for trying to penetrate British Intelligence was to help the Germans. Upon his release in September 1919 he was deported to his native Hungary.

The New Year of 1916 was to be one of change for the Branch; it was also to be the year of an historic confrontation between the head of Special Branch and Mata Hari, and the first civil treason prosecution of the war.

The changes experienced by the Yard were chiefly caused by their own successes in the counter-espionage field. As well as having been responsible for the arrests of nine enemy agents who had been executed (and a much greater number of other suspects who had merely been detained), they had recorded the location of more than 30,000 enemy aliens and participated in the programme of civilian internment. A number of experienced Branch officers, such as John Macarthy, James MacBrien and William Melville, had been drafted into the Security Service which, on 1 January 1916, was formally redesignated MI5 as part of Lord Kitchener's reorganisation of the War Office. As part of his recommendations a post of Director of Military Intelligence (DMI) was created. Prior to this innovation the province of military intelligence had been a sub-section of the Directorate of Military Operations and Mobilisation, headed by Major-General Sir Spencer Ewart. The new DMI was Major-General Sir George Macdonogh, and at his instigation a

* McBride & Co, New York, 1916.

further ten Branch officers were attached to the newly formed Intelligence Corps and given counter-espionage responsibilities on the Continent. By the end of the war MI5 employed some eight hundred staff, while some six thousand other personnel were engaged on counter-intelligence duties. A very limited number of volunteers, among whom was Detective Inspector Ginhoven, were selected for "Special Intelligence" work which involved reconnaissance missions behind the enemy lines.

The Special Branch contingent in France was led by Detective Inspector Martin Clancy, and was based at the British Expeditionary Force's GHQ at St Omer. Among the first to arrive there was Detective Sergeant Daniel Maclaughlin who was the Branch's first casualty of the war. He was assigned the job of bodyguard to the Secretary of State for War, but on 6 June 1916 he died beside Field-Marshal Lord Kitchener when HMS *Hampshire,* en route to Russia, was sunk off the Orkneys.

The loss of HMS *Hampshire* and Lord Kitchener was a shattering blow to morale at home and in the Forces, and an intensive investigation was launched to establish the exact circumstances of the disaster. Rumours abounded of Bolshevik sabotage and betrayals by enemy agents. The enquiry's conclusions (which were subsequently published in a government White Paper) decided that the *Hampshire* had been sunk by incompetence rather than espionage. Nevertheless there remained an air of mystery surrounding the tragedy which, inevitably, was exploited by several self-publicists. A seaman who had served on the U-22, Heinz Hickman, later claimed in America that his submarine had torpedoed the cruiser, whilst a self-styled "uncaptured German spy" suggested he had signalled details of the *Hampshire*'s route to another German submarine. Perhaps most bizarre of all was Frederick Duquesne's story of having smuggled himself aboard *Hampshire* to guide a U-boat into the attack with a torch.*

The evidence tends to support the theory of the cruiser striking a mine in extremely heavy seas. In any event only sixteen of the crew survived the incident, and of them two subsequently died of exposure. It was later established that the U-75 had recently laid a string of twenty-two mines between Marwick Head and the Brough of Bersay. This area would, under normal circumstances, have been regularly swept by minesweepers but on this occasion the appalling conditions had kept the mine-sweepers in the shelter of Scapa Flow. For the Branch, Dan Maclaughlin's death was a bitter, and possibly avoidable blow, and deprived it of a very popular officer.

* *The Man Who Killed Kitchener*, Clement Wood, *1932*.

One of the survivors reported seeing Maclaughlin and his charge on deck soon after the ship had been struck, and Captain Savill had apparently ordered a boat to be lowered for them. The heavy seas had, however, prevented one from being launched successfully.

The name of Sir Roger Casement first achieved worldwide recognition in July 1912 when his report on the ruthless exploitation of the of the Congo by the Belgian government was published by the British Foreign Office. Casement was a career Consular Service officer, born in Dublin to an Ulster Protestant. In August 1902, after more than five years in West Africa, Casement was asked to investigate alarming accounts describing the terrible conditions of the Congo. This land-locked, equatorial state was owned and ruled, almost as a private fiefdom, by King Leopold of the Belgians. An estimated twenty million natives lived in the region, apparently in abject slavery. The Belgian government had denounced the stories of systematic oppression that had filtered out as exaggerated and inaccurate so the Foreign Office appointed Casement to conduct his own eye-witness report. In January 1906 Casement returned to London to present his report personally to the Foreign Secretary, Lord Lansdowne. He handed him a dossier documenting atrocities on a gigantic scale; he described wanton killings, slavery, mutilation, torture and dozens of other acts of inhumanity which the Belgian government were apparently aware of but unwilling to stop.

The report caused diplomatic uproar in Europe, with the Belgians accusing the Foreign Office of wishing to promote British commercial interests in Africa. As the storm grew Casement took a well earned leave in Ireland and then accepted a Consular appointment in South America.

It was while Casement was British Consul in the Brazilian port of Para that reports reached London of a second, Congo-syle operation being conducted in the Amazon basin. On this occasion the stories had come from Barbados, whose islanders had been recruited to work on rubber plantations in the Putumayo district of the Amazon. In July 1910 Casement was instructed to visit the area and check on the allegations of ill-treatment of British subjects.

If anything Casement found conditions in Putumayo worse than those he had experienced in Africa, with the indigenous native population having to suffer rather worse atrocities than those practised on the imported labour from Barbados. Casement prepared a damning indictment and forwarded it to Sir Edward Grey, Lord Lansdowne's successor, in January 1911. At the end of June 1911 a grateful British monarch rewarded Casement's work with a knighthood. The report of the exploitation in Putumayo created a second scandal, but it was short-lived. When Casement returned to the region in October he discovered that arrest warrants had been issued against the two hundred worst offenders, but no other action had been taken by the Peruvian authorities. This news brought further public indignation, and American opinion was mobilised to bring pressure to bear on the government in Lima.

Casement's frequent travels through the tropics had taken their toll on his health, and in the spring of 1912 he retired from the Consular Service and went to live in Ireland. His retirement was not to be a quiet one. In spite of his Protestant Ulster background Casement firmly allied himself with the increasingly militant Irish Nationalist movement and, in particular, the Irish Volunteers.

When war finally broke out in August 1914 Casement's hostility to English politicians had become translated into a sympathy for the German cause, and this was no doubt encouraged by calls for Britain to go to the aid of neutral, defenceless Belgium. Casement had, after all, spent several years and all of his health trying to expose Belgian atrocities and persuade English politicians to impose sanctions on those responsible. Late in September 1914 Casement wrote a letter to the *Irish Independent* from New York urging all Irishmen to fight against the English rather than the Germans. Casement's former colleagues in Whitehall were aghast, and Arthur Nicholson, the Permanent Under-Secretary at the Foreign Office wrote to him to obtain confirmation that he was indeed the letter's author. In fact Casement was en route to Norway when his letter was published in Dublin, and by the time Nicholson had reacted Casement was in Berlin negotiating with the German government to raise a Nationalist army to drive the English from Ireland.

The Branch had known of Casement's pro-German attitude from reports received from the British Embassy in Washington. Casement had had frequent meetings with the German Ambassador there throughout the summer of 1914 and had distributed Nationalist propaganda. None of these acts had been of a criminal nature, but his letter to the *Irish Independent* sealed his fate, at least as far as the Branch were concerned. His name was added to a list of suspects to be detained under the Defence of the Realm Act, and further signed publications urging a German victory ensured that a prosecution for treason would follow his arrest... if such an event were ever to take place. In an attempt to obtain further evidence Superintendent Quinn authorised a search of Casement's London address. Among his belongings were his diaries covering the previous eleven years, and they made extraordinary reading. Casement had documented, in minute detail, his homosexual experiences and proclivities. They were to prove a useful weapon.

The likelihood of Casement's arrest on British territory grew more and more as his schemes to raise an army in Germany collapsed. His visits to German PoW camps to recruit Irish followers met with disappointment and he eventually persuaded the German government to let him land secretly in Ireland and start the rebellion.

Casement's negotiations with Berlin were followed avidly in England by the Royal Navy's codebreakers. Captain Hall, the DNI, was thoroughly convinced of the value of a cryptanalysis service even if some of his colleagues were somewhat less enthusiastic. The Shore Wireless Service's network of intercept stations had expanded beyond its four original coastal sites and had taken over all the Marconi Company's commercial receivers and transmitters. By the time the German Admiralty was exchanging telegrams on the subject of Casement's impending voyage to Ireland the SWS was relaying the traffic to Room 40 of the Admiralty where teams of decrypters transformed even the most secret signals into understandable text.

Throughout February and March 1916 Thomson and the DNI held regular meetings to discuss developments in Ireland, for Casement had chosen Easter Sunday for the date of a general insurrection. The Germans had agreed to provide the necessary arms and ammunition, and had also undertaken to divert attention away from the landing area by mounting a combined air and sea attack on another part of the coast. The Admiralty decrypters had succeeded even in identifying the codeword which was to herald Casement's embarkation at Wilhelmshaven so there was little chance of the operation going according to the Germans' plan. In the event the submarine carrying Casement, the U-20, broke down in the North Sea and the fourteen Admiralty direction-finding stations along the east coast were able to monitor the resulting wireless traffic. A second U-boat was summoned to help and Casement and two Irish volunteers continued their journey around the north of Scotland, twenty-four hours behind schedule and under the closest Royal Navy scrutiny.

Late in the night of 21 April, Casement stepped ashore in Tralee Bay, County Kerry, from a small canvas dinghy with his two companions, Captain Monteith, and a Corporal in the Royal Irish Rifles named Bailey. By dawn the following morning, Good Friday, Casement was under arrest at the Police Barracks in Tralee. Within forty-eight hours of his arrival he had been escorted by train to Dublin, and at ten o'clock on Easter Sunday he was ushered in to Thomson's office at Scotland Yard.

The DNI's counter-measures at sea were almost as effective as

Thomson's arrangements on land. The German vessel carrying Casement's munitions, the *Aud,* was spotted by HMS *Bluebell* and, after a shot across the bows, complied with an order to make for Queenstown. She was disguised as a Norwegian tramp steamer and was flying the Norwegian flag, but as the *Aud* approached the harbour she struck her colours and was scuttled. All the crew were picked up and in due course they too were escorted to London for interrogation. Bailey, one of Casement's two companions, was arrested in Tralee on Easter Saturday, following a tip-off to the police, and he promptly betrayed Monteith's hiding place. The rebellion, scheduled for Easter morning, was postponed until the next day, and was then suppressed after some intensive fighting around the Dublin Post Office.

At his first interview with Thomson, Casement declined to make any statement with the Branch short-hand writer present but was voluble as soon as the officer left the room. He claimed that he had returned to Ireland to prevent the insurrection rather than to lead it, and denied having tried to suborn British PoWs. He defended his actions by saying that he had simply tried to recruit Irish prisoners for an Irish Brigade. He had never attempted to persuade any to join the German army. According to some accounts of this first meeting between the head of the Branch and his prisoner, Thomson arranged for a Branch officer to place one of Casement's diaries before him. Although he did not appear to recognise it, his solicitor, George Gavan Duffy, wrote to the Yard soon afterwards, asking for its return. The request was denied.

Casement was lodged at the Tower of London, under military jurisdiction, until 15 May when he appeared at Bow Sreet Police Court on a charge of treason. The committal proceedings lasted three days, during which time the prisoner stayed at Brixton. At the conclusion of the hearings Casement was remanded to Brixton and sent for trial.

The case for the prosecution was opened by the Attorney-General, Sir F.E. Smith, (later Lord Birkenhead) before the Lord Chief Justice, Lord Reading. Former detainees from an internment camp in Limburg testified that Casement had urged them to join his Irish Brigade, and a code book found among Casement's possessions at his arrest was proof enough of his intention to lead a pro-German rebellion in Ireland. At the end of a trial lasting three weeks the jury deliberated for just an hour before finding Casement guilty. After the foreman had announced the verdict the Irishman made an impassioned political harangue and then stood silent for Lord Reading to pronounce the death sentence.

Casement duly lodged an Appeal which was heard in June, but

in the meantime public sympathy began to mount for the prisoner. A petition was handed to the Prime Minister, Mr Asquith, bearing the signatures of some forty distinguished figures, including those of Arnold Bennett, G.K. Chesterton, and John Galsworthy. There was also considerable pressure from America where Casement's trial had received tremendous publicity. None of this suited Thomson or Hall, who feared that a convicted traitor was in danger of escaping with his life. They therefore arranged to type up selected extracts of the diaries and had certain explicit passages photographed. These packages of vice were intended to be evidence of Casement's depraved homosexual indulgences and they had the desired effect. Support for Casement evaporated as soon as news of the diaries spread, and even those most vocal in his defence were silenced when confronted with photographs of Casement's immediately recognisable hand-writing. Hall's deliberate circulation of the diaries, which was only possible with Thomson's help, almost backfired on the two men. Shortly before Casement's Appeal was due to be heard his lawyers considered presenting the material as proof of Casement's insanity, but the idea was vetoed. The Appeal was dismissed on 19 July and Casement, stripped of his knighthood, was hanged at Pentonville on 3 August 1916.

One of the principal functions of the contingent of Branch officers at St Omer was one of liaison with the French Sûreté and, to a lesser degree, the military intelligence unit, the Deuxième Bureau. It was this liaison that led to Thomson's meeting with the legendary Mata Hari in November 1916.

Contrary to her legend, Mata Hari was neither beautiful nor Eurasian. In fact she was born in Leeuwarden, Holland, on 7 August 1876, the daughter of a moderately prosperous hat shop owner named Adam Zelle. She was christened Margaretha Gertrude and in 1894 married Captain John MacLeod of the Dutch colonial army. As his name suggested, MacLeod was of Scottish ancestry. The marriage, however, was not a success and, after the death of their young son, they were divorced. Soon afterwards Margaretha MacLeod took up the profession of an "exotic dancer" and created a mythical, oriental past for herself.

In December 1916 Mata Hari (the name was Hindi for "eye of the morning") completed a dancing engagement in Madrid and was due to return to Holland. Accordingly she embarked on the SS *Hollandia* at Vigo, bound for Rotterdam via Falmouth. When the ship arrived in Falmouth the passengers underwent a routine passport inspection and search for contraband, and through some inexplicable blunder Mata Hari was mistakenly identified as Clara

Benedict, a suspected German spy, and detained by a Branch detective. She was escorted up to London and lodged at Holloway while further inquiries were conducted. Eventually Mata Hari lost patience and demanded to see the Dutch Minister in London. He drew her case to the attention of Basil Thomson who interviewed her (via an interpreter) at the Yard. Of that meeting he was later to recall: "Of all the people that I examined during the course of the War she was the quickest on the uptake". The confusion over her real identity was quickly sorted out but she was not immediately released because she claimed, among other things, to be working against the Germans under the protection of the French Deuxième Bureau.

Instead of returning Mata Hari to Holloway Thomson gave her a room at the Savoy Hotel. He then cabled the Deuxième Bureau to establish the truth of her claim. In any event the Branch realised that they had no grounds for keeping her in custody. Her self-confessed espionage had taken place abroad and she had not willingly landed in England. In Paris Thomson's request for information on Margaretha MacLeod landed on the desk of a certain Captain Georges Ledoux who had, the previous August, interviewed her about her contacts with German Staff officers. The exact nature of her relationship with Ledoux remains unclear but evidence presented at her subsequent trial suggests that she was under suspicion of being a German agent and had agreed to supply the Deuxième Bureau with information. When Thomson pressed her on the subject of her German contacts she said that she had extracted valuable intelligence from two German Service attachés in Madrid, Major Kalle and Lieutenant-Commander Hans von Krohn.

The French answered the Branch's request for information somewhat ambiguously and advised Thomson to return Mrs MacLeod to her port of embarkation. Thus, with a few words of fatherly advice Thomson placed Mata Hari on the next ship bound for Spain. Once back in Spain Mata Hari took up residence at the Ritz Hotel and made plans to travel overland to Holland via Paris. The local French Consul granted her a visa and early in January 1917 she arrived in the French capital by train. It was later alleged that her journey had been financed by Major Kalle who had signalled Berlin for permission to supply "Agent H-21" with the necessary cash. The cable was monitored by an intercept station on the Eiffel Tower. When the Deuxième Bureau learned of Mata Hari's return they arranged for her to be arrested on 12 February 1917 at her hotel in Paris, the Plaza- Athénée. Commissaire Albert Priolet of the Sûreté charged her with espionage and, despite her protestations of being a Dutch subject, lodged her at the women's prison of St Lazare.

The German signals intercepted by the French were to provide damning evidence of Mata Hari's duplicity. One decoded cable addressed to a German Intelligence sub-station in Cologne reported that "H-21" had managed to get herself recruited as an agent of the Deuxième Bureau. Another requested a payment be sent to a certain Anna Lintjens in Holland. Miss Lintjens was subsequently identified as Margaretha MacLeod's elderly maid.

Mata Hari's trial, which was held *in camera* before a Military Tribunal, opened on 24 July 1917. She was found guilty less than a day and a half later. She was condemned to death and the sentence was carried out by a firing squad at dawn on 15 October 1917. Soon after her death Captain Ledoux was denounced as a German spy by his chauffeur and he was arrested. He was eventually able to prove his innocence and was awarded the Légion d'Honneur. The chauffeur was then found to be in the pay of the Germans and he was executed.

After the war Thomson said of Mata Hari: "The only graceful thing about her was her walk and the carriage of her head. She made no gestures and, to say truth, time had a little dimmed the charms of which we had heard so much, for at this time the lady must have been at least forty."

Mata Hari's conviction as a spy was almost entirely the fault of Major Kalle, the German Assistant Military Attaché in Madrid, whose lack of discretion in his cables to Berlin enabled the French to identify the dancer as H-21. What, one is tempted to remark, is the point of disguising agents with codenames if the system is to be abused? Although the French publicised her execution they were, of course, rather more security-conscious about the nature of the evidence presented in the case. This enabled them to continue to intercept and decode German signals.

Germany's lack of a secure diplomatic code eventually led to the release in America of the famous Zimmermann telegram which in turn effectively brought America into the war. The original Zimmermann telegram had, of course, been cracked by the famous Admiralty decrypters of Room 40, but rather than announce the source it was considered prudent simply to pass the method or key to the US State Department. Thus it appeared, at least for a time, that the Americans had acted on their own. This subterfuge was intended to disguise the fact that the Allies had been reading much of the German traffic but inevitably they took swift action to cut off the source.

If the Germans were prompt in this instance, it was uncharacteristic, for even at this late stage of the war their agents were dispatched to England with secret ink and a collection of cover-addresses in neutral countries. In January 1917 George Bacon, a German-American journalist, arrived in England and began mailing newspaper articles home. Unknown to him two of his addressees in New York, named Sander and Wunnenberg, had already been added to the Suspects Index so Bacon was interviewed by Detective Inspector Fitch. Fitch noticed that the journalist owned an expensive manicure case, yet his hands were obviously in need of attention. A more thorough search of his hotel room revealed a bottle of secret ink and a novel that had been scored with tell-tale pin pricks, the kind made to transform an ordinary book into a code-book. At his trial at the Guildhall in February 1917 Bacon was convicted of espionage, having admitted to posting reports of London's air defences to his contacts. The Branch were particulary sensitive about German air raids at this time as Chief Inspector Ward, the officer who arranged for Lincoln's extradition, had been killed during a Zeppelin attack. Bacon's death sentence was later commuted to life imprisonment, and he was deported back to the US to testify against his two contacts, Sander and Wunnenberg. Both men pleaded guilty to breaking the Neutrality Act and were imprisoned for two years. They also paid a hefty fine.

One of the last German agents to be caught by the Branch was Alfred Hagn, a Norwegian also working under a journalistic cover. Hagn first came to London in October 1916 and returned to Norway as soon as his money ran out. He returned on 17 April 1917 and found lodgings in Tavistock Square. Hagn was evidently an inept spy for he was denounced the following month by an Italian academic who had rooms in the same building. When challenged by Branch detectives Hagn admitted his guilt and produced some ammonia and a bottle of mouth-wash, both ingredients of his secret ink. He was tried on 27 August, found guilty and, like Bacon, had his death sentence commuted. On 13 September 1919 he was released from Maidstone prison and deported because his mental condition had deteriorated.

Only a few of the German agents arriving in England stuck to their cover stories in the face of a hostile interrogation from the Branch, but none confessed quicker than Jose de Patrocinio who landed at Gravesend from Flushing in September 1917. De Patrocinio was the son of an influential Brazilian journalist, but the previous autumn he had found himself in Amsterdam with virtually no money. Up until that time he had been a Press Attaché at the Brazilian Consulate but when his appointment came to an end he was not offered a further term. Patrocinio had then been recruited by the German Intelligence Service and had been provided with a list of cover-addresses in Denmark and Switzerland. As it turned out the Germans had made a disastrous choice, for he was panic-stricken by the time his ferry reached Gravesend and poured out his story to a Branch detective on routine Port Control duties. He was subsequently deported to Brazil without a trial.

Of all the cases dealt with by the Branch during the Great War, the most remarkable was that of Sir Joseph Jonas, the former Lord Mayor of Sheffield. Jonas had been born in Germany and in 1876, aged thirty-one, had become a naturalised British subject. In 1905 he was a millionaire knight and the head of Jonas, Colver & Co, one of Sheffield's largest steel-makers. According to the Branch's information in 1918, he was also a source of information for the German Intelligence Service. One of the more difficult aspects of the case was the fact that there was not one shred of admissible evidence against the man. Another was his close friendship with the Royal family. The Branch organised a raid on Jonas's office in Sheffield on 1 May 1918, and it was led by Herbert Fitch. Jonas was astonished by the intrusion but eventually surrendered the keys to his private safe. Inside was a collection of five-year-old correspondence, all of which related to the supply of armaments to the Ministry of Munitions. The addressees were his former business agent in London, an engineer named Charles Vernon, and a Vickers foreman named Richard Zieschang. All three had strong German connections. As well as having been born in Germany, Jonas had been the German Consul in Sheffield; Vernon's real name was Carl Hahn, but he had become a naturalised British subject in 1884 and on the outbreak of war had changed his name by Deed Poll to Charles Vernon-Hahn. He had subsequently dropped the Hahn. Zieschang had been born in England of German parents, and it was he who had denounced Jonas to the Branch.

The Jonas letters revealed that prior to August 1914 one of Jonas's principal customers was a German firm headed by a certain Paul von Gontard. Von Gontard was extremely inquisitive by nature and required to be kept fully up to date about the manufacture of arms in the Midlands. The letters seized by Fitch showed that Jonas and Vernon had kept their client well informed.

At his trial at the Old Bailey in July 1918 Jonas claimed that he had committed no breach of the Official Secrets Act because all the letters had been written when Britain was not at war with Germany. The prosecution insisted that even if Germany had not then been an enemy, she had certainly been a potential enemy. The second charge related to information concerning a new rifle that Vickers had been testing at their factory in Crayford, Kent. Vernon had questioned Zieschang about the experiments because he worked as a Vickers foreman.

After a long trial Jonas and Vernon were acquitted of the more serious charges but the jury found them guilty of a misdemeanour in that Vernon had, in November 1913 sought information from the Vickers site, and that Jonas had aided and abetted him. The judge, Mr Justice Lawrence, pointed out that even a technical breach of the law some years past was still a serious matter and fined Jonas £2,000 and Vernon £1,000. They were also ordered to pay the huge costs of the case. In addition, the King announced the following month that Jonas had been stripped of both his knighthood and his British citizenship. It was a heavy price to pay for having tried to please an overseas customer more than five years earlier.

Although counter-espionage work was an important part of the Branch's wartime work, it was by no means their only responsibility. The greatest number of Branch officers were attached to eighteen Port Units where they examined incoming visa holders. The Aliens Restriction Act also charged the police with several duties in relation to aliens and, more particularly, enemy aliens. These duties were mainly logistical in nature although it invariably fell on the Branch to serve many of the Internment Orders on the named individuals. Aliens of military age came under the jurisdiction of the War Office while the police dealt with the frequent cases of breaches of orders which restricted the movements of aliens without prior permission.

The advent of war certainly eclipsed the domestic political scene but the Branch retained its brief to monitor political extremism at home. Among the organisations coming under its scrutiny was the Women's Suffrage Movement, led by Mrs Pankhurst. As can be seen from this comment by Detective Inspector Edwin Woodhall in *Guardians of the Great*, (Blandford, 1934), the Branch had no quarrel with the Movement's aims:

> Let it be said, here and now, that the men of the Special Branch were, from the point of view of duty, the suffragists' avowed antagonists. Many of us openly declared our sympathy with their aims, but they were fighting against the Government, and if the State did not see its way clear to give women the vote, that ended the argument so far as we were concerned.

The threat presented by the women suffragettes was perceived in terms of the personal protection that was to be afforded to senior political figures. On the outbreak of war the suffragettes had declared a truce for the duration. Several politicians, as we have seen, had been the subject of attacks, and Lloyd George was protected by no less than four Branch officers during the war. They were Detective Sergeants Andrews, Nalty, Randall and Sandercock. The royal family also required protection and on one occasion before the war DI Reilly had intercepted Emily Davidson as she approached the King and Queen on a visit to Westminster City Hall. She was later to commit suicide by throwing herself in front of the King's horse on Derby Day.

The suffragette truce was greeted with relief at the Yard because it freed the Branch's twelve short-hand writers who had attended most of the rallies and political meetings before the war. They were re-assigned to interrogation work at the Port Units.

The detectives with short-hand had traditionally been rewarded with an extra allowance of three shillings a week so the job had always been a popular one. The suffragettes, however, strongly objected to notes being taken of their public utterances and on more than one occasion a Branch officer was roughed up by a mob of women. They then resorted to the subterfuge of posing as newspaper reporters but, as Patrick Quinn reported to the Home Secretary in October 1913, this too was unsatisfactory:

> I have the honour to report, for the consideration of the Secretary of State, that officers of the Special Branch have lately had great difficulty in obtaining admission to meetings of Syndicalists and Suffragettes, and have more than once been recognised and molested during the course of such evenings. When they have attended as Pressmen objections have been raised by the reporters.

Apart from the suffragettes the Branch's chief political headaches were caused by various pacifist organisations which acted as fronts for revolutionary groups. Some tried to disrupt the munitions industry while others attempted to foment dissent in the ranks. These activities were by no means limited to small collections of agitators or malcontents. One of the anti-war movement's leaders was Colonel Cecil Malone, a former Coalition Liberal MP for East Leyton. He was arrested by Branch detectives after addressing a rally at the Albert Hall, and was imprisoned for six months after being found guilty of sedition. Fortunately many of the groups of Russian exiles who had been active in London returned home during the first years of the war, thus reducing the Branch's surveillance activities. It was in an effort to exclude such militants that Lenin had been refused re-entry into the United Kingdom from his exile in Switzerland in 1917. Instead he travelled to Petrograd via Germany in a sealed railway carriage.

One unique episode in which the Branch acted as a political police was in the arrest and detention in August 1918 of the "Plenipotentiary for Great Britain of the Russian People's Government", Maxim Litvinov. There was no precedent for such an arrest, for Litvinov was deemed to possess diplomatic immunity. The arrest of Litvinov and his staff of twenty was intended as a reprisal for the seizure of the British Consulate in Petrograd. During the attack on the building, following an attempt on Lenin's life, the British Naval Attaché, Captain Francis Cromie DSO RN, had been murdered. The senior British diplomat in Russia, the British Agent Robert Bruce-Lockhart had then been imprisoned. Herbert Fitch oversaw the Branch's operation and escorted Litvinov to Brixton prison. Six days later he was released and Lockhart was deported to Finland.

The prospect of a Soviet-style revolution in England was never far from the government's attention during the latter part of 1918 when large numbers of demobbed servicemen were being returned to civilian life with little chance of employment. The climate in England was one of discontent and, war or no war, the Metropolitan Police had their share of troubles. So too did the Branch.

In December 1917 the pay of a Constable in London was increased to thirty-eight shillings a week with a War Bonus of twelve shillings a week. In addition, men with fifteen years service had a further one shilling a week, while men with twenty-one years were earning two pounds.

This level of pay was recognised by virtually everyone as being completely inadequate and early in the New Year of 1918 the Commissioner, Sir Edward Henry, obtained the Home Secretary's consent for the preparation of a new pay structure which would raise the income of both the police and the police widows. In February 1918 an unofficial Police Union, led by PC Thiel, sent the Commissioner a letter outlining the plight of the badly paid Constables. Sir Edward responded to the letter by having Thiel sacked for participation in an illegal organisation (the union) and insisted the matter was under review. Five months later, on 27 August, the National Union of Police and Prison Officers, with less than a thousand members, issued an ultimatum. If Thiel was not reinstated and if a payrise was not forthcoming, the Metropolitan Police would strike on 30 August 1918. Incredibly, at this time of crisis the Commissioner was on holiday in Ireland. He sent no reply to the Union, and at midnight on 29 August police Superintendents throughout the capital sent telegrams to the Yard telling of the large numbers of their men that had failed to report for duty. At the Yard itself there was strike action, and even the Branch was affected. Twenty-five Detective Sergeants and sixteen Detective Constables met in the Branch's briefing room to discuss their grievances, and refused to obey orders.

The government was evidently as unprepared for the strike as the Commissioner, and the Prime Minister dispatched General Smuts to mediate with the executive committee of the Police Union. He also requested the army to guard Downing Street with a force of five hundred men who were to be concealed in the Foreign Office quadrangle. On the third morning of the strike he conceded virtually all of the Union's demands, including the reinstatement of Constable Thiel. That night the Commissioner submitted his resignation to the Home Secretary, and it was accepted "with regret" and sweetened with the offer of a baronetcy.

The unexpected resignation of Sir Edward Henry had almost been followed by that of the Home Secretary, Sir George Cave, but apparently Lloyd George held the former solely, and doubly, to blame: he was at fault for not being at hand to stop the mutiny, and he was at fault for not even knowing it was going to happen.

The man called on by the Cabinet was the Adjutant-General at the War Office, Sir Nevil Macready. Macready had little prior experience of police work, with the exception of once having commanded a combined force of soldiers and police in South Wales during an industrial dispute, but he was determined to restore the police to normality. For the following eighteen months the Commissioner's attention was entirely taken up by the endless negotiations that eventually led to the creation of the Police Federation.

While these events were taking place Basil Thomson decided to completely separate the Branch from the CID and the rest of the Force. In April 1919 he himself took the title "Director of Intelligence" and, on Quinn's retirement on 31 December, oversaw the Branch's operations personally, even though James McBrien had nominally been appointed the new Commander. The Branch also abandoned their rooms in Scotland Yard and established themselves in nearby Scotland House.

The person who was most affected by the new arrangement was Thomson himself. He was now in a position to deal on equal terms with Kell, who had also received a knighthood in the New Year Honours, along with Quinn. Thomson saw the Branch as a bulwark against a growing tide of Bolshevism and its isolation from the rest of the Force would, he believed, protect it from the spreading mutinous influences. Instead of being answerable to the

Commissioner, Thomson reported directly to the Home Secretary, and initiated proceedings by preparing a Report on Revolutionary Organisations in the United Kingdom. The Report was updated by weekly summaries which Thomson personally presented to the Cabinet. These replaced Thomson's previous offering, the Fortnightly Report on Pacifism and Revolutionary Organisations in the United Kingdom and Morale Abroad.

One particularly fertile area of discontent had been discovered by Leftist political activists in the various groups of demobilised servicemen who had returned to civilian life but had been unable to find jobs. Several pressure groups had sprung up, like the National Federation of Discharged and Demobilised Sailors and Soldiers which had been set up in April 1917 under the presidency of James Hogge, the Liberal MP for Edinburgh East. Such organisations, and there were many, were ideal targets for the militants and Thomson employed informants in most so the Branch could monitor them from both the inside and outside. Even the "safe" bodies were, at times, in danger of being taken over. An example is the Comrades of the Great War, a charity sponsored by the Earl of Derby, who had been Secretary of State for War between 1916 and 1918. The Chairman of the Comrades' Executive Committee was Colonel Wilfred Ashley, the Conservative MP for the Fylde Division of Lancashire, yet even the Comrades were the subject of a disquieting Branch report in November 1918.

The militant take-over was fought off, but the War Office's blind eye attitude to the recruitment of "Honorary Members" from among serving soldiers left a useful loophole for some of the other, more overtly political, organisations to exploit. The practice was against regulations but the War Office authorities had taken what they saw as an opportunity to stabilise a threat from malcontents. Instead the effect was to enable the development of a Soldiers', Sailors' and Airmen's Union, a Leftist group which had ties to such Communist front organisations as the *Hands Off Russia* movement.

The CPGB's forerunner, the British Socialist Party, was at the forefront of a campaign to launch a general strike late in January 1919, but the strike, which had been intended to spark off a nationwide stoppage, collapsed. On 31 January the police foiled an attempt to take over the municipal buildings in Glasgow by occupying the premises themselves. A new Defence of the Realm Act was passed to outlaw strikes in selected industries and, according to Thomson's thirty-third report, dated 10 February 1919, the revolutionary plotters failed "partly because the government dealt firmly with rioters".

Matters came to a head early in May 1919 when the Directorate

of Intelligence learned of further wide-scale plots for a general
strike. It was at this point that Thomson warned that "we might be
forced to enrol some sort of Civic Guard to keep order in the streets,
as has recently been done in Holland and Switzerland". His agents,
who were positioned all over the country also reported a "self-
demobilisation" campaign to take place in England and in the
major military towns of France. It was scheduled to begin on 11
May 1919, so the Branch raided the Soldiers', Sailors' and Airmen's
Union on 8 May and seized their files. When the day itself came,
there were only a few isolated incidents. Disillusioned, the more
militant factions set up two new radical bodies, the National Union
of Ex-Servicemen and the International Union of Ex-Servicemen.
In mid-1919 the agitation reached a climax of public demonstrations and covert approaches from the Communist International.
Thereafter the campaign lost political cohesion and, after the
formation of the British Legion in 1921, disintegrated as a platform
for the revolutionaries.

The period between the Armistice in November 1918 and the
Branch's raid of 8 May 1919 remains the closest that the United
Kingdom ventured in modern times towards a violent overthow of
the established order. It is worth noting that at no time during this
period did the Branch act as *agent provocateur* or seek to undermine
the more radical pressure groups. Instead their objective reports to
Thomson enabled him to keep the Cabinet fully informed and
enabled the Prime Minister to remove the grievances upon which
the agitators had capitalised.

Despite Thomson's demonstrable ability in the field of intelligence-gathering his days at the Directorate of Intelligence were
numbered. Thomson's style of recruiting agents and circulating
their reports was not appreciated by the Prime Minister and in
October 1921 Lloyd George got his opportunity to dismiss the
Assistant Commissioner. Four Irishmen had succeeded in breach-
ing the minimal security of the Prime Minister's residence at
Chequers in Buckinghamshire and had painted the words "Up
Sinn Fein" on a summerhouse in the grounds. Lloyd George
reported the matter to his Home Secretary, Edward Shortt who, in
turn, confronted Thomson with an alleged example of the Branch's
ineffectency. The Commissioner, General Sir William Horwood, had
been unhappy with the ambiguous existence of the Directorate of
Intelligence over which he had no control and declined to support
his Assistant Commissioner. Thomson was given the choice of
retirement or dismissal and he opted for the former. His departure
resulted in the closure of the Directorate and the termination of the
Branch's semi-independent status. Henceforth the Commander of

the Branch reported to the Assistant Commissioner (Crime) who in turn reported to the Commissioner rather than directly to the Home Secretary. The Thomson regime had lasted eight years, and was at an end.

CHAPTER VI

Policing the Peace

There is a dividing line between ordinary and
political crime. In normal times the function of the
Criminal Investigation Department is to unravel
crimes that have been committed, and of the Special
Branch to foresee and to prevent political agitators
from committing crime in order to terrorise the
community into granting them what they want.

Sir Basil Thomson in *Queer People* (Hodders, 1922)

The most extensive and ambitious operation ever conducted by the
Branch began early in the morning of 14 October 1925 when Chief
Inspector Parker appeared before the Chief Magistrate, Sir
Chartres Biron, at Bow Street and asked for warrants to arrest the
entire Executive of the Communist Party of Great Britain. The
charge was that of sedition.

The application had been approved by the Commissioner, Sir
William Horwood, the Assistant Commissioner for the CID, Sir
Wyndham Childs, and the Home Secretary, Sir William Joynson-
Hicks (later Lord Brentford). As well as marking the start of a
campaign to show the Communist doctrine to be unlawful, it also
represented a triumph for Childs. Five years later he remarked in
his memoirs, *Episodes and Reflections*, published by Cassells:

I spent the seven best years of my life trying to induce various
governments to allow me to use the full force of the law, or if the
law was not suffcently comprehensive, to give me legislation. I
have come to the conclusion that I wasted those seven years in
fruitless endeavour. I have never been able to comprehend why
the successive Governments I served always refused to strike one
overwhelming and final blow against the Communist organisation.

Childs undoubtedly found Ramsay Macdonald's administration
reluctant to take on the CPGB but the new Home Secretary, swept

78

into power by the Zinoviev fiasco, was a determined anti-Communist and perfectly amenable to Childs' plan to remove the CPGB from the English political scene once and for all. A previous attempt, in May 1921, had been something of a damp squib. On that occasion Parker had raided the CPGB headquarters and had seized nearly three tons of Communist literature in an operation ordered by Sir Basil Thomson. It was to be one of his last acts as Assistant Commissioner and the administrative head of the Branch. The subsequent prosecution at the Mansion House before the Lord Mayor centred on the subversive nature of the magazines, newspapers and pamphlets. If it could be shown that the contents of the material was subversive then the printers, the National Labour Press Limited of Salford, were in breach of the 1921 Emergency Regulations. More importantly, the CPGB would also be guilty of procuring the printers to break the law.

The case was heard on 21 June 1921 and Albert Inkpin, formerly the Secretary of the British Socialist Party (which had been absorbed into the CPGB), was the defendant. The Lord Mayor read several of the pamphlets selected by the Branch and concluded that they "advocated violence and that one class of the community should be armed to overawe the rest – civil war in fact". They were, he decided, calculated to cause sedition and disaffection and so he sentenced Inkpin to six months' hard labour. The National Labour Press Limited were fined £200 with costs, and their undertaking "never again to print that sort of literature" was accepted by the Court.

In November 1921 Thomson was summoned before Lloyd George's Home Secretary, Edward Shortt, and was advised to resign. If he did not, he was warned, he would be sacked and would forfeit his pension. Thomson stepped down and was succeeded by Sir Joseph Byrne, who had, until the previous year, been the Inspector-General of the Royal Ulster Constabulary. Byrne had resigned his post after less than four years because he found it too political, and had been replaced by a tough army veteran, Major-General Sir Hugh Tudor. The choice of Byrne proved to be a controversial one, and it also proved one impossible to sustain. Virtually every politician with an interest in Irish affairs voiced an objection and the government were forced to withdraw Byrne. Instead he was offered the job of Governor of the Seychelles, a tiny colony of idyllic islands in the Indian Ocean. Byrne accepted the alternative and the Home Secretary cast around for another, more acceptable, candidate. The man he decided on was Major-General Sir Wyndham Childs, who had recently retired as Deputy Adjutant-General at the War Office. Childs was so

anxious to take the job that he did not wait to inquire what the
salary was.

Childs may have been appointed by Shortt, but his political
sympathies were rather more in line with the Home Secretary's
successor, Sir William Joynson-Hicks. It was Joynson-Hicks who, in
October 1925, gave Horwood and Childs the go-ahead for a second
major raid on the CPGB. It was less than a year since the General
Election and for the fortnight leading up to the raid the Branch's
surveillance on the CPGB, led by Detective Sergeants Foster and
Rogers, had been intensified.

Sir Chartres Biron granted the warrant, which charged the
defendants with

> having, on divers days since January 1, 1924, unlawfully
> conspired together to utter and publish seditious libels and to
> incite divers persons to commit breaches of the Incitement to
> Mutiny Act, 1707, against the peace of our lord the King, his
> Crown and Dignity.

That afternoon the operation began in earnest. Chief Inspector
Parker raided the King Street headquarters of the CPGB while
other Branch officers made simultaneous visits to other CPGB
organisations. Detective Inspector Norwood went to the Young
Communist League's office at 38 Great Ormond Street and
Detective Sergeant Albert Foster went to the *Workers' Weekly* office
in Dr Johnson's Building in the Temple. All the detectives were
armed with copies of pamphlets and other documents which
named the CPGB's Executive.

The raids were a qualified success. Parker found Albert Inkpin,
the Secretary of the CPGB, in his office in King Street and arrested
him. It was less than three years since he had been released from
serving the six months' sentence, with hard labour, for his earlier
offence. Parker also arrested Ernest Cant, the London Organiser of
the CPGB.

Foster, for his part, found Tom Wintringham and Ross
Campbell, both assistant editors of the *Workers' Weekly* and arrested
them. Meanwhile Norwood detained William Rust, the Secretary
of the YCL and Harry Pollitt, Secretary of the National Minority
Movement. Both men were well known to the Branch. Rust had
once served two months' imprisonment for criminal damage, and
Pollitt had been convicted in June 1921 of making a speech
"calculated to cause a breach of the peace". He had been fined £10.

Two other executive members, Thomas Bell and William
Gallacher (later Communist MP for West Fife) were detained in
Scotland by Branch detectives who had travelled up to Glasgow by

train. Gallacher, of course, was an old customer of the Branch's. He had twice been imprisoned for making seditious speeches (and, on one occasion in April 1919, for incitement to riot) and had done twelve months' imprisonment during the war for publishing seditious articles. Bell was arrested just before midnight at his lodgings in Glasgow, and Gallacher was arrested at his home in Paisley early the next morning. The pair made a brief appearance in court and were then escorted down to Euston by train.

The arrests were followed by thorough searches of the CPGB premises in King Street (by DS Renshaw) and Great Ormond Street. Then Branch detectives visited the homes of those arrested and seized whatever CPGB literature they could find. DS Hockley went to Cant's home in Stamford Hill and DI Hawkins to Pollitt's address. Vast quantities of propaganda were recovered and taken to the Yard for examination.

Only four executive members escaped arrest, and they were picked up in a second round of raids on 22 October. Parker arrested Arthur McManus and John Murphy at King Street while Foster met Walter Hannington's train at Paddington Station. As soon as Hannington was arrested DS Ginhoven went to his rooms in Hampstead and searched them for evidence. The last to be arrested was Robert Arnot, the Director of *Labour Research* at their offices in Mecklenburgh Square.

The twelve CPGB executive members represented the top level of the organisation which itself then only numbered some five thousand members. Rust, Pollitt, Gallacher, Murphy, Bell, McManus, Arnot and Hannington had all attended the Communist International held in Moscow the previous year and the Security Service took the view that the Party was effectively directed and financed from Russia. The arrests carried out by the Branch were the first step in an exercise designed to prove that the CPGB's principal aims, the overthrow of parliamentary democracy and the destruction of capitalism, were unlawful. If the courts were to outlaw the CPGB then both MI5 and the Branch would be given a virtual *carte blanche* to dominate Soviet activity in England. The actual charge, alleging offences under the 1797 Incitement to Mutiny Act, was simply a convenient device to bring the CPGB's doctrines under the scrutiny of a court.

The next step in the proceedings was the appearance in court of all twelve defendants for committal on 23 October 1925. The Director of Public Prosecutions, Sir Archibald Bodkin, who had observed the initial stages in court, now left the prosecution to Sir Travers Humphreys. As well as the Incitement to Mutiny offence, they were also charged with "conspiracy to utter and publish seditious libels". All pleaded not guilty, and Sir Henry Slesser, KC, defended seven of the twelve, with Pollitt, Campbell, Rust, Gallacher and Bell conducting their own defence. The hearing, before Sir Chartres Biron, lasted five days, during which Branch detectives gave evidence of the arrests made and described a few of the documents seized in the raids. Several of the letters removed from the correspondence files at King Street were presented to the court by DS Renshaw. The first was a carbon copy of a letter to the Secretariat of the Communist International in Moscow, signed by "The General Secretary". It read:

> Our Political Bureau further wishes me to direct your attention to the somewhat unnecessary reference made in the letter, such as the transmission of money by the secret channel, and to suggest that if the letter is authentic the comrades responsible may be warned of the necessity of being more discreet in their communications.

A second letter on the subject of the CPGB's finances read:

> As you see in the Budget, the total indebtedness of the bureau is £257 14s. Had we received the full amount promised us for the six months ending December 31 we would not now be burdened with this deficit. We were promised £150 every month for the six months ending December – a total of £900 . . . a further sum was promised for wages of the president and secretary.

One of the more curious items recovered from King Street was a letter from a certain Mr G.W. Middleton in Glasgow, seeking the Party's attitude to members who wished to join the police. The carbon of the reply stated that the CPGB had

> no objection to members of the party joining the Police Force if they are thoroughly reliable members. Before any action is taken in this direction it is desirable that the record of any such members be carefully considered and their complete trustworthiness be established. A half-dozen good party members in a Police Force in one of the bigger towns like Glasgow would certainly be very useful.

The letters were scene-setters for the main evidence of sedition, the first of which was a document found in Pollitt's house by DI Hawkins. It stated:

> Our task towards the State – (1) To expose its real nature. (2) To undermine its authority. (3) Ultimately to destroy it. Examples – (1) Attempt of Poplar Guardians to exercise their powers for the

benefit of the working class produced conflict with central authority. (2) Class system is reflected in the Army and the Services generally. Division between officer class and rank and file must be exploited for the purpose of undermining the authority of the officer class.

The next items were from DS Kitchener's collection of *Workers' Weekly*. The issue dated 5 June 1925 carried an article entitled PARALYSIS OF INDUSTRY UNTIL DEMANDS ARE GRANTED which suggested that:

> In the event of the military being drafted into any industrial centre the workers must fraternize with the soldiers and convince them that they must only use their arms on behalf of their own class.

The 7 August edition went further:

> The main thing is personal contact with soldiers and sailors. If you have friends in the forces keep hammering away at them until they realise that soldiers have no interest in fighting wars for their bosses' profit. Write his name on a piece of paper and give it to some responsible member of the Communist Party – the local secretary for preference. Give your own name as well. It will come to us quite safely. Communists do not correspond on these matters through the post. Do not be disappointed if it takes weeks for the letter to come through. Help us to smash the war men. If you don't know a soldier, sailor or airman, and your neighbours and friends do not, get to know one. If you don't know how to tackle him when you have got him apply to the Communist Party...

This documentary evidence was supported by certain observations made by Branch detectives. DS Wilson presented a transcript of a speech given to the North-West London branch of the CPGB by John Campbell in September and DS O'Connor offered his short-hand notes of a harangue made by Walter Hannington at a demonstration in Trafalgar Square the previous June. Both were highly inflammatory. The Branch were also able to shed some light on the Party's internal finances, having traced no less than four separate bank accounts with the Co-operative Wholesale Society in Manchester. During one period of a few months the Party had been credited with more than £11,000, but it proved impossible to identify the source of the money. The defendants claimed the cash came from the sale of books and pamphlets, but the Crown suggested it had come from Moscow.

Occasionally the proceedings hit a lighter note. William Galla-cher, who was not represented by Counsel, recognised one of the Branch detectives giving evidence as one of a pair of men who had been caught hiding underneath the stage of the Bedford Street rehearsal theatre some eighteen months earlier. DS Hockley was in the witness box describing various papers he had taken from Cant's home when Gallacher challenged him about the incident. Reluc-tantly Hockley admitted that he had indeed been discovered eavesdropping on a CPGB meeting, and had then been escorted to Bow Street police station.

At the end of the committal proceedings Sir Chartres Biron found there was a *prima facie* case for the defendants to answer and they were all sent for trial at the Old Bailey. When the question of bail was raised there was further light relief for among those standing surety for the defendants were such celebrities as George Bernard Shaw and the Countess of Warwick. The magistrate asked Shaw whether he was worth £100 and Shaw confirmed that he did indeed have that much money, but Lady Warwick was not so sure.

The Old Bailey trial opened twelve days later, on 17 November, before Mr Justice Swift, with the Attorney-General, Sir Douglas Hogg KC MP leading for the Crown. By this time Bell and Rust had taken on William Pringle, formerly the Liberal MP for Lanarkshire, to defend them, leaving only Pollitt, Campbell and Gallacher to conduct their own cases. The trial itself was relatively unsensational and there were few heated exchanges. The judge intervened only once, and that was during Campbell's final speech to the jury. Whilst denouncing the Branch's evidence he claimed it was "an organisation which looked after political developments exclusively, and which did not exist in this country before the war and which people would have considered intolerable". Sir Douglas Hogg protested that this was both untrue and irrelevant, and the Judge agreed. Campbell was told that if he wanted to make statements like that he could do so from the witness box, and would have to produce his evidence for cross-examination. Campbell declined the invitation.

The trial ended on 25 November 1925 with the jury convicting all the defendants. The five who had previous convictions (Inkpin, Pollitt, Hannington, Rust and Gallacher) were sentenced to twelve months imprisonment. The remaining seven were offered a choice: to be bound over to be of good behaviour, or six months imprisonment. A brief discussion followed in the dock, which concluded in a refusal to be bound over. Thus all twelve went to gaol.

The case was remarkable for a number of reasons, not the least of

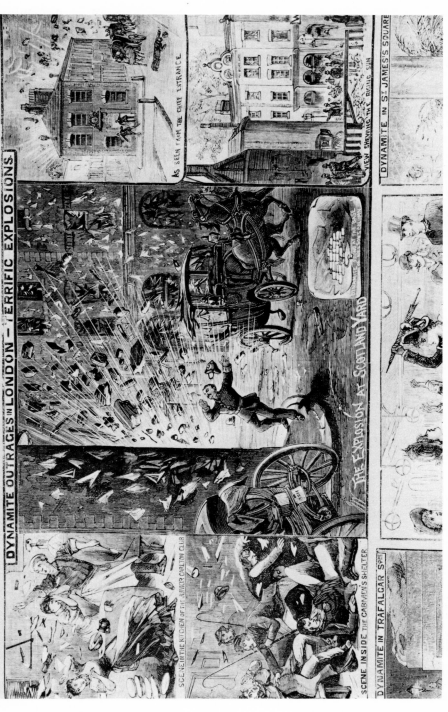

The Fenian terrorist bombing campaign in London, 1884, as recorded in the *Illustrated Police News* of 7 June 1884.

(BBC Hulton Picture Library)

The procession of monarchs at the funeral of King Edward VII in 1910 with a Special Branch escort (two detectives marked with arrows): left, Superintendent Patrick Quinn; right, Superintendent Spencer.

(BBC Hulton Picture Library)

A phalanx of armed police at the siege of Sidney Street, Hounsditch, on 3 January 1911.

(BBC Hulton Picture Library)

In the first days of the 1914–18 war ten French-speaking Metropolitan Special Branch officers were seconded to the Intelligence Corps and despatched to France. All returned safely in due course. *Back row, from left to right*: PC Cuthbert Park, Sergeant Pat Barrett, Inspector Charles Frost, Inspector Jack Bannon, Sergeant Albert Canning. *Seated, left to right*: Sergeant Leo Gough, PC William Palmer, Sergeant Lionel Kirchner, Sergeant Bob Brown, PC Durkin.

The cheque paid to Horst von der Goltz, alias Bridgm[an] Taylor, by Captain Franz von Papen, the German M[ili]tary Attaché in Washington. It was one of many in[cri]minating items seized by the Branch when von Pape[n's] liner docked at Falmouth in January 1916, and it nea[rly] brought von der Goltz before a firing squad at the To[wer] of London.

Carl Hans Lody, executed for treason in November 1914.

Haicke Janssen (*left*) and Willem Roos (*right*) used their business as cigar importers as a cover for their spying for the Germans. They were executed by firing squad in July 1915.

Lizzie Wertheim and Georg Breeckow were found guilty of espionage in 1915. He was executed at the Tower of London in October 1915; she died insane in Broadmoor in 1920.

To Whom It May Concern!

My name is Anton Küpferle nee to Sollingen A. Rastatt i.B. I am a soldier with rank which I not desire to mention in regards on my behalf lately. I can say that I have had a fair trial of the U. Kingdom but I am unable to stand the strain any longer and take the law in my own hand. I fought many a battles and death is only a saviour for me. I would have prefered the death to be shot, but don't wish to ascent the scaffold as a xxx and hope the Almighty Architect of the Universe will lead me in the unknown land. I am not dying as a Spy but as a soldier. My fate I stood as a man but cant be a liar and perjur myself. Kindly I shall permit to ask to notify my uncle Andros Troll Sollingen A. Rastatt i.B. Germany; and all my estate shall belong to him. What I done, I have done for my country. I shall express my thanks, and may the Lord bless you all.

Yours,
Anton Küpferle

My age is 31 years and I am born June 11/1883

The suicide message written on a prison slate by Anton Küpferle. Arrested on a charge of espionage in May 1915, he hanged himself in his cell during his trial.

Anton Küpferle.

Mata Hari (Margaretha Gertrud Zelle), one of the most notorious First World War spies. Her cover was blown because of German lack of a secure diplomatic code, and she was executed by firing squad in October 1917.

(*BBC Hulton Picture Library*)

Superintendent Patrick Quinn during the trial of Sir Roger Casement at Bow Street Police Court, May 1916.

(*BBC Hulton Picture Library*)

Some Heads of the Special Branch.

hief Constable Albert Canning,
VO, OBE, 1936–46.

Commander Leonard Burt, CVO, CBE, 1946–58.

Commander Evan Jones, CVO, 1958–66.

uty Assistant Commissioner Robert Bryan,
E, 1977–81.

uty Assistant Commissioner Victor Gilbert,
E, 1972–77.

The scene outside 49 Moorgate after the City Police and Special Branch raid on the Arcos (All Russian Co-operative Society) offices there on 12 May 1927.
(*BBC Hulton Picture Library*)

Armed police, December 1975, surrounding 22A Balcombe Street, where two IRA gunmen had barricaded themselves in with their hostages. After five days the gunmen released the hostages and surrendered.

(*BBC Hulton Picture Library*)

which was its overtly political nature. Sir Travers Humphreys had
stated as much at Bow Street when he had opened the prosecution's
case:

> This is not a prosecution of an individual for an individual act.
> The case for the prosecution is that all the accused are engaged
> with others – many others – in an illegal conspiracy – a con-
> spiracy to do an act, or achieve an end by unlawful means. They
> are concerned in different capacities in teaching the doctrines of
> what they call Communism.

The defendants claimed that whatever had been written, no one
had actually been subverted or incited to mutiny, and that it was
their ideals which were actually on trial. Clearly the jury did not
agree, for they had taken just twenty minutes to reach their verdict.

The judge then told the defendants:

> You are members of an illegal party carrying on illegal work in
> this country, and it must stop. Five of you – Inkpin, Rust, Pollitt,
> Gallacher, and Hannington – have been convicted before. You
> have had your warning as to breaking the laws of this country,
> and I can do nothing now other than send you to prison. Because
> you are not of the ordinary criminal class you shall not be dealt
> with in the ordinary way, but be put in the second division. The
> sentence upon you five is imprisonment for 12 calendar months.

The 1925 Communist Party of Great Britain convictions were
indeed a triumph for the Branch although the sentences imposed
on the defendants were light. Nevertheless it confirmed in law the
seditious nature of the CPGB... and confirmed Edward Parker's
succession on James McBrien's retirement.

The remainder of the 1920s was a quiet period for the Branch.
Even the General Strike of May 1926 turned into a routine exercise
for the Branch who limited their activities to the preparation of a
news-sheet for internal distribution. By the end of a week the
General Strike was over. In spite of the strike the strength of the
Branch remained at its usual peacetime level of 150 officers and
clerks.

The first half of the decade had been consumed by routine
surveillance on the CPGB and other potentially subversive
organisations, and the IRA militants had been too busy fighting the
Free State to launch operations on the English mainland. Childs
and McBrien had scotched such plans as might have existed in a
series of raids early in the morning of Sunday, 11 March 1923
which resulted in the deportation of more than a hundred IRA
suspects to the Free State.

The operation had been sparked off by the interception of correspondence addressed to a known IRA activist in London referred to simply as "Officer Commanding, Britain". The Home Secretary took the opportunity to order the arrests of all Irish suspects and later read one of the intercepted letters to the House of Commons:

> I could not promise you grenades at present. It is impossible to keep the foundry open here. Hence, the the output is very small; but I am having some aluminium light grenades made, and packed with shrapnel, which, I hope, will be effective.

McBrien assigned two detectives to each suspect and within two hours had detained thirty-three suspects, including ten women, at local police stations. Twelve buses were then used to collect all the prisoners and transport them to Hunter Street police station. At Euston a specially chartered train carried them to Liverpool where a warship was waiting to ship them to Dublin.

A total of 110 people was removed to Ireland in the cruiser *HMS Castor* and interned at Mountjoy Prison on arrival. Surprisingly, considering the quantity of documents seized in the raids, there was only one immediate prosecution; that was the case of Francis McCarthy, on 15 April 1923. He was found in possession of an unloaded revolver at his home in Jamaica Road, Bermondsey, by Detective Inspector Haines of the Branch. McCarthy was fined one pound.

The daring operation, carried out under the authority of the Restoration of Order in Ireland Act, was also an illegal one. The House of Lords later ruled that this operation had been conducted illegally, and some £50,000 compensation was paid to the deportees. On 17 May ninety of the deportees were returned to Holyhead where sheepish Branch detectives issued them with free railway warrants to their homes. Seven of the returning deportees were found to be carrying weapons and re-arrested, so the exercise was not entirely wasted.

For the rest of McBrien's tenure there was to be little excitement for the Branch, but there was just the faintest whiff of scandal in the air.

On 12 December 1925 two young constables on patrol in Hyde Park came across a man "fondling" a woman on a bench. Constables Hancox and Lawrie arrested them both for a breach of public decency and effectively opened a hornets' nest. The woman, who was a known prostitute, gave her name as Thelma de Lava, and the man identified himself as Sir Basil Thomson, the former Assistant Commissioner.

Thomson and Miss de Lava were escorted to Cannon Row police station to be charged, and on the way Thomson tried to persuade PC Hancox to drop the case, promising him that he could "leave the police and never have to work again". He also expressed his regret that the Deputy Commissioner, Sir John Olive, had recently retired. When these attempts failed to move the policemen, Thomson got the duty Inspector, George Duncan, to enter his name on the charge-sheet as "Mr Hugh Thomson". It was also agreed that Thomson should appear at Marlborough Street Magistrates' Court on 14 December before the arrival of the press. This plan failed when Thomson went to Bow Street Court on the appointed day, and discovered his mistake too late. To complicate matters further, Miss de Lava also failed to appear so a warrant had to be issued for her arrest.

The case eventually came to court in January the following year. Thomson protested his innocence and claimed that he had been carrying out important research for a newspaper article on the topical subject of "Hyde Park offences". He denied asking to use the name "Hugh Thomson" but his defence was undermined when the Cannon Row charge sheet was presented in evidence. Thomson had clearly signed his name "Hugh Thomson". The defence was altogether weak. Under cross-exmination Thomson suggested that he had entered the Park after dinner to meet a secret CPGB informant (whom he could not name) at Speaker's Corner. He agreed he had been approached by Miss de Lava, and had paid her a few shillings because he felt sorry for her. He had been adjusting his clothing when the two police officers had arrested him. He denied kissing the prostitute and insisted that his behaviour had been entirely proper. In his defence he called Admiral Hall, the former DNI and now a Tory MP, and Reginald McKenna, the former Home Secretary who had originally appointed him Assistant Commissioner in 1913. In spite of these important witnesses, the magistrate found him guilty and fined him five pounds.

The incident effectively ruined Thomson's career and he never fully recovered from it. Afterwards he was to claim that he had been framed by General Horwood, who had originally accepted his resignation in 1921, and the police establishment whom he had criticised on numerous occasions. He appealed against his conviction but the Court of Appeal upheld it. In the future his involvement in police and intelligence matters was strictly limited to that of an observer and newspaper commentator. This was not to prove the case for Admiral Hall, who had so stoutly defended Thomson in the House of Commons in 1919.

Hall maintained his close interest in counter-intelligence even after he had left the Admiralty, and in March 1927 he stumbled on what he believed to be an example of Soviet espionage in England. An acquaintance reported to him that a young man named Wilfred Macartney was actively seeking information about shipments of arms to Finland. Macartney had apparently boasted that he was working for Moscow so Hall referred the matter to Kell. The Security Service embarked on a prolonged investigation which led to them supplying Macartney with an RAF document marked "secret". Macartney was then observed to pass it to an official of the Soviet Trade Delegation, based in offices in Moorgate.

The confirmation that the Russians had taken possession of the document and had stored it in their London headquarters was enough for MI5. They presented the case to the Home Secretary who in turn agreed to seek the Prime Minister's approval for a full-scale raid on the Soviet premises in Moorgate. The plan was for a raid on the afternoon of 12 May 1927.

Once MI5 had obtained clearance they brought the Commissioner and the Assistant Commissioner into the picture. They were informed that "a certain confidential military document was missing, believed stolen, and that there was reason to think the document itself was somewhere in the offices of the All Russian Co-operative Society (known as Arcos) in Moorgate Street". Scotland Yard's job was to mount the raid with expedition.

When the Assistant Commissioner was informed of the plan he pointed out certain complications. For a start, Moorgate was in the City of London and was therefore outside their jurisdiction. There was also the matter of the Diplomatic Immunities Act. The Soviet Trade Delegation enjoyed diplomatic protection and therefore was deemed to be foreign territory, so far as the police were concerned. These difficulties were quickly ironed out by MI5 who agreed that the Commissioner of Police in the City, Colonel Turnbull, should have nominal control over the raid although most of the participants indoors would be Branch officers led by Tommy Thompson. The problem of diplomatic immunity would be overcome by obtaining a warrant to raid Arcos which, as a limited company, did not enjoy diplomatic immunity. The fact that it shared the premises with the Trade Delegation was coincidental. It was thus agreed that the head of the City CID, Chief Superintendent Halford, would apply for a warrant under the Official Secrets Act. This he did on the morning of 27 May. Meanwhile Childs instructed McBrien to gather thirty of his men together for a special operation which was to take place at various different ports. The detectives were to report to the conference room at four o'clock that afternoon equipped for an overnight stay.

At the appointed time the Branch officers gathered in the Conference Room and learned of the raid for the first time. They were issued with revolvers and then instructed to travel by tube to Moorgate Station. Once there they met a force of City policemen who secured the outside of the Soviet premises. They then forced their way into the building and seized every document they could find. The operation took place in the presence of the Assistant Commissioner, Sir Wyndham Childs, and the Deputy Assistant Commissioner (Crime), Colonel John Carter. The raid lasted for three days, during which every safe, strongroom and filing cabinet was opened and its contents examined by experts from MI5 and the Foreign Office.

Although the raid failed to turn up the RAF document it did uncover a vast amount of information about Soviet espionage and in particular revealed the cover addresses of Soviet networks in Canada, Argentina, Colombia, Guatemala, Uruguay, Mexico, Brazil, Chile, South Africa, Australia and the United States. It also prompted similar raids in Berlin and Paris.

The only remaining loose end of the Arcos raid was Wilfred Macartney who had been panic-stricken when he had first learned of the police action, but his confidence returned when no one came to arrest him. In fact his case had been given to the Branch as MI5 had no further use for him and they proceeded to build a case against him. After prolonged surveillance lasting six months Macartney arranged to meet his new Soviet contact who called himself "Mr Johnson". On 16 November an elaborate trap was set outside the agreed rendezvous, a café opposite Hampstead tube station. "Mr Johnson" was arrested inside the café by Detective Inspector Cosgrove and Superintendent Byrne while Macartney was detained in the tube station by Superintendents Parker and McBride. Both prisoners were then escorted back to the Yard where they were interrogated by Branch detectives in the presence of the Deputy Assistant Commissioner, Colonel Carter. "Mr Johnson" turned out to be a German student named Georg Hansen, although he denied having acted as Macartney's courier and pay-master.

On 16 January 1928 Macartney and Hansen appeared before the Lord Chief Justice at the Old Bailey and pleaded not guilty to a variety of offences under the Official Secrets Act. The trial lasted three days, at the end of which both defendants were convicted and sentenced to ten years' imprisonment.

The Macartney-Hansen case marked a new era for the Branch, one in which its attention would become increasingly focused on espionage. The IRA were apparently no longer a threat in mainland England and the CPGB were under routine observation. There was only one further Official Secrets case for McBrien to deal with before his scheduled retirement in November 1929.

The case was a minor one, and had begun when a Bond Street photographer reported in February 1926 that he had recently copied some blueprints for a client. Detective Inspector Kirchner was assigned the case and he quickly discovered from the negatives that the blueprints had come from the Admiralty and showed the design of a submarine known as the "K2". A check in Portsmouth revealed that the originals were intact so the Branch set about tracing the photographer's client who had given his name as "Mr Jenkins".

While Kirchner was trying to identify "Mr Jenkins" the Admiralty received a surprising communication from an American entrepreneur, Albert Charbonneau. He expressed his interest in buying obsolete submarines which the Admiralty had decided to scrap, and asked if he might also obtain their original construction plans. The Admiralty explained that they only sold their obsolete vessels for scrap, and never let their old submarines go to foreign governments. Furthermore, their policy was to refuse to release plans which, they said, invariably contained details of secret equipment. Such equipment was, of course, always removed before vessels were scrapped.

When Kirchner learned of this exchange he interviewed Charbonneau who admitted that he had accompanied "Mr Jenkins" to the Bond Street photographic studio to have the plans copied. He claimed that he had been worried by his companion's haste to return the originals to Portsmouth and had therefore checked with the Admiralty to see if they were classified. As soon as he had heard the Admiralty's reply he had burned the photographs. Charbonneau identified "Mr Jenkins" as twenty-eight-year-old Sam Goode, from Portsmouth.

Kirchner returned to Portsmouth to interview Goode, but the young man refused to say from whom he had received the K2 blueprints. He was arrested, and when his case came before Mr Justice Salter at the Old Bailey in July 1928 he was sentenced to six months' imprisonment.

Despite intensive inquiries the Branch were never able to establish who had borrowed the plans for Goode, but in the event little harm had been done as the copies had been burned. Charbonneau was never charged with any offence.

In the last year of McBrien's tenure there were several major changes at the Yard. The Commissioner reached his retirement and the Home Secretary, Herbert Samuel, announced that in November 1928 Sir William Horwood would be succeeded by Field-Marshal Lord Byng who, for the previous five years, had been Governor-General in Canada. The Assistant Commissioner (Crime), Sir Wyndham Childs, also announced his resignation, but it was not prompted by any consideration of age. He resigned to fight a libel action against the *New Statesman* magazine which published an article attacking his handling of the Savidge case. In a similar incident to the one that ended Sir Basil Thomson's career Sir Leo Chiozza Money was arrested in Hyde Park with a Miss Irene Savidge. On this occasion the police evidence was disbelieved by the magistrate and the two defendants acquitted. Miss Savidge was then escorted to the Yard for a further statement to be taken, but soon afterwards she claimed that she had been bullied. A public outcry ensued, and the Home Secretary set up a formal Inquiry headed by Sir John Eldon Bankes, a former Lord Justice of Appeal. The Inquiry exonerated the police, leaving Childs free to pursue the *New Statesman.* In his place the Home Secretary promoted Norman Kendal.

For the past ten years Kendal had been the Deputy Assistant Commissioner for the CID. He had been called to the Bar in 1906 and had joined the Yard having been invalided out of the 5th Cheshire Regiment.

The remaining months of McBrien's tenure were not to pass without controversy. In March 1929 he was witness to an important internal investigation carried out inside the Branch. Two detectives, Detective Inspector Ginhoven and Detective Sergeant Jane, were found to have passed information from the Special Branch's registry to a former policeman who had been dismissed from the force. Furthermore, they had both falsified their regulation CID diaries to conceal the fact that they had met with the man. Such a leakage was considered a very grave offence, especially since Macartney had once claimed to have paid a Scotland Yard officer for advance warning of the Arcos raid. A Disciplinary Board of Inquiry presided over by the new Deputy Commissioner, Rear-Admiral Sir Charles Royds, was convened and the two officers dismissed without a pension. Ginhoven had been a particularly popular member of the Branch and his service stretched back to 1910. Known to other detectives as "Gin", he had undertaken many adventures behind enemy lines in Germany, Turkey and Austria during the Great War. One of his wartime colleagues, Edwin Woodhall described him as "a brilliant linguist and a master of disguise". A few years earlier, in February 1926, McBrien had tried to obtain an increase in his language allowance of three shillings a week, stating that it was "totally inadequate for Officers such as PS Ginhoven, who has a knowledge of 11 languages".

Detective Sergeant Jane was also an important loss to the Branch. He was one of the Branch's twelve qualified short-hand writers and had worked in a team with DCs Waldram, Jempson and Davies to record many of the political speeches made since before the Great War.

Finally, after forty years of service in the police, Superintendent James McBrien retired. He had commanded the Branch for more than ten years and had been instrumental in moulding a thoroughly professional Branch. Most of his officers spoke at least one foreign language and several specialists had a command of some unusual ones. Detective Constable Phelan spoke Gaelic and Detective Constable Dorey was a qualified interpreter and translator in Russian.

On 30 October 1929 *The Times* announced McBrien's departure (spelling his name incorrectly) and described him as "the bodyguard of kings" because of his duties with King Edward and Queen Alexandra, and with King George and Queen Mary.

McBrien was succeeded by his deputy, Detective Chief Inspector Edward (Teddy) Parker, the man who had directed the CPGB raids. He was, however, only a few years younger than McBrien and had just four years less police service. As a result his tenure was to be only five years, the quietest five years, in operational terms, in the Branch's history. Parker had held the post for under two years when, in November 1931, the Commissioner, Lord Byng, announced his retirement on health grounds. The new Commissioner was to be Lord Trenchard, "the father of the RAF". Nevertheless, even in this short period, Parker had played his part in the historic 1931 negotiations of what was to become known as "The Treaty of Westminster". Before dealing with this important development, however, we should first review the Irish scene.

CHAPTER VII

The Treaty of Westminster

They call the officers of the Special Branch the Yard's
"Hush-Hush Men". That is because their activities
are seldom brought to light in open court. And it is a
fact that this group of the Yard's detectives is the
nearest thing to Continental secret police organiza-
tions Britain has.

Stanley Firmin in *Scotland Yard: The Inside Story*,
(Hutchinson 1948)

The first IRA outrage in London since the "Troubles" had taken
place in June 1922, almost six months after Sir Wyndham Childs
had taken up his new position as Assistant Commissioner in charge
of the Special Branch. He later described the assassination of Field-
Marshal Sir Henry Wilson as "a break in a fairly long period of
peace".

Wilson had been Chief of the Imperial General Staff until 1918
and after the war had been elected an Irish MP. Thereafter he
divided his time between his home in County Longford, in Ireland
and his house in London, in Eaton Place. He was a fierce opponent
of the Irish Republican movement and as such was an obvious
target for the IRA. News of his murder reached Scotland Yard
early in the afternoon of 22 June 1922. This was quickly followed
by more news of the incident: two armed men fleeing from the
scene had been apprehended by members of the public and some
Police Constables. Police Constables March and Sayer had been
wounded whilst giving pursuit.

The fact that the murderers, James Connolly and John
O'Sullivan, had been caught was little consolation for the Prime
Minister who promptly called a meeting of his Cabinet and
summoned the Commissioner and Childs to Downing Street.
Childs was obliged to admit that Wilson had only been guarded by
the Branch when he had been CIGS. On his retirement his
detective had been assigned to the new CIGS, and it had

apparently been the responsibility of the Irish Office to request another bodyguard. They had never done so, and the Home Office had never added his name to their list of prominent figures requiring Branch protection. Horwood and Childs insisted the fault lay with the Irish Office and both men escaped with their jobs.

Connolly and O'Sullivan both had direct links with the IRA, even though neither was Irish; they were, however, of Irish extraction. Connolly was identified as Reginald Dunn, and O'Sullivan, who had a wooden leg, was identified as Joseph O'Brien. When Dunn was searched at Gerald Road police station he was found to be carrying IRA literature. Both men claimed that they had been incensed by one of Sir Henry's speeches in which he advocated extending to women the existing penalty of a flogging for carrying weapons. The assassins were hanged at Wandsworth Prison the following August. On the morning of the execution Branch officers mingled with a crowd of Sinn Fein supporters who gathered, in error, outside Pentonville Prison.

The advent of the Irish Free State effectively transferred the problem of the IRA to the newly formed Royal Ulster Constabulary in the remaining six counties in the north. The IRA, of course, had continued to pursue its aims in the Republic but operations in mainland England were evidently low on their list of priorities. This, naturally, had been something of a relief for James McBrien, who had dealt with only a minimum of incidents before he had handed over, in November 1929, to Edward Parker. During this period the IRA had been in constant conflict with the Republic's own Special Branch, headed by Superintendent Neligan and his successor, Colonel Eamon Broy. Ironically Broy's "S-Branch", which had come to be known as "Broy's Harrier's", had largely been staffed by armed former IRA men. As one might have expected, there had been virtually no co-operation between Dublin and London so the Branch at Scotland Yard had been obliged to rely entirely on the Royal Ulster Constabulary for intelligence about the IRA and the occasional tip-off.

The IRA's pre-occupation with affairs at home allowed the authorities in London to convene a conference in 1931 to discuss the security of the Empire. Fifty Chiefs of Police from all the British territories overseas gathered in London and met with the two hundred and fifty Chief Constables representing the English county forces. Also present were Sir Horace Williamson, the recently appointed Director of the Indian Political Intelligence Department, and the Director-General of MI5, Sir Vernon Kell. The Yard was represented by the Commissioner, the AC (Crime), Norman Kendal, and the Head of the Branch, Edward Parker. The purpose of the gathering was to restructure Britain's security affairs and create definite areas of responsibility which would prevent wasteful duplication and, at the same time, centralise records.

According to the calculations of the Deputy-Director of MI5, Sir Eric Holt-Wilson, those who attended the secret conference commanded "over one hundred thousand police, including over seven thousand detective officers, all of whom were working in instant response to guidance from the headquarters of the Security Service, which itself numbered some six hundred officers, officials and technical experts".

As a result of the conference the Treaty of Westminster was drawn up which defined the interests of the various British domestic agencies. Henceforth, it was agreed, the Yard's Special Branch would have sole responsibility for the IRA and the Security Service would take over surveillance of the CPGB. Accordingly, the Branch's three senior Comintern experts, Captain Guy Liddell, MC, Miss Bunty Saunders and Miss Millicent Bagot, transferred their office to the headquarters of the Security Service at 124 Cromwell Road in west London. A Central Record Office was introduced, and a Registry to cover the entire Empire.

This division of labour was long overdue for the Branch were ill-equipped to deal with the Comintern whose subversive activities were international in nature. An activist from India might well be reported as having attended a course in Moscow, and might equally well be spotted some months later in London. This kind of monitoring job was beyond the means of the Branch, and the Security Service was infinitely better able to cope. The decision to transfer responsibility for CPGB surveillance to MI5 was to prove particularly fortuitous later in the thirties when it was discovered that the Soviets were using some CPGB personnel for espionage.

The welcome hiatus in IRA activity on the mainland continued until the outbreak of the Spanish Civil War in 1936, the year which also saw Edward Parker's retirement from the Branch, to be succeeded by his deputy, Albert Canning. In December 1936 Frank Ryan, a veteran IRA leader, took eighty-one of his men to Spain to form the James Connolly Battalion of the Abraham Lincoln Brigade. During the course of the civil war more than four hundred Irishmen travelled to Spain to fight in the International Brigades. Forty-two were killed and over a hundred were wounded. Ryan and eleven others were captured by the enemy.

The war in Spain served to distract the IRA leadership from launching any attacks in England and it also reduced their effectiveness in Northern Ireland. The IRA in the six counties had always been dominated by volunteers from the south. The Belfast

IRA had been thoroughly infiltrated by the RUC who, at one moment, were running both the local Commanding Officer and the Intelligence Officer. The Belfast CO was murdered in December 1936 when his dual role was discovered by the leadership in Dublin, and the following month the IO was shot four times on his way to church. He died in hospital on 27 January 1937.

Meanwhile the IRA in London were undergoing an internal power struggle. One faction, led by Peadar O'Flaherty, mounted a coup and sacked the OC Great Britain. In his place he appointed Jimmy Joe Reynolds. A few months later a counter-coup was staged and Reynolds was replaced by Jack Lynch, an IRA veteran who had adopted the name Buckley. As well as suffering the debilitating effects of this internecine struggle, the IRA's will to fight the English was undermined by the Anglo-Irish Agreement of 25 April 1938 in which Britain granted Ireland her remaining naval bases in Ireland. The Treaty, signed by Neville Chamberlain and Eamon de Valera, would allow Ireland to remain neutral in any future world war. Apart from the six counties in the north, there was little left to fight for.

That attitude, however, was not allowed to survive. The militants were anxious to end partition by taking a bombing campaign to England but there were serious problems ahead to complicate their ambitious plans. American financial support for the IRA had been reduced to a trickle after a series of squabbles. Very few of the IRA membership had any experience with explosives and the condition of such gelignite that had been stock-piled turned out to have deteriorated to a dangerous level. Furthermore, any "Active Service Units" sent over to conduct the sabotage would be vulnerable to arrest because they would not have any cover jobs. In spite of these drawbacks the IRA's Army Council decided to press ahead to take advantage of the British Prime Minister's policy of appeasing aggression. Bomb-making ingredients were accumulated and Jim O'Donovan, the IRA's principal strategist, prepared a plan of attack.

The acquisition of material proved, initially at least, to be somewhat hazardous and led to the arrests in London of Jimmy Joe Reynolds and Denis O'Connell. Owing to a slip-up at the Branch they were subsequently released, apparently because no-one realised their motive for possessing such a large quantity of potassium chlorate.

When O'Donovan presented his "S-Plan" to the IRA Chief of Staff, Sean Russell, it was greeted with enthusiasm. He had carefully defined the IRA's best targets in England and had suggested suitable tactics. It was a sophisticated document, the preparation of which was later thought to have been helped by some assistance from German Intelligence.

Throughout the summer of 1938 the IRA laid the framework for their attack. They recruited new faces who were completely unknown to the Branch and organised a series of bomb-making courses. Safe-houses were established on the mainland and, where possible, IRA Commanding Officers were covertly appointed to existing networks of sympathisers. This allowed organisers to travel among various different IRA groups without having their identity revealed to the general membership. According to the S-Plan, this precaution would lessen the danger of betrayal by a police informer.

On the night of 28 November 1938 the IRA tried a full-scale exercise to test their men and equipment. Three volunteers were selected to blow up the Customs posts at Clady and Strabane. The operation proved a disaster with all three men being killed by a mine that exploded prematurely. Jimmy Joe Reynolds (the CO Great Britain), and Charles McCafferty were blown to pieces while John James Kelly was badly injured and was found by the police muttering deliriously: "stand back John James... there's a wee mistake". These, evidently, had been Reynolds' last words. He died soon afterwards in hospital. The RUC launched a major investigation into the affair (as did the IRA) and came to some perceptive conclusions: the IRA were still active, and they were planning a major campaign. Their response was swift. On 22 December the RUC swept through Belfast arresting all known IRA activists on warrants issued under the Special Powers Act. Those arrested were taken to the Crumlin Road prison and served with formal Internment Orders.

During interrogation a number of the IRA internees acknowledged that a major campaign had been planned but the RUC believed that their pre-emptive raids had crushed any chance of an IRA revival.

There was little clue that this was not the case until 12 January 1939 when the Foreign Secretary, Lord Halifax, received an unusual communication. It read:

> The Government of the Irish Republic believe that a period of four days is suffcient notice for your government to signify its intentions in the matter of the military evacuation and for the issue of your Declaration of Abdication in respect of our country. Our Government reserve the right of appropriate action without further notice if upon the expiration of this period of grace, these conditions remain unfulfilled.

The note was signed "Oglaigh na h-Eireann (Irish Republican Army) General Headquarters" and bore the signatures of Sean Russell, Peadar O'Flaherty, Stephen Hayes, Thomas Grogan, Patrick Fleming and George Plunkett. The IRA had declared war, but the RUC had advised the Branch that the IRA was dead.

The Foreign Secretary passed the ultimatum to the Branch, and they were still examining it when, on Monday 16 January 1939, seven bombs went off in England. An overhead electricity cable close to Willesden power station was badly damaged and there was an explosion outside the control room of Southwark power station. Three bombs went off in Manchester, one in Birmingham and one in Alnwick. There were more explosions the following day, by which time the Branch were on full alert.

The Branch's first reaction was one of disbelief, partly prompted by the RUC's assurance that the IRA had already been defeated, and partly because it seemed that the Prime Minister had already conceded most of Dublin's demands. Port Units at Fishguard, Liverpool and Holyhead were reinforced and raids were planned on the homes of known IRA sympathisers. During the week following the bombings thirty-three Irishmen were rounded up.

The Branch raids were carried out on the authority of search warrants and executed early on Wednesday morning. The operation was timed to take place simultaneously at six in the morning. By ten past six Detective Inspector William Rogers and Detective Sergeant Coveney had reported their first success. They had raided rooms in Roundwood Road, Willesden rented in the name of "Turner" to a carpenter called Lawrence Lyons. They found a 6mm rifle and twenty-four rounds of ammunition. Lyons was traced to his place of work, a power station construction site, near Dartford in Kent, and arrested the same morning on a firearms charge. After some other suspects had been interrogated four drums of aluminium powder were traced to an address in Petherton Street, Islington, where a french polisher named James Lyons was arrested.

Another gun, this time a Mauser automatic, was found at 6.40 am at rooms occupied by Brendon Kane in Harold Road, Sutton by Detective Inspector Arthur Newton. Kane, a butcher's roundsman, was promptly arrested. At about the same time DI Frank Bridges searched a flat rented to a porter named Joseph Casey in Viaduct Street, Bethnal Green. He recovered two Colt revolvers, a Mauser pistol and seventy rounds of ammunition. There were also a number of incriminating letters including one dated May 1938 and signed by Wharton. In it he said:

Owing to unforeseen circumstances I regret I will be unable to

accept the position of T/O suggested at the last CC meeting.
Meantime it is not advisable to arrange for any further meetings
at the above address as I shall be there only at irregular hours for
some months.

Casey was escorted back to the Yard and charged with possession
of weapons and bomb-making equipment. DI Harold Keeble and
DS McDougall were particularly successful in Mornington Cresent.
They found Jack Logue, Francis Burns and Daniel Fitzpatrick all
asleep in the same rooms, and after shaking them awake the Branch
officers realised they had stumbled into a bomb factory. They
found eighty-eight sticks of gelignite in an attaché case and
seventeen detonators. There were coils of fuse wire, a suitcase of
white powder, some kitchen scales and all the other paraphernalia
needed to make explosives. There were also five copies of the IRA
ultimatum. All three men were arrested, and when Fitzpatrick was
challenged by DS McDougall about an empty shoulder holster he
replied: "If I had it in bed with me you would all be unlucky." The
last London raid was conducted by DI Tommy Thompson and DS
Evan Jones who went to Camden Road, the address found on one
of Casey's letters. There they arrested a scaffolder, Gerald Wharton,
for possession of a large quantity of potassium chlorate and iron
oxide and more than one hundred balloons. Wharton told
Thompson that the balloons were left-over Christmas decorations.
    The Branch raids were considered a triumph and it soon became
clear that the police in Manchester had achieved equally good
results by turning over known or suspected IRA dens. Superintendent William Page had been up all night supervising raids and had
arrested seven Irishmen. He had also recovered six one hun-
dredweight barrels of sodium chlorate, forty sticks of dynamite,
three matchboxes packed with a mixture of sodium chlorate, sugar
and paraffin, and a handful of candles.
    As a result of the Branch's examination of Preston's diary the
Cardiff police were asked to make one further raid which, on 28
January, resulted in the arrest of a further four IRA suspects,
including Timothy Dacey, the owner of a cycle repair shop who
was found with twenty sticks of gelignite and sixteen detonators.
Further information led to another set of raids in London. DI
Tansley and DI Cooper arrested Michael Preston of Cambridge
Street, Pimlico; John Mitchell was taken into custody in Brentford
by DI Baker for possession of bottles of poison and DI Whitehead
arrested Peter Stuart at an address in New Oxford Street. All the
men had large numbers of the IRA proclamation and more than a
thousand rubber balloons between them. Stuart was evidently a

bomb-maker who specialised in manufacturing "airships". These were balloons filled with an ingenious incendiary formula which ignited as soon as the acid content had eaten away the rubber protection and exposed the mixture to air.

When John Healy was arrested by DI Charles Buckle at his Irish social club in Kilburn High Road, West Hampstead, no less than a ton of iron oxide and two tons of sodium chlorate were recovered. He claimed he had bought it all the previous September "to make pastilles". His name and his home address had been found on a letter dated 11 January and addressed to the "Commandant, London Unit". It read: "Make sure no stuff has been left over at Healy's, Fordington Road."

It was when DI Sydney Barnes arrested Michael O'Shea at Clewar Cresent, Harrow Weald, that the Branch really began to make progress. As well as finding four revolvers, a rifle and thirty-eight rounds of ammunition, they discovered a copy of Jim O'Donovan's S-Plan, the IRA's strategy document. There were also several other incriminating letters lying around his rooms.

As soon as the Branch examined the S-Plan they realised that the bombs of earlier in the month were just the first part of a major campaign. If anyone doubted this conclusion, they did not have long to wait for confirmation. Early on Saturday 4 February two bombs went off in London underground stations. Suitcases packed with explosives and timers had been deposited at the left luggage offices at both Leicester Square and Tottenham Court Road Stations. Two people were seriously injured, the first casualties of what was to be called the English Campaign. The next day there were more explosions in London and several fires in Coventry.

The new attacks made it clear that the arrests to date had been insufficient and urgent steps were taken to analyse all the papers recovered to see if there were other members of the IRA identifiable. Peter Stuart was unquestionably the "Operation Officer, Britain" for his handwriting matched some of the signatures found on the documents. There were also orders for "B Company, London" from a senior GHQ officer named Mason. In one circular he stated:

> If you think an operation cannot be carried out without men being arrested or civilians killed you are at liberty to call the operations off.

In another he gave advice on how to avoid being spotted as an Irishman. The members of the Battalion should not have a typical Irish accent, should not wear trench coats with their hands in their pockets, green scarves or hats worn at rakish angles. The only consolation for the Branch was contained in a telegram from "P Area" which suggested that operations in Bristol, Bath and the Welsh border country "would create the impression that a large number of units was in existence in this country".

The messages from "Mason" were traced to a twenty-nine year old engineer's fitter of Great Nelson Street, Liverpool, and at the Branch's request a raid was organised by the local CID. In Michael Mason's flat the police found another IRA suspect, Joseph Walker, and both men were taken into custody along with a collection of electrical fuses which had been adapted to work off alarm clocks. Information from John Healy led to the arrests, also in Liverpool, of three Irish dockers, James, Patrick and John Hannan. Guns were found on all three. Some of the potassium chlorate recovered in London was also traced to a Liverpool tobacconist and he too was arrested, along with three other suspects. The Branch, however, were only interested in Mason and Walker, and they were escorted down to London on 7 February for interrogation at the Yard. Earlier the previous night an explosive device had gone off beside the perimeter wall of Walton Gaol. Luckily there had been no casualties.

Meanwhile the Branch were accumulating more information from their suspects and informants and another set of raids was organised. Molly Gallacher, who was arrested by DI Whitehead at a rented room in Thornhill Square, had two rucksacks containing white powder in her room. Her address book had entries for Peter Stuart and Brendon Kane. At a house in Sixth Avenue, Manor Park, DS Arthur Cain and DS Golding found two tins of detonators, timing devices and nearly a hundred balloons. The occupiers were Charles McCarthy and his two sons Thomas and Daniel. Much to Cain's astonishment McCarthy's daughter stepped forward and denounced her brother Daniel as a member of the IRA. She added that her father and other brother were innocent. At a simultaneous raid in Ashmore Road, Paddington, DI Bridges had found traces of aluminium powder in two drums stored in John Ryan's basement. He too was arrested.

On 17 and 18 February the Branch made their last arrests. Detective Sergeants Cain and Golding raided a house in Belle Vue Terrace, Hendon, and found a suitcase containing several timing devices. The owners, Thomas and Daniel McCafferty, were arrested. An apparently empty school exercise book found in a bedroom was later to prove an important piece of evidence linking them to Wharton.

On the following morning DS Arthur Fretwell searched a house in Hargrave Park and found yet more bomb-making materials. He arrested James Connolly and Francis McGowan.

Once this second sweep had been completed the Branch began a thorough examination of all the seized documents. Considerable attention was given to the S-Plan, especially by Cecil Liddell of MI5, because it was so unlike the usual run-of-the-mill IRA literature. It was a sophisticated, well-prepared summary of the English Campaign and betrayed several clues that led MI5 to believe that it might have been written with German help. If that was indeed the case, then the development was a particularly sinister one. The author confidently predicted the outbreak of a European war and was advocating that the IRA should concentrate on specially selected targets, such as the electricity grid, that would cause maximum disruption for minimal risk.

All the accused were tried at four different hearings, three of which were held in London. The first took place in Manchester, where Mr Justice Stable meted out some stiff sentences. Five defendants received twenty years and a sixth fourteen years. The only woman in the group, Mary Glenn, whose brother got twenty years, went to prison for seven years. Only one man, Patrick Walsh, was acquitted.

On 28 March the first of the London bombers were convicted at the Old Bailey. Michael Mason, who had been identified as OC Great Britain in succession to Jimmy Joe Reynolds was sentenced to seventeen years' imprisonment. When Mr Justice Humphreys asked if he had anything to say Mason declared that his real name was Cleary, and then promptly sat down again. Michael Preston, who had received twelve years, then stepped forward and declared that his real name was Fleming. Neither Mason, Preston or Stuart had said a word to the Branch throughout their interrogations although it had been established that "Peter Stuart" was really Peter Walsh, the son of a Glasgow policeman. He was sentenced to fifteen years imprisonment. The remaining six defendants received terms ranging from ten years for John Healy, the Irish club proprietor, to eighteen months for Joseph Walker. Michael O'Shea, who, according to the seized documents, was "OC Sutton & Epsom", got five years. At the end of the case the judge congratulated the Branch for showing "acumen and celerity" in making the arrests. Such praise was to prove a trifle premature, for the following day the IRA attempted to blow up Hammersmith Bridge. Two explosions rocked the bridge but they caused no structural damage. On 30 March seven bombs went off in London and there were other explosions in Liverpool, Birmingham and Coventry. There was evidently still plenty of work for the Branch to do.

While the Branch reeled from this new onslaught the Courts dealt with the remaining IRA suspects. On 4 April Mr Justice

Humphreys sentenced a second batch of seven defendants. Gerald Wharton, who was described as "the worst and most dangerous" of the conspiracy, received ten years' imprisonment. According to the Branch's records, Wharton was a known IRA activist who had previously served two years' hard labour for offences against the Defence of the Realm Act in 1920. He had been freed from Wormwood Scrubs in February 1922 following a general amnesty, and thereafter his activities in Ireland had earned him another two year sentence in Ireland, part of which had been spent in the notorious Curragh Internment Camp, from which he had unsuccessfully tried to escape by building a tunnel. Mr Justice Humphreys branded him a "hypocrite" after a lengthy defence statement made from the dock, and sentenced him to ten years' imprisonment. Daniel Fitzpatrick, another known member of the IRA who had previously been convicted in Belfast received eight years. The remaining defendants were sentenced to terms of imprisonment and, for the two youngest, borstal training. Only Charles and Thomas McCarthy were acquitted, and they were immediately congratulated by DI Tommy Thompson who shook them both warmly by the hand. The evidence against them had been less than clear although it was enough to convict Daniel McCarthy.

The next day the last of the IRA suspects were convicted and sentenced. The two McGowans, Francis and James, both received long sentences from Mr Justice Humphreys. The two McCafferty brothers, James and Daniel, were convicted by some important technical evidence from DS Salter of the Yard's Photographic Department. The exercise book found in their bedroom appeared to be completely blank, but with the aid of "oblique lighting" the experts had managed to highlight and photograph handwriting impressions. One of the pages examined using the technique revealed the names and addresses of several IRA activists and described Wharton as "Gerald Wharton, Camden Road, N. – Waterford City Unit". When confronted with this damning link with the IRA Daniel McCafferty proclaimed that "everything he had done had been done as a soldier of the Irish Republic". He received four and a half years' imprisonment while his elder brother received five.

The judge completed his sentencing by sending Molly Gallagher to a borstal for three years for possession of sodium chlorate at her flat. In less than a week the judge had sentenced twenty-one members of IRA Active Service Units to a total of a hundred and fifty-two years of penal servitude. He described the Branch's efforts as displaying "very great diligence and very great intelligence without much assistance from any other body in bringing to justice these dangerous people".

The only person known to have escaped the Branch's net was Margaret Edgeworth, Molly Gallagher's flatmate. She had disappeared once news of the Branch's operation had spread, and she was subsequently spotted in Dublin with Molly Gallagher's brother, another IRA activist.

These convictions were undoubtedly a severe blow for the IRA leadership but the Hammersmith Bridge operation and the bombs of 30 March proved they had other volunteers available to plug the gaps. The Branch were determined to keep up the pressure and continued a policy of routine raids on known IRA sympathisers. Detective Sergeants Morrison and Jordon uncovered a few minor cases of Irishmen (and women) concealing illegal firearms, but it was not until DI Whitehead and DS Hugh Scott raided John Keane's home, just a few doors away from Gerald Wharton's address, that the Branch were able to recover more bomb-making equipment. They found a hamper packed with potassium chlorate, sulphuric acid and some thirty rubber balloons. The two detectives simply waited for Keane, a porter, to return home. On the same day DI Cooper arrested Denis and Joseph McGillycuddy for possession of gelignite, fuses, aluminium powder and a Webley revolver at their room in Burns Road, Harlesden.

Progress, too, was being made in Birmingham. A bomb factory in Trafalgar Road, Moseley, blew up on the night of 30 March. The explosion took place in a bedsit rented to an Irishman named Gerard Lyons who had escaped injury in the blast and fled before the police arrived to investigate. When they did finally arrive they discovered nearly two hundred sticks of gelignite and seventy-six pounds of potassium chlorate. An alert was sounded for Lyons but he got clean away. Nevertheless some fingerprints were discovered on a bottle of acid, and these identified "Lyons" as an IRA activist from Belfast named Gerard Dunlop.

Although the Branch had to wait some weeks before they could catch up with Dunlop they were able to identify more members of the IRA in England. An outline of the command structure had been pieced together from documents seized during various arrests but some of the key figures proved elusive. None more so than John Martin, the man who had apparently taken delivery of various purchases made by John Healy the previous December. Healy had admitted buying tons of sodium chlorate and several gallons of sulphuric acid, claiming that they were for a textile business in Ireland. Some of the order had been delivered to Healy's home address, where the Branch had discovered it, but other consignments had been sent to another address in Acton Lane. A surveillance operation here had eventually led the Branch to two young Irishmen, John Martin and James McGuinness, who lodged in Gower Street. The Branch were convinced that Martin and McGuinness were the people who had taken delivery of some of the potassium chlorate but none of the witnesses were able to pick either of them out at identity parades organised by DI Rogers. Eventually the Branch were able to link Martin to two quantities of explosive materials and on 5 May he was convicted and given ten years imprisonment by Sir Gerald Dodson. When the defendant heard the sentence he announced that his real name was Pearse McLaughlin. His fellow-defendant, James McGuinness, was acquitted.

By early May 1939 the strength of the Branch had been considerably increased from its establishment of one hundred and fifty officers by the Commander, Albert Canning, who had requested the transfer of regular CID detectives. The Commissioner, Sir Philip Game, considered the hunt for the surviving IRA Active Service Units to be a top priority and approved a plan of saturation coverage on known IRA haunts. Dozens of possible suspects were under observation, and it was one of these surveillance operations which was to prove immensely profitable on the night of 4/5 May.

Two Branch policewomen were assigned to watch two Irishmen living in Sidmouth Street, Patrick Dower and Patrick McAleer. Dower was believed to be quite senior in the IRA hierarchy whilst McAleer, who was in poor health, remained an unknown quantity to the Branch. At six in the evening of 3 May the two policewomen trailed their suspects to the Tottenham Court Road where they joined up with three friends. They then began a tour of the West End, during which one of the group would break off and loiter in a doorway for a few moments before rejoining his friends. The two detectives made copious notes and then followed two of the group home to an address in Acton Street. By six the following morning no less than four bombs had gone off along the route taken by the Irishmen and two unexploded devices had been recovered from shop doorways. Fortunately only two people were injured. The rooms in Sidmouth Street and Acton Street were quickly raided and the four taken into custody. When DI Frank Bridges arrested McAleer he found him to be still carrying two electric detonators. The fifth man, Timothy Murray, was picked up in Paddington and charged with causing explosions the previous evening.

There was a surprise in store for the Branch when they interrogated the two men from Acton Street. One gave his name as

Gerard Bradford, but he was identified as Gerard Kirk, a well-known IRA explosives expert. The other turned out to be Gerard Dunlop, the man who had so recently destroyed his own bomb factory in Birmingham. On 1 July all five were sentenced to twenty years' imprisonment by the Common Serjeant, Cecil Whiteley, QC. The two policewomen, whose identities remained secret throughout the proceedings at the Old Bailey, were given a commendation.

On the same night that the Branch were stalking Dower and his friends the IRA received another setback in Birmingham. A huge explosion shook Cliff Rock Road, Rednal, and destroyed part of a house there. When the police arrived on the scene they found a young man, Martin Clarke, and three women picking their way through the debris. The three women, an Irish woman of seventy-seven and her two daughters, gave their names as Mary, Elevelyn and Emily Higgins. Emily Higgins was found to be nursing two sticks of dynamite in her blouse, and all four were arrested. The women were subsequently identified as members of the Furlong family, well-known as IRA sympathisers.

Although the IRA had managed to destroy a second major bomb factory in the Midlands their attacks continued, apparently unhindered by the increasing number of Branch raids on lodging houses. On 19 May fires were started by incendiaries left in eight hotels and ten days later several cinemas were attacked with magnesium bombs. After a lull during the remainder of the month, the IRA stepped up its attacks with Post Offices becoming the principal targets in June. On 24 June three banks in Piccadilly were bombed and Madame Tussaud's Chamber of Horrors suffered damage from a balloon-type incendiary device. To the public the Yard seemed powerless to prevent the outrages and public opinion called for stronger measures from the government.

In fact the Branch had not completely lost control of the situation. A group of six Irishmen based in Harlesden had been kept under observation during the night of 24 June and two of them, Thomas Nelson and Patrick Donaghy were spotted distributing time-delayed incendiaries into pillar-boxes. Both men were later sentenced to twenty years' imprisonment.

On 24 July, Sir Samuel Hoare, the Home Secretary, addressed the House of Commons in support of the Prevention of Violence Bill. During 1939, he stated, there had been 127 terrorist outrages which had resulted in the death of one person and injuries to a further fifty-five. In all, sixty-six people had been convicted in connection with these crimes, but the police required greater powers. In particular the Bill would enable the Branch to detain suspects for questioning without charges being preferred and all

Irish subjects would be required to register with the local police. In addition, the Branch officers at the ports would have greater discretion to refuse entry to suspects. These measures were rushed through both Houses in three days, but not before another wave of bombs had hit London, and on this occasion the mainline stations were the target. On 26 July a man was killed at King's Cross when a suitcase bomb in the left-luggage office detonated, and a similar device went off at Victoria injuring five people.

The scale of the new attacks was unprecedented and it was obvious that the IRA had succeeded in replenishing themselves without interference. Nevertheless the Branch was able to make some useful arrests during these troubled days. On 22 July DI Charles Allen set a trap for three Irishmen at a house in Brunswick Square which was being used to cache detonators. John O'Regan, Herbert Moore and Edward Stapleton were later sentenced at the Old Bailey to ten years imprisonment.

In spite of these successes pressure built up on the Yard to achieve results and it was decided to eliminate what was believed to be the IRA's command centre in London. The Branch had long since identified the OC London as Gary Jones, a twenty-four year old labourer. A permanent watch on him had led detectives to the Wembley home of Charles Woods, an engine driver. His wife, Ella Woods, was an active IRA supporter and member of the fiercely Republican Roger Casement Club. Their house was raided by DI James Holmes and DS Cain, and a quantity of bomb-making equipment recovered. The garden shed revealed an unlicensed Webley revolver, and when the garden was dug up more explosive chemicals were found in jars. Meanwhile Gary Jones was arrested in a flat belonging to two sisters, Ann and Rose Conway. They were jointly charged with possession of some two hundred sticks of gelignite and detonators.

Their cases came before the Common Serjeant at the Old Bailey on 22 September, more than a fortnight after war had broken out with Germany, which was particularly unfortunate for John Woods. He alone was acquitted of all charges and discharged, but as he left the dock he was intercepted by Branch detectives and detained under the Emergency Powers Act. His wife and the others were all sentenced to ten years imprisonment.

Between the arrest and conviction of Gary Jones and his fellow conspirators the IRA committed their worst act of terrorism, the bombing of Broadgate in Coventry. This single act on 25 August killed five people and left a further sixty badly injured. It was to prove the IRA's last shot in the so-called English Campaign.

CHAPTER VIII

The Branch At War

MI5 was closely allied with Scotland Yard's Special Branch of the Police. In fact upon occasion the two agencies had interchangeable agents, and their relationship was usually of the kind which should exist between bureaux of government, something which did not always obtain between MI5 and MI6.

Lauran Payne in *Britain's Intelligence Service* (Robert Hale, 1979)

Those responsible for the IRA bomb in Coventry were quickly apprehended. They were Peter Barnes and James Richards, both described as labourers. They admitted being members of the IRA and were sentenced to death by Mr Justice Singleton at Birmingham Assizes. Three others living in the same house, Joseph Hewitt, his wife Mary and his mother-in-law Brigid O'Hara, were all acquitted.

The prosecution of the Coventry bombers was unsatisfactory in that the person who had actually placed the bomb in Broadgate had escaped to Ireland. Apparently Barnes and Richards (whose real name turned out to be McCormack) had manufactured the bomb and then given it to a third individual who was supposed to deliver it to its target, a power station. The man, who rode across Coventry with the bomb in his carrier basket, panicked and left the bicycle and bomb near the entrance of a shop in Broadgate. He then made his way to Ireland where he later underwent psychiatric treatment in a mental hospital.

The night before Barnes and McCormack were hanged at Winson Green prison in February 1940 a few incendiaries had been dropped into postboxes, but that was the limit of the reaction in England. The English Campaign had been defeated and other events had intervened to preoccupy the Branch.

First among these was the matter of enemy aliens in Great Britain, of whom there were nearly eighty thousand registered with the police. More than half had taken up residence since the beginning of 1938. In spite of this seemingly huge number, only half a percent, four hundred and fifteen, were interned on the actual outbreak of war in September 1939. The majority of these arrests were identified German espionage suspects whose names had been circulated to the Chief Constables up and down the country in sealed envelopes which were only to be opened on receipt of a particular codeword from the Security Service. Those on the Yard's list were taken into custody by Branch detectives while elsewhere the regular CID executed their Chief Constables' orders.

A large number of Austrians and Germans decided to quit the country once hostilities had been declared, and within two months the total number of enemy aliens was 73,355. Each of these cases was categorised as "A" (high security risk requiring immediate internment), "B" (those of uncertain loyalty who were subject to restriction orders) and "C", the more than 60,000 enemy aliens who had demonstrated their hostility to the Nazi regime in Germany and who were left at liberty. The plans for dealing with the enemy aliens had been long prepared by a special sub-committee of the Committee of Imperial Defence. The Branch itself played little part in drawing them up although the Commissioner, Sir Philip Game, had submitted various papers to the Committee on the practical aspects of enforcing the proposed regulations. It was generally believed that the 1914 programme of wholesale internment of civilians would probably not have to be adopted because so many of the Germans and Austrians in England were refugees who had come to England to escape persecution at home. Nevertheless MI5 identified a number of German intelligence sources within the refugee communities and pointed out that several senior *Abwehr* officials were themselves Jewish.

Before embarking on an account of the Branch's wartime role the opportunity should be taken to review the Branch's counter-espionage role since the Macartney-Hansen case of 1928 (see pages 89 and 90).

In the intervening years there had been surprisingly few incidents of espionage. The first hint of the Germans operating in England arrived at the Yard on the morning of 24 October 1935. The Kent County Constabulary reported that one of their detectives, Frederick Smith, had searched a bungalow in Stanley Road, Broadstairs, at the request of the landlady, and had found it full of the paraphernalia of espionage. The notes, maps and diaries found in the bungalow left no doubt about the occupation of the tenant, a middle-aged German named Hermann Goertz.

Goertz had rented the bungalow from a Mrs Florence Johnson for a period of six weeks from 14 September. She had called the police after her tenant had failed to reappear from a brief trip to the Continent. She believed he had decamped without paying the rent. The Security Service despatched Lieutenant-Colonel Hinchley-Cooke to investigate, and he confirmed that the evidence suggested that Goertz was a German intelligence agent who had been surveying most of the RAF airfields in the south of England. Goertz's name was added to the Suspects Index, but no further action could be taken until 8 November 1935 when Goertz turned up at Harwich. The Branch's Port Unit at Harwich, headed by Superintendent Webb, promptly arrested Goertz and escorted him to Broadstairs where he was charged with numerous offences under the Official Secrets Act.

There was no denying the incriminating evidence gathered from his bungalow, and on 9 March the following year Goertz was sentenced to four years' imprisonment. The Branch had only marginal involvement in the case but it served to remind both the Yard and MI5 that the Nazi regime was preparing an espionage offensive against the United Kingdom.

Following the Goertz case were several other incidents of German espionage. In June 1937 a German-born housewife in Dundee, Mrs Jessie Jordan, was discovered to be running an *Abwehr* post office, in much the same way that Gustav Ernst had done in 1914. She was allowed to continue her work until March 1938, by which time MI5 had accumulated enough evidence to arrest her, and to allow the FBI to trap several of her correspondents on the other side of the Atlantic. Once again, the Branch was hardly involved, although Inspector Gagen later arrested a journalist named Donald Adams for writing to German cover addresses identified by the interception of Mrs Jordan's mail. Adams was sentenced on 25 September 1939 to seven years' imprisonment.

Perhaps surprisingly, the major pre-war case of espionage in England was not a German case, but a Russian one. The affair was the culmination of nine years' work by MI5, and in particular Captain Maxwell Knight. He had infiltrated a woman agent into the CPGB in 1931, and by January 1938 she had accumulated enough proof against the CPGB's National Organiser to have the Branch arrest him.

According to Knight's agent the Organiser, Percy Glading, had persuaded three of his former work-mates at the Woolwich Arsenal to supply him with blueprints of the latest 14-inch naval gun and other classified information. The Branch were instructed to set a trap for Glading at Charing Cross Station on the evening of 21

January when Glading was scheduled to hand over stolen secret documents to his Soviet contact.

The Branch detectives, led by Tommy Thompson, took their places around the station and waited for Glading to arrive. When he did so he was approached by a younger man and handed a parcel covered with a newspaper. At that moment Thompson stepped forward and arrested Glading, and DS Sydney Barnes arrested his companion. Inside the parcel were four blueprints classified as secret.

As soon as the arrests had been completed DS Evan Jones conducted a search at Glading's house and found further evidence of the prisoner's work for the Russians. Meanwhile Glading was escorted to Cannon Row and charged with offences under the Official Secrets Act. His contact turned out to be no Russian, but Albert Williams, an employee of the Woolwich Arsenal. His home in Woolwich was then searched by DI Bridges, and another Branch detective, DI Peel, was assigned the home of a third suspect identified by MI5, George Whomack. He too worked at the Woolwich Arsenal.

The case was a classic piece of counter-espionage work. MI5 had spent nine years waiting patiently to catch Glading red-handed, and when the time came they simply told the Branch whom to arrest and where to find them. When, in March 1938, the three defendants appeared at the Old Bailey they were convicted on the evidence found at their homes, and on the testimony of the Security Service "mole" who had warned her MI5 case officer of the rendezvous at Charing Cross Station.

Glading was sentenced to six years, Williams four years and Whomack three years. The Branch had failed to catch the Soviet organiser of the network, but no doubt he would have turned out to be a diplomat who would anyway have escaped prosecution.

Very shortly after the conclusion of this Old Bailey trial the Branch were presented with their own case to follow up. In June 1938 an employee of Vickers-Armstrong at Crayford, St John Burch, was approached by one of his former colleagues, an engineer named Robinson Walker. Walker boasted that he was an agent working for the Germans, the Italians and the Russians, and asked Burch to steal drawings for him. Burch was appalled by the idea and reported the matter to Vickers-Armstrong. They in turn contacted Detective Inspector Buckle of the Branch.

The Branch's plan was perfectly straightforward, and it worked. Burch was invited to remove a drawing of a fuse-setter from work and hand it to Walker. As soon as he did so the Branch would make their arrest. On 23 June 1938 Burch took the drawing home and then gave it to Walker who promised to have it photographed by the Russian Trade Delegation and return it the next morning. Needless to say, Walker was arrested by DI Buckle as soon as he left Burch's home.

When Walker's case came to trial at the Old Bailey in September 1938 the jury did not even bother to leave the Court before finding the defendant guilty. He was sentenced to three years' imprisonment by Mr Justice Wrottesley, so ending what was probably the least complicated investigation ever handled by the Branch.

As we have seen, the Germans had only taken to launching covert intelligence-gathering operations in England very late in the day. The pre-war cases of German espionage were of trifling importance and the Security Service were confident that the initial nationwide sweep had enjoyed the same kind of success as the operation they and the Branch had conducted in 1914.

It was this complacency which characterised the attitude of both the Security Service and the Branch during the so-called Phoney War, between September 1939 and May 1940. The political crisis that led to the fall of the Chamberlain government and the apparently unstoppable German onslaught caused Churchill to create a special committee to review the nation's security measures. Known as the Security Executive, this body was chaired by Lord Swinton, who had served the previous administration as Air Minister, and consisted of representatives from all the interested services... except the Branch.

The Security Executive was appointed by the Prime Minister in June 1940 and, according to the brief public announcement which was released the following month, consisted of Swinton, Sir Joseph Ball and William Charles Crocker. The reason for their appointment was not made clear, but it was in fact because Churchill had just sacked the Director-General of MI5, Major-General Sir Vernon Kell. Kell had held his job since 1909 but a combination of poor health and incompatibility with the new Prime Minister led to his summons to a final interview with Sir Horace Wilson, the Head of the Civil Service, on the morning of Monday 10 June. His services, he was told abruptly, were no longer required. His Deputy, Sir Eric Holt-Wilson, handed in his resignation in protest as soon as he heard the news. Kell's place was to be taken temporarily by Brigadier Jasper Harker, the Director of B Division (the counter-espionage department) and Captain Guy Liddell, MC, was promoted to his post as Director B (known simply as DB) in his place. This was a significant development for the Branch because, prior to the Treaty of Westminster, Liddell had been attached to the Branch.

The Security Executive's first task was to choose Kell's successor, but in the meantime they took over the day to day management of MI5. A business efficiency expert from Roneo Vickers, Reginald Horrocks, was taken on to reorganise MI5's Registry, and a recruiting campaign initiated to increase the number of MI5 officers.

The Branch too, were undergoing expansion with CID officers being transferred to the Branch's new offices in the North Building of New Scotland Yard to cope with the vetting of refugees. At the beginning of the IRA's English Campaign the Branch's strength was 156 detectives and administrative staff. This number was to increase slightly with the return of a few retired Branch officers. Plans were also prepared for a complete removal of the three Yard buildings (South, Central and North) to a more secure location, an old school near Wimbledon. As the war progressed some of the Yard's duties were given to other agencies, such as the Civil Defence organisation which took over the enforcement of the Air Raid Precautions. Moves such as this enabled the Yard to free CID officers for war emergency work.

So far as the Yard was concerned the Branch's increased staff was quite sufficient to carry out its many duties. The Security Service, however, did not agree, and saw the Branch's close involvement with them as a threat to MI5's security. The reasons for the deterioration in the Branch's traditionally good relations with MI5 are difficult to pin down. Very likely it resulted from friction involving the first important spy case of the war.

The case had begun in October 1939 with the transfer of a code clerk named Tyler Kent from the American Embassy in Moscow to the staff of the American Ambassador in London, Joseph Kennedy. From the moment that Kent arrived he associated with a group of Right-wing, anti-Semitic extremists who were, at that time, denouncing the war with Nazi Germany as a Jewish plot. At the centre of the group was a club called The Right Club which was headed by the Unionist MP for Peebles, Captain Archibald Ramsey. It so happened that Captain Ramsey, his wife, and a naturalised British subject named Anna Wolkoff were the subject of an investigation by MI5, who had planted several agents inside the club. MI5's operation proceeded throughout the spring of 1940 but failed to obtain any admissible evidence against the Ramseys or Miss Wolkoff.

Initially it was presumed that the MI5 operation, which was supervised by Max Knight, the officer who had cracked the Glading case, was of a counter-subversion nature. But, as soon as Anna Wolkoff had been spotted entertaining the Italian Assistant

Naval Attaché, espionage was suspected. As far as MI5 could discover, only Kent had access to secret information, and they were American secrets.

After months of surveillance it was decided to inform the American Ambassador of the situation and Max Knight sought an interview with Kennedy. Knight explained that the Branch were soon to be instructed to apply for a warrant for the arrest of Kent and Wolkoff. Kennedy was appalled to learn that his code clerk had been disloyal and, on his own initiative, withdrew Kent's diplomatic immunity. Two days later Branch detectives arrested Kent at his flat at 47 Gloucester Place in the presence of Max Knight and an observer from the Embassy. Copies of about fifteen hundred American diplomatic telegrams were found in his room. The case was to become a *cause célèbre* in America because of the secrecy surrounding Kent's trial in November. It was later alleged that Scotland Yard had deliberately suppressed news of his arrest, but this was not so. A public statement was made by the Home Office on 2 June concerning his detention, and details of his conviction on five charges, brought under the Official Secrets Act and the Larceny Act, were carried by newspapers on 8 November 1940. He was sentenced to seven years' imprisonment and Miss Wolkoff received ten years. Captain Ramsey was detained under Section 18(B) of the Defence of the Realm Act and released four years later.

Under cross-examination Kent admitted having lent Miss Wolkoff copies of highly secret telegrams sent between President Roosevelt and the new Prime Minister, but there was no evidence that she had passed this information on to anyone else except Captain Ramsey. MI5 suspected she had given them to the Italian Attaché, who in turn would have ensured Berlin was informed, but this part of the case had to remain unresolved. For his part Kent justified himself by saying that he acted to prevent Roosevelt from conspiring with Churchill to bring the United States into the war against the interests of the American people.

The sensitivity of the Kent-Wolkoff case is plain to see. The Branch had seized fifteen hundred American diplomatic telegrams, more than enough to decypher the State Department's "Grey" code. Their contents, whilst not betraying naval or military intelligence, did expose the Prime Minister's close relationship with the American President. In political terms it is difficult to imagine a more potent issue. The Security Service believed that only the tightest security could ensure that such investigations could be properly undertaken and some evidently considered the Branch's discipline unsuited to the task in wartime.

Whatever the exact substance of the debate, in the summer of 1940 the Security Service were anxious to acquire powers of arrest by directly employing Yard detectives. The Branch resisted the move as Canning thought that such a development would reduce liaison rather than enhance it. Instead of having the issue resolved by the Director-General of MI5, the Security Executive recognised the matter as one of general security policy and decided to adjudicate. Their decision was a compromise that was to have important implications for the Branch. The Executive approved the idea of introducing a small police unit into MI5, but because of the Branch's resistance the detectives would be selected from the regular CID.

This novel solution met with some resistance from Sir Norman Kendal, the Assistant Commissioner (C), and his deputy, Ronald Howe, but in the end the plan was approved both by MI5 and the Commissioner, Sir Philip Game. The only remaining question was: which policeman would be picked to go to MI5? In the end the Security Executive decided this issue too, and chose a senior CID officer, Chief Inspector Leonard J. Burt.

At the time Burt had more than twenty-five years' experience in the Metropolitan Police and had served in virtually every part of London, with the exception of North London. He had spent five years in the Murder Squad and had headed the Drug and Vice Squad at the Yard. His reputation as a formidable detective was made by such successes as the Grierson murder case in 1935 and the Nodder case of 1937. Convictions were obtained in both and the murderers sentenced to hang. During the English Campaign he had participated in the search for the IRA bombers in the Midlands. His name was known to the Security Executive because of a case he had investigated in 1938... with William Charles Crocker.

Crocker was one of the most successful solicitors of his day, having amassed a considerable fortune by delving into fraudulent fire claims for suspicious insurance companies. His investigations led to the conviction of many arsonists, among whom was Willie Clarkson, the famous wigmaker. In September 1933 Clarkson lodged a claim with Lloyds for loss suffered in a fire at his shop in Ramillies Place, Oxford Street. The claim was for nearly £37,000, and it turned out to be the eleventh such claim made by Clarkson in recent years. In October 1934, just as Crocker had accumulated enough evidence to prosecute Clarkson, his quarry suddenly died. Undeterred, Crocker managed to obtain a judgment declaring two of Clarkson's previous insurance claims fraudulent. This certainly did not suit the executor of Clarkson's will, a man named William

Hobbs with a string of criminal convictions. Crocker suspected that Hobbs had forged Clarkson's will, and persuaded Sir Norman Kendal to order an official police enquiry into the will's authenticity. The man Kendal chose for the job was Len Burt and, after a long and complicated investigation, Hobbs was convicted in March 1938 of forging Clarkson's will and sentenced to five years' imprisonment. As soon as his Appeal had been dismissed the insurance companies were repaid their money.

When the question of a selecting a suitable candidate for MI5 came to be discussed Crocker proposed Len Burt, and the Security Executive agreed. Accordingly, on 19 August 1940 Chief Inspector Burt was commissioned into the Intelligence Corps and took up his new post in B1(c), the Security Service anti-sabotage section headed by Lord Rothschild. Accompanying Burt was his deputy, Reginald Spooner, Detective Inspectors Donald Fish and Smith, and Detective Sergeant Jim Skardon, who had also assisted in the Clarkson will case. Burt later commanded the Branch, while Skardon opted to remain in the postwar Security Service.

During the First World War, as we have seen, the Branch's work involved close liaison with the Security Service and resulted in the successful completion of many joint operations. The majority of espionage cases were detected by vigilant censorship and the identification of enemy cover-addresses through the employment of double agents.

In the Second World War the position changed greatly, for two fundamental reasons. Firstly, with a squad of Yard detectives inside MI5 the Security Service had little need of the Branch's powers of arrest. Burt, Spooner and the rest kept their warrant cards and remained accredited to the CID in spite of their military ranks. This dual role enabled MI5 to arrest and detain suspects without reference to the Yard. Furthermore, they maintained their own interrogation centre, Latchmere House, at Ham Common, so there was rarely a need to trouble the Branch for the use of premises.

Of the sixteen enemy agents executed in England between 1939 and 1945 only one, Josef Jacobs, was shot in the Tower of London after a court-martial. All the rest were tried at the Old Bailey and hanged in civil prisons. Again, in contrast to the Great War, the Security Service established a nationwide system of Regional Security Liaison officers to co-ordinate MI5's activities with local Chief Constables, so there was little need to call upon the Branch to deal with the two hundred or so provincial forces. Very occasionally Branch detectives were invited to participate in an MI5 investigation but more often than not their role was limited to that of providing escorts for prisoners.

Instead of the Branch's traditonal duties, which no doubt some of the officers with Great War experience came to expect, the Branch was burdened with responsibility for security inquiries among the tens of thousands of aliens who had registered with the police. In May and June 1940, as the threat of invasion grew daily, the Branch were obliged to supervise the Home Office's programme of mass internment. Camps were hastily built in ill-suited requisitioned properties and reception centres sited on race-courses to enable the authorities to review each case individually. When one considers that eventually more than 27,000 men and women filed had to be served with internment orders and escorted to their nearest reception centre one begins to grasp the size of the task. In May 1940 the incoming government attempted to alleviate the situation by transferring large numbers of internees to the Isle of Man, and by initiating a programme of deportation to purpose-built camps in Canada and Australia. The following month Mussolini declared war and a further 19,000 Italian nationals living in Britain became liable to internment.

In addition to these vast numbers there was a smaller group of British subjects whose subversive activities had brought them to the attention of either MI5 or the Branch. Both the Fascists and the CPGB had been kept under close observation for several years, and both for their varying reasons opposed the war. The numerous pro-German organisations had been the object of MI5's investigations. Two sections in particular held a watching brief: the counter-espionage (B) Branch ran agents into the potential Fifth Columnist groups to identify those with contacts with the Germans, and the political (F) Branch received reports from agents inside the British Union of Fascists and other similar bodies.

As we have seen, it was through the infiltration of agents that B Division succeeded in breaking up the Right Club. For their part F Division concentrated their efforts equally against the many Communist front organisations and the Fascists. Responsibility for the Leftist groups was vested in F1, the MI5 section headed by Roger Hollis, a future Director-General of MI5. F2, headed by Graham Mitchell (Hollis' future Deputy Director-General), dealt with the other end of the political spectrum. Much of the information sifted by F Division originated from Branch short-hand writers who had attended, since the mid-1930s, almost all political gatherings, from the smallest CPGB branch meetings to the largest Fascist rallies. The presence of these conspicuously placed detectives busy taking notes invariably led to a moderation in the tone and content of the platform speeches.

By the end of 1940 the Branch had served fewer than fifty Detention Orders under the controversial Section 18(B) of the Emergency Powers (Defence) Act. By August the following year this number had grown to 1,428, the highest of the war, and a figure which included several policemen. Sir Norman Kendal, the Assistant Commissioner (Crime) commented: "It looks to me as though the country forces are overdoing it." The majority of those detained (as opposed to the foreign nationals who were, in general, interned) were arrested by Branch detectives in the latter half of May 1940. Several raids were carried out on suspect premises including, on 23 May, a massive operation at the British Union of Fascists' headquarters in Great Smith Street. Twenty supporters were arrested, and on the same day Sir Oswald Mosley was taken into custody on an Order signed by the new Home Secretary, Sir John Anderson.

No sooner had the arrests been completed than procedures were set up to release the detainees. The majority were freed within a matter of months although some were subject to a variety of Restriction Orders which imposed certain conditions. It can be said, however, that it was the Branch's action in May 1940 which effectively eliminated the Fascist movement from the political scene.

As well as having to cope with the various Fascist movements the Branch retained their traditional responsibility for monitoring the Communists. It will be recalled that the CPGB had been obliged to undergo a number of ideological somersaults to keep pace with directives from Moscow. Prior to Stalin's pact with Hitler the CPGB had urged an anti-Fascist line and had backed the government's resistance to the Nazis. Once the pact had been made public the CPGB changed tack (much to the amusement of the short-hand writers) and denounced the British government's anti-Hitler stance. These changes in policy naturally embarrassed the CPGB leadership, and in particular the General Secretary, Harry Pollitt. Suddenly the Party line was opposition to a war with Germany so local organisers concentrated on disrupting the manufacture of munitions. On 22 June 1941 the Nazis invaded the Soviet Union, thus causing another reversal in the CPGB's war policy. Overnight the Nazi allies became "Fascist enemies of the working class".

The CPGB's chief organs during this period were the official newspaper, the *Daily Worker* and Claud Cockburn's newsletter, *The Week*. In May 1940 the Defence Regulations had prevented either from being distributed abroad but no attempt had been made to stop their publication. Then, in July 1940, the Home Secretary Sir John Anderson had written to the editor of the *Daily Worker* to express his concern over some of his more aggressively anti-war articles. The paper heeded his message briefly, but in January 1941 Anderson ordered Canning to suppress the *Daily Worker* because of its "systematic publication of matter calculated to foment opposition to the prosecution of the war to a successful issue".

Shortly before dawn on 21 January 1941 Branch detectives led by Detective Inspector Whitehead surrounded the *Daily Worker*'s printing press in Cayton Street, Clerkenwell, and then burst into the building. All the machinery was switched off and the newsprint for the following day's edition confiscated. All the staff on the premises were interviewed before being released. By the end of the morning the building was empty, save a handful of uniformed constables to guard the gates. The presses remained silent until August 1942.

By the middle of 1941 the Branch's workload had been sufficently reduced to allow Sir Norman Kendal to release Branch detectives to fight in the armed forces. Most opted for the RAF, and of the group from the Branch who joined up, sixteen were killed on active service. A plaque in their memory today hangs in the Head of the Branch's office in New Scotland Yard.

Two remaining wartime roles of the Branch should be mentioned here: the guarding of prominent people and the work of the Port Units.

Arguably the most famous of all the wartime bodyguards was Detective Inspector C.R. ("Walter") Thompson. Churchill records in *The Gathering Storm* (Cassells, 1948) the first night of the war, which he spent at Chartwell.

> There were known to be twenty thousand organised Nazis in England at this time, and it would have been only in accord with their procedure in other friendly countries that the outbreak of war should be preceded by a sharp prelude of sabotage and murder. I had at that time no official protection, and I did not wish to ask for any; but I thought myself sufficiently prominent to take precautions. I had enough information to convince me that Hitler recognised me as a foe. My former Scotland Yard detective, Inspector Thompson, was in retirement. I told him to come along and bring his pistol with him. I got out my own weapons, which were good. While one slept the other watched. Thus nobody would have had a walk-over.

Thompson accompanied Churchill for the rest of the war and went with him to all the important "Big Three" conferences. His predecessor as Prime Minister, Neville Chamberlain, had been protected by Detective Sergeant Arthur Lobb, probably the only Branch detective to have met Hitler, which he did at Berchtesgaden in 1938.

Many of the personal protection duties undertaken by the Branch during the war years were remarkably dull. George Wilkinson and Detective Sergeant Les Golding, for example, were assigned to the Russian Embassy and supervised the security arrangements for such uninspiring Soviet personalities as the Foreign Minister, Vyacheslav Molotov, and the Ambassador, Ivan Maisky. When Molotov travelled to New York in October 1946 to attend the opening session of the United Nations, Wilkinson escorted his charge to Southampton, but at the last minute the ambassador asked him join him aboard the *Queen Elizabeth* for the sea journey across the Atlantic. Unperturbed, Wilkinson accepted the invitation and when Cunard protested there was no accommodation left for an extra passenger he shared a cabin with the ship's radio officer.

Another necessary but unrewarding wartime task for the Branch was the provision of a Branch detective to the Duke of Windsor. Prior to the abdication, Superintendent Storrier of London's "A" Division had been allotted the task of guarding Edward VIII, but soon after that traumatic event the Prime Minister requested the attendance of a Branch officer and Detective Sergeant Atfield was appointed. When the Duke was sent to Nassau as Governor in 1940 he was accompanied by a new Branch officer, Detective Inspector Harry Holder.

It could be said that during the First World War the Port Units had been of rather lesser importance, in security terms, than those created in September 1939. The front line in the 1914–1918 conflict remained in France and Belgium and the German espionage effort was concentrated in those countries. It was for this reason that so many Branch detectives had been seconded to the Inter-Allied Intelligence Bureau in 1915 to help identify enemy agents. By June 1940 the British front line had been relocated on the coast of Sussex, and the Port Units had acquired correspondingly crucial roles.

At the outbreak of war the Branch's Port Units were strengthened by military personnel from a newly recreated Intelligence Corps. A large number of territorials underwent a brief training course at Mytchett Place, near Aldershot, and were then posted as members of the Field Security Police to individual Port Units. Returning British nationals were carefully vetted, while foreign nationals and refugees were directed to various reception centres for more detailed examination before final "landing clearance" was granted. Most famous of these centres was the Royal Victorian Patriotic School, sited conveniently close to Wandsworth prison. If, after a lengthy series of interrogations (which could take up to three weeks) the examining officers remained dissatisfied, the detainee would either be passed to one of the Combined Services Detailed Interrogation Centres or simply served with an Internment Order.

The first enemy agent to be caught by a Port Unit was Alphons Timmerman, a twenty-eight year old Belgian who turned up in Gibraltar in the summer of 1941. He was cleared to travel to the UK but by the time he arrived in Glasgow on 1 September his name had been circulated as a known *Abwehr* spy. He was arrested and turned over to the Security Service for intensive interrogation. He was subsequently hanged at Wandsworth on 7 July 1942. Prior warning from London also accounted for the arrests of Johannes Dronkers, in Harwich, Franciscus Winter, in Gourock, Scotland, and Joseph Vanhove, at RAF Leuchars, Scotland.

Only three Britons were executed as German spies during the war. The first was George Armstrong, a Communist seaman who had been deported from Baltimore in the United States in February 1941. He was followed by Duncan Scott-Ford, another young merchant seaman who had volunteered his services to the enemy in a neutral port.

The last British case was that of Oswald Job, a fifty-eight year old manufacturer of glass eyes whose arrival was expected by MI5. He had arrived at Bristol airport from Lisbon on 1 November 1943, and had been allowed to "land" with the minimum of formalities. In fact he was acting as a courier for a German double agent MI5 had been operating since April 1940. The Branch were to keep him under discreet observation but after three weeks of surveillance Job realised his every move was being watched and challenged his "shadow". The wretched Branch detective had no alternative but to arrest Job and escort him to a police station. The Security Service officers in charge of Job's case were appalled by this blunder, but eventually enough evidence against him was found among his belongings to convict him of espionage. He was later hanged at Pentonville prison on 16 March 1944.

The Branch detectives who played a role in MI5's famous "Double-Cross System" were Detective Inspector Bill Gagen and Canning's three most senior officers, Bert Foster, Charlie Gill and Tommy Thompson.

Gagen was the Branch officer assigned the job of serving the more sensitive Internment Orders in September 1939. All the suspects were on MI5's Precautionary Index and were thus believed to be either enemy agents or potential enemy agents. One of Gagen's first tasks was to detain a Welshman named Arthur Owens, who was to become an outstanding double agent for MI5. Gagen's introduction to MI5 had taken place in July 1939 when he had been the arresting officer in the Donald Adams case. Adams, who described himself as a racing journalist, had been corresponding with cover addresses known to be used by the German *Abwehr*. He had been identified by MI5 when six of his letters had been intercepted, and late in September 1939 he pleaded guilty to eighteen Official Secrets Act charges. He was sentenced to seven years' imprisonment.

Canning's deputy, Bert Foster, also liaised closely with MI5's B Division which was, by June 1940, headed by Guy Liddell, himself a former member of the Branch. When Karel Richter parachuted into Hertfordshire in May 1941, it was Foster who acted as the "bridge" between the local police, who had made the arrest, and MI5, who had been expecting him. Richter was later hanged at Wandsworth on 10 December 1941.

Compared to the First World War, when Sir Basil Thomson and Patrick Quinn had ensured that the Branch had been at the very centre of the British counter-espionage effort, its role in the Second World War was demonstrably different. Neither Sir Norman Kendal nor Albert Canning were given the same opportunities to participate, partly because in September 1939 Sir Vernon Kell was arguably the most experienced man in his field anywhere in the world. After all, he had been doing the same job for more than thirty years, whilst Kendal had only joined the Yard in 1918, and was Kell's junior by seven years. In any event, MI5 was certainly not obliged to rely so heavily on the Branch's support and experience. Even when it came to the recruitment of personnel, MI5 did not call on the Branch. Instead, as we have seen, the Security Service simply selected six of the CID's most able detectives and gave them an Intelligence Corps rank. Whatever the reasons, and whether they were justified or not, some of the older officers in the Branch felt they had experienced a less than glorious war.

CHAPTER IX

Burt Of The Branch

> If you enquire, even in official circles, as to the exact
> functions of the Special Branch, about which so little
> authentic information is made available, no one will
> tell you. In fact, it may be said with truth that there
> are very few who could tell you all its secrets.
>
> George Wilkinson in *Special Branch Officer* (Odhams,
> 1956)

Even before the war in Europe was over, plans were laid at the
Yard for a peacetime Special Branch. The moving spirit in laying
the foundations was the Home Secretary and Minister for Home
Security, Herbert Morrison, MP.

In late 1944 Morrison set about tackling the question of a
successor for Sir Philip Game, who had been Commissioner for
more than a decade. At sixty-eight he was well over retirement age
and his release from service had been agreed for 1 June 1945. It was
inevitable that there would be something of a clean sweep at the
Yard since Sir Norman Kendal, the Assistant Commissioner in
charge of the CID, was also due for retirement, as was the Head of
Special Branch, Chief Constable Albert Canning.

Even though Morrison was known not to be a traditionalist his
choice for the new Commissioner took everyone by surprise, not
least the candidate himself, Sir Harold Scott, the Permanent Under
Secretary at the Ministry of Aircraft Production. Scott later
commented:

> To say that I was astonished was an understatement. The first
> joint Commissioners of Police of the Metropolis in 1829 were Sir
> Richard Mayne, a lawyer, and Colonel Sir Charles Rowan, an
> army officer. Since that time it had become traditional for the
> Commissioner to be chosen from among senior officers of the
> armed forces and it was expected that when the then Commis-
> sioner, Air Vice Marshal Sir Philip Game, retired, tradition
> would be followed.

Scott saw the opportunity to "escape from the burden of paperwork which bears ever more heavily on the high officials of Whitehall" and accepted the offer. He served his political masters well and the Police College at Hendon, which had proved such a success in producing an officer corps within the force, was closed down. The College had long since been a *bête noire* of the Labour Party, for no-one could rise beyond the rank of Inspector unless he passed through the course. This selection process had been roundly condemned by Attlee as elitist, so it was not a surprise when Hendon was scrapped.

There were, in 1945, two other important jobs to be filled: Assistant Commissioner (Crime) and the Head of the Branch. Sir Norman Kendal's replacement was found simply by promoting his deputy, Ronald Howe.

Howe had come to the Yard from the DPP's Prosecutions Department in 1932. He was a barrister, and since his transfer he had held the title "Chief Constable, CID". His thirteen years in the top echelons of the Metropolitan Police had given him remarkable influence, perhaps only matched by his mentor, Sir Norman Kendal. Howe, who had been billeted with Sir Arthur Conan Doyle at Crowborough during the Great War, once described his job as "the most fascinating post in the world".

The Branch proved a more difficult proposition. Most officers in the Branch itself believed that the Deputy Head of the Branch, Tommy Thompson, would be selected, a pattern that had been established in 1903 when John Littlechild had retired. The new administration, however, had other ideas. Thompson was told that Lieutenant-Colonel Len Burt would be returning from MI5 to take up the post of Head of the Branch with the police rank of Detective Superintendent. Jones was to remain at his post at the Branch, for Burt's chief assistant in MI5, Reg Spooner, had opted to return to normal CID duties. When Thompson did eventually retire Burt selected Evan Jones for his deputy.

The appointments brought general consternation throughout the Yard and the Branch. Burt was indeed a highly experienced and popular detective, but the top job had always been filled from within the Branch. Burt had not had one day's experience of Special Branch work from the inside. His experience had been from the outside and, worse in some people's eyes, had been from an MI5 standpoint. At the time of his move in 1940 from the Yard to the Security Service he had been in the Murder Squad.

Burt took up his post on 1 January 1946 and within three months the Yard underwent its first reorganisation, with the introduction of a new rank of Deputy Commander. His immediate superior,

Deputy Assistant Commissioner Hugh Young, had his job redesignated "Commander (Crime)" with Ronald Howe remaining as Assistant Commissioner (C).

Burt's return to the Yard took place after an absence of more than four years, during which he and his chief assistant, Reg Spooner, had been involved in the arrest and interrogation of several controversial cases. In May 1945, before transferring to the Branch, Burt had flown to Rome to deal with John Amery and escort him to London. Amery had subsequently been found guilty of treachery and sentenced to death. Another of his cases was that of William Joyce, "Lord Haw-Haw", whom Burt questioned in Brussels before bringing him back to London to face trial at the Old Bailey. Amery was executed in Wandsworth prison on 19 December 1945; Joyce was hanged on 3 January 1946.

At the time of Burt's succession Sir Findlater Stewart was completing a detailed enquiry for the Prime Minister on the structure of the postwar security and intelligence services. Over the years there had been calls at various times for MI5 and the Branch to be incorporated into a single, unified command structure, but Sir Findlater's report, which was delivered to Clement Attlee in November 1945, recommended that the existing division of labour between MI5 and the Branch continue, as defined by the 1931 Treaty of Westminster.

Burt really had very little time to cope with such bureaucratic issues for there were more pressing matters to deal with. On 15 February 1946 he and Reg Spooner interviewed Dr Alan Nunn May, the atomic physicist and thus completed their last direct case for MI5. Nunn May's secret work for the Soviets had been discovered following the defection of a code clerk from the Russian Embassy in Ottawa the previous September. Although the clerk himself was of small interest the documents he purloined as his "meal-ticket" were of great importance and revealed, among other things, the existence of an extensive spy ring in Canada. As soon as Nunn May's identity had become known to MI5 the scientist had been placed under discreet observation, and it had been Burt and Spooner (then still in the Security Service) who had been selected for the task.

The surveillance had failed to spot Nunn May at any of the meetings which MI5 knew had been arranged with his Soviet contacts, so, rather than risk waiting any longer, Burt and Spooner interrogated him at the London headquarters of the Atomic Energy Authority. The meeting was a flop because there was little direct evidence with which to confront the physicist and he simply denied ever having disclosed classified information to any

unauthorised person. Nunn May left Shell-Mex House a free man,
but for the next five days he was put under increasing pressure by
some deliberately heavy-handed surveillance work by Branch
detectives. By 20 February Nunn May had had enough and signed
a statement admitting his contacts with Soviet intelligence officers.
A few days later, on 4 March 1946, he was formally arrested by
DCI William Whitehead at the conclusion of a physics lecture at
King's College, London.

Nunn May pleaded guilty to Offical Secrets Act charges at the
Old Bailey on 1 May and was sentenced to ten years' imprisonment
by Mr Justice Oliver.

The immediate postwar preoccupations of the Branch concerned
routine duties, such as the protection of the Soviet Foreign
Minister, Vyacheslav Molotov, when he visited Britain in
December 1946 and November 1947. On these two occasions Burt
assigned Superintendent George Wilkinson as his Branch bodyguard. There was, however, a growing threat from Jewish
extremism in Palestine.

In 1940 a Jewish terrorist organisation had been formed under
the leadership of Abraham Stern. He had been shot two years later
whilst attempting to escape from prison, but his right-wing
followers, estimated at some five hundred in number, continued an
underground war for the creation of a Jewish state. The Stern gang
were just one facet of the movement which included Haganah,
which represented the more moderate Jewish opinion, and the
Irgun Zvai Leumi, the most militant group. The Palestine Police
were aided in their fight to maintain the status quo by the fact that
their three major opponents spent as much time plotting against
each other as they did against the 100,000 peacekeeping troops in
the region.

The incident which sparked off the Branch's interest in Jewish
terrorism took place at the British Embassy in Rome, the
headquarters of a covert Secret Intelligence Service operation to
dissuade further illegal immigration into Palestine. The operation
was conducted by a former Special Operations Executive sabotage
expert, Colonel Harold Perkins, who arranged for limpet mines to
be attached to the hulls of ships carrying the illegal immigrants.
The ships, packed with refugees, invariably sank in the Mediterranean with terrible loss of life. In retribution the Irgun planted a
bomb in the Rome Embassy.

On 15 April 1947 a young woman called at the Colonial Office
and asked if she could use a cloakroom as one of her stockings was
falling down. The bemused gatekeeper escorted her to the

cloakroom where she adjusted her dress and deposited a time-bomb wrapped in an old copy of the *Evening Standard* and that day's *Daily Telegraph*. The following afternoon the bomb was found and the police called. It had failed to explode because the hands of the wristwatch timer had been pressed against the face, thus preventing the small hand from reaching the appointed hour and detonating the explosive. On the reverse of the watch was a thumb print belonging to a known member of the Stern gang named Albert Eliav. A "stop and detain" order was sent to all the Branch's Port Units but the delay in finding the bomb had allowed the perpetrators to escape abroad. All was not lost, for a few days later the Belgian police reported the arrest at Mons of a man and a young woman on the Paris-Brussels Express for carrying twenty sticks of gelignite. George Wilkinson was quickly despatched to investigate and he turned up several clues to link the two suspects to the Colonial Office bomb. Among them was a false French passport in the name of Elizabeth Lazarus which' had been stamped in Dover on 11 and 15 April.

Under normal circumstances both would have been extradited to England to stand trial, but there were grave complications. The woman turned out to be a French Resistance heroine from Toulouse named Betty Knout, and her maternal grandfather to have been Molotov's brother. She had been decorated with the Croix de Guerre. Her companion denied any knowledge of her or the explosives although he was found in possession of a watch similar to the one found in the Colonial Office bomb. The Belgian authorities refused the Branch's request for extradition on the grounds that their alleged crime was of a political nature. Instead they were tried in Mons for the illegal importation of explosives and found guilty. Betty Knout was sentenced to twelve months' imprisonment, her companion to eight months.

The conviction of Knout and Eliav enabled the Branch to close the file on a series of letter-bomb attacks carried out from France. An examination of Knout's suitcase revealed a false bottom in which a number of similar letter-bombs were found. There was only one further spate of Jewish letter-bomb attacks before the end of the Mandate in May the following year. Rex Farran, the younger brother of a British SAS officer who had been tried for, and acquitted of, the murder of a Jewish suspect in Palestine was killed when a bomb addressed to his elder brother Roy went off. Another bomb had been delivered to the home of a former GOC Palestine, General Sir Evelyn Barker, but it failed to go off.

Since the detonator of the device sent to Sir Evelyn Barker was of French manufacture George Wilkinson and Tom Barratt travelled to Paris to trace its origin. Coincidentally, Princess Elizabeth and the Duke of Edinburgh were due to visit the French capital and extra precautions were taken to improve the royal party's security arrangements which, under normal circumstances, would have been limited to the presence of Tommy Thompson and the Princess's Personal Protection Officer (PPO), Inspector Aleck Usher. Shortly before the visit was scheduled to start, however, the French authorities reported that the Stern gang had offered a temporary truce so the Branch contingent were able to enjoy their visit to Paris to the full.

By this stage Burt was satisfied that the Jewish extremists had ended their short-lived campaign in England, but in July 1948 Detective Inspector George ("Moonraker") Smith gave him some disturbing news. One of his informants, a Jewish aircraftsman doing his National Service in the RAF, had told him that he had been asked to desert from the RAF and join the Irgun in Palestine. The young man had been non-committal but had later attended a meeting in a Brewer Street restaurant at which it was suggested that he might remain in the RAF but commit acts of sabotage. The Irgun would provide him with all the necessary explosives.

The aircraftsman had agreed to think the idea over, and had contacted Smith. Burt and Smith instructed the informant to take the matter a stage further, so a further rendezvous was arranged at a bus-stop at Lea Marshes, near Hackney. Observation was kept by a team of detectives, including DC Winifred Sherwin, an attractive woman officer attached to the Branch. The informant met his contact and then accompanied him to a disused shop at 14 Gravel Lane, Houndsditch. When the two men emerged Branch detectives trailed the second man to his home in Southgate. By the following day he had been identified as a twenty-three year old Jewish grocer named Monti Harris.

The Branch established an observation post directly across the street from his business in Gravel Lane and Harris was placed under intensive surveillance for a period of three weeks. On Saturday, 28 August the Branch decided to raid the building before Harris had a chance to plant any bombs. There was a limited amount of evidence to indicate that he had been tinkering with them. On one occasion the Branch detectives had been alarmed to see smoke pouring from the basement and Harris emerge looking shaken. Apparently one of his experiments had gone badly wrong. Smith led the raid and arrested Harris as he was locking up for the night. Inside they found twelve primers, ammunition, reels of safety fuse, cylinders of gun-cotton, twenty-five detonators and other bomb-making equipment.

Harris was escorted to Bishopsgate police station where he was charged with offences under the Explosive Substances Act. His reply was remarkable:

I am in the cart and I know it. This is a political and a national matter. I am caught red-handed and I am not giving you any sob-stuff. What about the ammunition and the other things you have found? I do not want you to bring a second charge. I am guilty and only want it to be cleared up.

Harris was tried before Mr Justice Stable at the Old Bailey and sentenced to seven years' imprisonment. In the meantime Smith had arrested a second man, Nathan Burns, and charged him with being Harris' accomplice. It was always suspected that a third man might have been involved, but he was never identified.

Burt's tenure at the Branch continued until September 1958, but during that period surprisingly few cases of espionage were referred to the Branch for action.

Burt's first was that of Klaus Fuchs, the atomic physicist who had spied for the Russians both in England during the war and at Los Alamos where he had worked on the development of the atomic bomb. Fuchs' case was handed to the Branch complete in almost every respect. He had signed a confession and had already undergone more than a month of interrogation at the hands of Jim Skardon, the CID officer who had taken up a permanent job with Security Service. All Burt had to do was to turn up at the appointed time on 2 February 1950 and arrest the scientist. This he did, and Fuchs pleaded guilty at the Old Bailey a few days later. The Lord Chief Justice, Lord Goddard, sentenced him to fourteen years imprisonment.

Although Burt had been involved in the investigation of Nunn May five years earlier, he had done so as an MI5 officer. Now back at the Yard he learned that the Branch were only consulted about a case when it was nearing its conclusion. If it was an eerie experience having a case presented in its final moments, it did not matter, for this was to be the pattern for most of the postwar prosecutions.

Spy fever gripped Fleet Street in the days following the flight of Burgess and Maclean late in May 1952. The Foreign Office and the Security Service were extremely anxious to handle the case with maximum discretion and failed even to use the Branch to get a search warrant for Burgess' flat in Chester Square. Instead MI5 called in one of their former officers, Anthony Blunt, who had access to the flat. It could be argued that if Blunt had not been given this golden opportunity to destroy compromising letters his own confession would not have been delayed for a further decade.

Rather than concern themselves with the Foreign Office's discomfort over Burgess and Maclean the Branch were concentrating their efforts on a case which enjoyed less notoriety, but one that did end in a good "result". MI5 had been investigating a rather more junior Foreign Office employee, William Martin Marshall, since mid-June 1952, when he had been spotted in the company of a Soviet diplomat. The young man was a wireless operator at Hanslope Park, the headquarters of the Diplomatic Wireless Service. His job was to receive and transmit messages to and from British Embassies around the world. For a twenty-four year old it was a sensitive position of responsibility, but according to MI5 Marshall had betrayed his country by selling details of his work to a man who held the rank of Third Secretary at the Russian Embassy. They had been keeping him under surveillance since the previous April.

The Branch operation, led by Detective Chief Inspector William Hughes, began at Marshall's home in Elborough Street, Wandsworth. It was designed to catch Marshall in the act of giving classified information to his Soviet contact. The wireless operator was followed the entire day, but it was not until dusk that he sat on a bench in King George's Park, just a short distance from his home. Suddenly a second figure approached and sat down beside him. They sat talking for about half an hour and then got up to leave. At that moment Hughes and his colleagues stepped forward and arrested both men. When Hughes told them he had reason to believe they were in breach of the Official Secrets Act, Marshall shrugged and replied, "It's up to you to prove your suspicions." They were escorted to Wandsworth police station and searched. The older of the two men identified himself as Pavel Kuznetsov and claimed diplomatic immunity. He was found to be carrying a large amount of cash. At first he had complained that he had been arrested while walking alone in the park, but when his statement was read back to him he altered it to read that he had been arrested while walking in the park with a stranger. When the text had finally been agreed he was released.

Marshall, of course, was not so lucky. An examination of his wallet revealed a piece of paper with various handwritten notes about his work at Hanslope Park. His diary contained a note of Kuznetsov's telephone number and there were several entries recording meetings with the Russian.

Marshall's case was sent to trial at the Old Bailey and on 10 July 1952 the judge, Mr Justice Barry, directed the jury to acquit him of a charge of deliberately obtaining secret information for

Kuznetsov. The jury retired to consider their verdict on the remaining offences relating to the unauthorised disclosure of information. After twenty minutes they returned and convicted the defendant; the judge sentenced the prisoner to five years' imprisonment.

Marshall's conviction was a good "result" for the Branch, and it was followed in March the next year by another: President Tito's incident-free official visit to England. This was the first visit to England ever made by a Communist head of state and there were considerable fears for Tito's safety. Accordingly, the Yugoslavs sent over a security expert, Anton Vratusa, to review the Branch's preparations at the end of January 1953. He brought with him a list of possible exiles who had threatened Tito's life and Burt found that it corresponded very closely to the Branch's own list. Arrangements were made for those identified as potential assassins to be placed under Branch surveillance. In the immediate postwar period there were more than 132,900 aliens registered in the Metropolitan Police District, of whom approximately 47,000 were refugees from behind the Iron Curtain. Many of these émigrés were less than sympathetic to the totalitarian regimes in their homelands, and the Yugoslavs were no different from the rest. All were the Branch's responsibility. Vratusa also inspected and approved the Branch's plans to secure White Lodge in Richmond Park which was to house the President and his entourage.

Tito arrived in London on 16 March aboard a Yugoslav sail training vessel and stepped ashore at Westminster Pier where he was met by the Duke of Edinburgh and members of the Cabinet. He was guarded by seven of his own bodyguards and a squad of five Branch detectives under William Hughes. So thorough were the security arrangements that, when Tito visited the ballet at Covent Garden, the name of every ticket-holder was compared with the Branch's Registry of known and suspected extremists. The visit lasted five days and passed off without incident.

This success was followed the same year by the bizarre case of John Clarence, a petty criminal who had, from time to time, provided Detective Chief Inspector Ward and DI Rhodes with information about his contacts with Soviet Embassy personnel. He had originally come to the Branch's attention in January 1953 for distributing Russian propaganda at Speaker's Corner. He had then claimed to have been asked by the Russians to spy on groups of Soviet émigrés. Clarence's record did not inspire confidence and the Branch detectives failed to take him seriously. However, in October the following year Clarence lost a briefcase containing military information about Britain's air defences. Since last seeing the detectives, Clarence had briefly obtained a civilian job with an anti-aircraft regiment. It only lasted four months but evidently Clarence had taken copious notes of everything he had seen. When the briefcase was handed in to Catford police station the desk sergeant made a routine examination of the contents to find the name of the owner. When he saw the information, together with what appeared to be some Soviet Embassy letterheading, he called in the Branch.

Clarence's trial in December 1954 had several moments of humour, not the least being a description of the defendant's military career. He had been discharged from the army after being found wandering in France in a home-made uniform, claiming to be the Duke of Clarence. The trial, before Mr Justice Hilbery, lasted four days, at the end of which the prisoner was found guilty of various Official Secrets offences and sentenced to five years' imprisonment.

Burt's first six years as Commander of the Branch had not given him any need to worry about the IRA, which had been largely inactive in England since the ill-fated English Campaign of 1939. Suddenly, in July 1953, the situation changed overnight.

Evidently there was a group of militants within the IRA who were determined to reopen hostilities against the mainland, and to do this required large quantities of arms and ammunition that the IRA simply did not have. They therefore decided to steal all they needed from the British Army.

Their first attempt, in July 1953, was a fiasco. Three volunteers chose the Officers Training Corps School at Felstead in Essex as the target and on the night of the twenty-fifth broke in without being detected. They filled their elderly van with arms and then discovered it had been so overloaded that it would not move. The IRA men then unloaded half their haul and, still dangerously overloaded, set off for London. They got as far as Bishop Stortford before losing their way, and were intercepted by a mildly curious police patrol car. As soon as the police officers checked the contents of the van they realised they had stumbled onto an arms raid, and arrested the three men in the van.

The IRA volunteers were not, in fact, all Irish. Sean Stevenson, for example, had been born in London and had served in the RAF. His companions were Cathal Goulding, senior IRA leader, and Manus Canning from Londonderry. All three were later sentenced to eight years' imprisonment for the burglary. Goulding was considered such an important figure in the IRA hierarchy, that whilst serving his sentence, he was transferred to different prisons nine times.

The Felstead raid was followed by another fiasco, this time in Omagh in Northern Ireland. A raid on the British Army barracks in the town ended in the capture of eight IRA men. Once again, the target had been the armoury.

The abortive raid in Omagh meant little to the Branch and had been investigated by the RUC, but their interrogations confirmed the widespread rumours. The IRA were acquiring weapons to launch a new offensive. When this intelligence was relayed to the Yard, Burt called a conference of the senior Operations detectives. Detective Chief Inspectors George Smith and Arthur Cunningham were assigned the task of activating all their old IRA informants, but none appeared to know about any forthcoming raids. Clearly the IRA were going to supervise whatever they had in mind from Dublin, rather than rely on the well-penetrated IRA network in London. In any event the War Office was warned that security at all armouries in the United Kingdom should be tightened.

The long-awaited IRA raid eventually took place at Hazebroucke Barracks, a REME training centre located in Arborfield, Berkshire. Early in the morning of Sunday 13 August a group of IRA volunteers, all dressed in REME tunics, took over the guardroom. Altogether twenty-one soldiers were blindfolded and tied up with bandages. The raiders then proceeded to empty the armoury into two Austin two-ton covered vans which they drove away. The haul consisted of fifty-five sten guns, ten bren guns, an assortment of other weapons and more than sixty thousand rounds of ammunition. One of the guards freed himself just before 6 am and alerted the CID in Wokingham and the Branch were then informed.

Detective Chief Inspector Williams was the Branch officer assigned to investigate the Berkshire end of the raid, but by the time he arrived there had been further developments. Shortly before an alert was broadcast to all patrol cars, two uniformed PCs, George Kerr and George Phillips, chased and stopped a speeding lorry outside Ascot. The driver gave his name as Joseph Doyle, but the Irish driving licence he offered was in the name of Richard Wall. His companion, Donal Murphy, presented a similar licence in the name of Robert Russell. They claimed they had just collected a consignment of batteries from Newbury and were on their way to London, but neither policeman knew of a likely source of such a load in Newbury... so early in the morning. When they opened the rear of the truck they found sixty-three steel cases of weapons and ammunition.

Kerr and Phillips arrested the two Irishmen and escorted them to Ascot police station. When the cab of the Austin was searched two loaded revolvers were found beside the seats. The two men refused to answer any questions but the documents they carried made up for their silence. For example, both men had kept a receipted hotel bill from the National Hotel, Bedford Way, in London, dated 11 August. A visit by a Branch detective revealed that eight Irishmen had stayed in the hotel, so an alert was sounded for all except "Robert Russell" and "Richard Wall". All had given addresses in Dublin.

There was also a receipt for rent paid by a James Murphy of 16 Winkfield Road, Wood Green, for a lockup garage in a mews near Harley Street. Detective Inspector Garrett raided the address in Wood Green and arrested James Andrew Murphy, who admitted being a member of the IRA.

The Austin van turned out to have been rented on 12 August to one Anthony Magan who had given a false address. Telephone calls were made to other van hire companies and one in the Gray's Inn Road confirmed that they had just had one of their Austins returned. When it was searched a sten gun magazine was found jammed between two floorboards.

The police now had three of the Active Service Unit in custody and concentrated their efforts on the missing weapons and the six remaining Irishmen: Anthony Magan, Joseph James Ryan, John Reynolds, James Garland, Pat Connor and William Martin Roche. All the Branch's Port Units were strengthened but they had little luck. However, through interrogation they learned the address to which Murphy had delivered the contents of the second van: 237 Caledonian Road. The landlord, a tailor named Lewis Apostal, was traced and he agreed that a few days earlier he had let his empty shop to an Irishman named Murphy. George Smith rounded up a large team of armed Branch detectives and, late on Tuesday 15 August, raided the premises with the minimum of noise. All the guns and ammunition had been transferred to new cases, all neatly stacked in the basement. For the next twenty-four hours Smith and his men camped in the basement hoping that the rest of the IRA men would walk into a trap.

The trap failed, but at least the Branch had recovered all the stolen weapons. As recognition of this the Commissioner, Sir John Nott-Bower (who had succeeded Sir Harold Scott in August 1953) and the Deputy Commissioner, Sir Ronald Howe, were given a guided tour of the IRA safe-house by Burt and Smith.

The evidence against Doyle and the two Murphys (who were not related) was, of course, overwhelming. All three men were tried at Berkshire Assizes in Reading in October before Mr Justice Cassels, and were convicted on a variety of charges connected with the Arborfield raid. They were each sentenced to life imprisonment.

In all probability the raid would have succeeded if PCs Kerr and Phillips had decided to ignore a speeding van. A military inquiry was later held to establish why none of the sentries on guard at Arborfield had been wearing the regulation whistles or carrying the pick-axe handles with which they were usually armed. Fortunately for the military, the judge at the trial limited his comments to praise for the police.

On 19 February 1959 James Murphy made a successful escape from Wakefield Gaol and returned to Eire. It was later rumoured that Klaus Fuchs, who was also serving a sentence at Wakefield, had been involved in the plot.

Burt's departure from the Yard closed an important chapter in the Branch's history. He had been promoted into the Branch's top job from the outside and, as he himself later admitted, his lack of a foreign language made his selection an unusual choice. Nevertheless he had run the Branch for more than twelve successful years.

CHAPTER X

The Troubled Years

Few, if any, of the Special Branch look like policemen, or even detectives. Many of them wear soft collars and sports jackets, though others might be taken for ordinary business men.

Stanley Firmin in *Scotland Yard: The Inside Story* (Hutchinson 1948)

The Special Branch inherited by Evan Jones on Burt's retirement in April 1958 had remained at the same strength (approximately two hundred officers) for the past decade. Burt had supervised such major public events as the funeral of King George VI and the Queen's coronation without trouble, and had been able to escort members of the royal family on their visits abroad. In 1947, for example, he had escorted Princess Elizabeth to South Africa. For Jones, and his deputy Douglas Grant, such trips were to be luxuries they would be virtually unable to afford. Jones himself made only one such trip, to Ghana in 1961 to review the local security arrangements there prior to the Queen's arrival.

Jones also had to deal with a new regime at the Yard. Sir Harold Scott retired in August 1958 and the Home Secretary, R.A. Butler, appointed Sir John Nott-Bower as the new Commissioner. The Assistant Commissioner (Crime), Sir Ronald Howe, had been promoted Deputy Commissioner in 1953 and his post had been taken by the former Secretary of the Metropolitan Police, Sir Richard Jackson. As well as these changes at the top of the Yard, Jones found another perceptible difference in the Branch's work.

Apart from the IRA and the occasional Indian nationalist, the Branch had never really been required to involve itself in international terrorism. The brief Irgun campaign was the first sign of a new tendency. Other signs had followed. In April 1955 Greek Cypriot terrorists began the EOKA campaign to secure union with Greece, and there were indications that other groups planned to

136

bring their grievances to London. One part of the evidence had come from a young student named Konrad Da-Riff.

The Da-Riff case had started on 7 November 1956 when nearly two hundred detonators and sticks of dynamite were found in an open wood store in Park Road, Kingston-on-Thames. Detective Chief Inspector Ewing from the Branch was called in to investigate and he made quick progress. The explosives were wrapped in a newspaper, and just legible on one corner was the name "Henry" written in pencil. This clue was followed up by an appeal to newsagents to report any newspaper customers surnamed Henry. A newsagent in Crawley identified the paper as one delivered on his rounds to a Middle-Eastern student who had since gone abroad. Further inquiries revealed that Mr Henry had, until 1954, been named Konrad Da-Riff. In that year he had changed his name by deed poll. Da-Riff was routinely added to the Branch's Port Watch list and there the matter stayed until 24 January 1957, when Da-Riff flew into Heathrow from Beirut.

Da-Riff was intercepted by the Port Unit and questioned about the dynamite found in Park Road. The prisoner explained that he had been walking on the Lancashire fells near Rochdale the previous summer and had come across a store hut near a quarry. According to the signs on the hut it contained explosives so Da-Riff returned three weeks later and broke in. He stole the dynamite and carried it back to his lodgings in Crawley. He claimed that he was an ardent supporter of President Nasser and had decided to take a language course of Arabic in Syria. Before going abroad he had dumped the gelignite in Kingston.

Da-Riff pleaded guilty to theft and possession of the explosives and was sentenced in March 1957 to seven years' imprisonment. The case was a minor one for the Branch but it was not without its significance, for it was the first sign of Arab militancy on the streets of London.

Although the investigation of espionage cases is, as we have seen, one of the Branch's traditional roles, there had been few to deal with during the Fifties. All this was to change in the summer of 1960.

Early in August 1960 Evan Jones was invited to a conference at Leconfield House, the Curzon Street headquarters of the Security Service. When he got there the Deputy Director-General, Graham Mitchell, introduced the Director of the counter-espionage, D Branch, and the head of the Soviet counter-espionage section who was known simply as the D1. When the group had assembled Jones was let in on an extraordinary story: MI5 had identified a major Soviet spy network based on the Admiralty Underwater Weapons

Establishment in Portland, Dorset, and they believed they were on the brink of catching that most elusive of prizes, a Soviet "illegal". The investigation was already well advanced but now certain complications had arisen which required the Branch's involvement.

The major complication was the "illegal", a Canadian passport holder living in London named Gordon Lonsdale. The Royal Canadian Mounted Police Security Service had already confirmed the validity of the passport but an MI5 observation post in the flat next door to him was convinced he was transmitting messages in code on a short-wave radio. The D1 believed that the solution to many of their queries about him could be answered by a search of a briefcase which Lonsdale had been seen depositing in the Midland Bank in Great Portland Street. The bank would be unlikely to allow MI5 to have access to it unless they had a warrant.

The necessary search warrant was obtained by Detective Chief Inspector George Smith and taken to the bank on 24 September 1960. There Smith introduced himself to the manager, Mr Len Easter, and swore him to secrecy. Easter examined the warrant and agreed that Smith could remove the briefcase and replace it later. Smith told Easter than his customer would never learn of the search because he was safely abroad for at least a fortnight.

Smith delivered the case to Curzon Street where MI5 broke the seals. It contained conclusive proof of espionage, such as one-time cypher pads and various items used to conceal the pads and transmitting schedules. Nevertheless the Security Service were in no hurry to pass the investigation on to the Branch. They were particularly anxious to identify other members of Lonsdale's ring, and when eventually they allowed the Branch to move in they had succeeded in tracing two further "illegals", Peter and Helen Kroger.

MI5 were also concerned about protecting the source of their information. It was only after the source, a well-placed Polish intelligence officer, had defected to the West that MI5 instructed the Branch to move in. Altogether five people were to be arrested: Harry Houghton, a civilian employee of the Navy, the first spy to be identified; his girlfriend, Ethel Gee, who supplied Houghton with more secrets; Gordon Lonsdale, the suspected Soviet case officer who had been spotted by MI5 watchers at a rendezvous with Houghton; Peter and Helen Kroger, a further two suspected spies to whom Lonsdale led MI5.

The Branch operation was scheduled for Saturday 7 January 1961, the date of Houghton's and Gee's next meeting with Lonsdale. The Security Service knew this to be the correct date because they always met on the first Saturday of each month. On the appointed day Branch detectives followed Houghton and Gee from Waterloo Station, by bus, to a street market near Walworth Road. After wandering around the market for about twenty minutes Houghton and Gee returned to Waterloo and met Gordon Lonsdale. As soon as he removed a packet of documents from Ethel Gee's basket the detectives, led by George Smith, closed in and arrested all three.

Houghton, Gee and Lonsdale were escorted back to the Yard while Ferguson Smith, George Smith and Woman Detective Sergeant Winterbottom went to Cranley Drive in Ruislip to supervise a raid on the remaining two suspects, Peter and Helen Kroger. They were arrested without a struggle although Mrs Kroger asked permission to "stoke the boiler". This was agreed, provided her handbag remained with the police. Inside it was a six page letter in Russian ready to be encrypted and reduced into a microdot.

The five arrests turned out to be even more important than the Branch had dared hope. Lonsdale was a Soviet intelligence officer (masquerading as a Canadian who had died many years earlier) the Krogers' fingerprints identified them as Morris and Lona Cohen, both wanted by the FBI for questioning in connection with the leakage of atomic information from Los Alamos. The bungalow in Cranley Drive proved to be a goldmine of espionage parapher-nalia and the experts spent several weeks returning to the property to literally dig out further compromising evidence. Branch detectives found radio transmitters, false passports, cypher equip-ment, one-time pads and a variety of household items specially prepared to conceal microfilm and microdots.

Both the Branch and the Security Service were delighted with the success of the operation and preparations were made for the five spies to be tried together at the Old Bailey. Meanwhile a second major case was about to be handed to the Branch.

Only a handful of people in England were aware that George Blake was under suspicion of being a long-term, ideologically motivated, Soviet agent. Those who did know worked for either MI5 or the Secret Intelligence Service, in which Blake himself was a career officer. Attention had been drawn to Blake by various statements made in Germany by defendants in another spy case. The statements suggested that Blake, who had been posted to Germany as a technical operations director attached to the Secret Intelligence Service's Berlin Station, was a Soviet spy. He had since been transferred to a language course in the Lebanon, but he had been called back to London to face a hostile interrogation from his superiors. MI5 were informed that this was to happen and they alerted their watchers to keep him under constant observation.

Their surveillance had given the interrogators the ammunition they needed to "break" Blake, even though they had been unable to find any admissible evidence against him. Once Blake had signed a confession, in which he admitted spying for the Russians for a decade, Evan Jones was called in to complete the formalities. His deputy, Ferguson Smith, and Detective Chief Inspector Louis Gale were assigned the task of arresting Blake, which they did on 4 April 1961.

The Old Bailey experienced two remarkable spy trials that spring. The first, in March 1961, lasted six days and resulted in all five "Portland Case" defendants being sentenced to long terms of imprisonment. The following month Blake pleaded guilty to Official Secrets Act offences and was sentenced to a record term of forty-two years' imprisonment.

Soon after Blake had recovered from the shock of Lord Parker's sentence the Branch were informed by MI5's D Branch of a third espionage investigation, this time centred on the Admiralty in London. This third case had proved a major headache to MI5 because their source, another defector, had been unable to name the spy. He had provided some scanty circumstantial evidence but not enough to lead the Security Service directly to him. After several months of fruitless investigation MI5 concentrated on one man, John Vassall, who was then working as a civilian employee in the office of the Civil Lord of the Admiralty.

Vassall may have been the prime candidate, but evidently MI5 had been unable to trap him meeting his Soviet contact or catch him with unauthorised possession of secret documents. They therefore warned the Branch that they would be conducting a special operation, after which the Branch would have to move in at short notice for the arrest. In the meantime the Branch kept a selected group of Soviet diplomats under observation. The long-awaited call came on 12 September 1961, and George Smith was dispatched to the Admiralty to intercept Vassall after he left work the same afternoon. Vassall showed surprising calm as he was arrested and agreed to hand the keys to his Dolphin Square flat over to Smith so the Branch could search it. Smith was probably not entirely surprised when a representative of MI5's D Branch advised him where to concentrate his search. A wooden bookcase received particularly close attention and it was found to conceal a hiding place for spools of film. The evidence was damning, but Vassall needed no persuasion. He made a full confession and pleaded guilty when his case reached the Old Bailey later in the year. He was sentenced to eighteen years' imprisonment.

The upshot of these cases was to return the Branch, and in particular George Smith, to the limelight. A not inconsiderable amount of the Branch's work is remarkably dull fare and concerns such mundane matters as vetting applicants for naturalisation. Nevertheless the press turned them into masters of international espionage and dubbed the Detective Chief Inspector from Wiltshire "Spycatcher" Smith. This public attention was not entirely welcome and inevitably led to reporters pressing Branch detectives for tips. On one occasion a freelance journalist misinterpreted a remark made by Smith that the file on the Portland case had not yet been closed. This led to a newspaper story alleging that the Branch were still pursuing clues from the Krogers' house and were hot on the trail of two further spies. Fleet Street received a drubbing from the government Inquiry that was set up to review the Vassall case.

The problem about such newspaper speculation is that it might well be rather more accurate than anyone cared to admit, albeit for entirely the wrong reasons. By the time Lord Radcliffe's Tribunal had submitted its report in April 1963 the Security Service had indeed passed two further cases over to the Branch for prosecution.

The first, in October 1962, concerned a senior civil servant at the Central Office of Information. Evidently Barbara Fell had been identified by the same source who had guided MI5 to Vassall. She had been interviewed over a period of many weeks by Jim Skardon's successor as the Security Service interrogator, Tony Healey, and had finally agreed to confess to passing some confidential documents to her lover, who happened to work in the Yugoslav Embassy. As was customary, the case was handed to the Branch on 30 October and Detective Chief Inspector David Stratton received her written confession. Early the next month she pleaded guilty to Official Secrets Act charges at the Old Bailey and was sentenced to two years' imprisonment. This further case was to be the last of 1962, but a few short months later MI5 provided the details of yet another suspected Soviet agent.

Meanwhile, the Branch had become entangled, albeit reluctantly, in the case of a call-girl and a routine CID prosecution. The name of the girl was Christine Keeler.

On Thursday 7 February 1963 Commander Evan Jones visited the headquarters of the Security Service and informed the Director-General, Sir Roger Hollis, that earlier the previous week detectives from Marylebone Lane police station had taken a statement from

Christine Keeler in which she made a number of startling allegations, not the least of which was that she had once had an affair with the Secretary of State for War, John Profumo. She also claimed that she had been asked by the Soviet Naval Attaché, with whom she had also been friendly, to obtain details of any deliveries of atomic weapons to West Germany.

Jones revealed that Keeler had made her statement on 26 January to a Detective Sergeant Burrows from Marylebone Lane police station. Burrows had called on a routine visit to serve her with a notice to attend the forthcoming trial of a West Indian named John Edgecombe for malicious wounding and possession of a gun. Keeler was due to appear as a witness for the prosecution. Keeler had then volunteered her extraordinary story, and as soon as the detective had returned to his office he had informed his immediate superior, Detective Inspector Anning, who had read Burrows' startling notes of the interview and promptly telephoned the Branch. His call had been received by Detective Inspector Morgan. Both men had discussed the allegations and had arranged to interview Keeler on the following Friday, 1 February.

Evan Jones had learned of this on the morning of the interview and, after debating the matter with his Deputy Commander, Douglas Grant, had decided to instruct Morgan not to attend. Accordingly Grant had conveyed the order to Morgan and the meeting had been cancelled. Christine Keeler had told Burrows that she was already under contract to the *Sunday Pictorial* and Jones was sure that news of any Branch involvement would leak out. He had no desire to become entangled in what was bound to become a major political scandal. Unfortunately the local CID had interpreted the Branch's cancellation of the interview as an order from them to keep away from Keeler and this is exactly what they had done. Detective Sergeant Burrows had telephoned Keeler and said, without elaborating, that he would not be visiting her that afternoon. He had promised to be in touch again at some unspecified date in the future. Lord Denning, who was to review the police's role in the Profumo affair later criticised this "lack of co-ordination".

Stephen Ward was not unknown to the Branch. According to the Branch's Registry, MI5 had requested the Branch to check their record of Ward on 31 July 1961. The Branch had replied that Ward did not have a criminal record and nothing was known to his discredit. In April the following year the Branch had passed on various reports to MI5 concerning Ward's alleged sympathy to Communism, in accordance with MI5's instructions to be kept informed of any information relating to him. The basis of these reports were various sightings of him at Russian diplomatic parties. When, in December 1962, Ward's address had been the scene of the Edgecombe shooting incident, the Branch had also sent a routine message to Curzon Street. As was their custom, the Security Service had not offered any explanation for their interest.

The next stage in the affair had taken place on 5 February 1963, when Stephen Ward had called at Marylebone Lane police station to allege that a journalist had stolen some photographs belonging to him, including one snapshot of Mr Profumo with Christine Keeler. This report had reached the Yard two days later and Evan Jones had immediately telephoned MI5 for the meeting on that day, at which he also gave them a copy of a police report summarising Ward's allegations. Jones apparently asked if there was anything MI5 knew that might have an influence on the CID's inquiry. MI5 denied there was any security or intelligence aspect to the case and told Jones that Profumo was already well aware of the situation.

When Jones returned to the Yard he drew up this remarkable memo:

> The facts given in the police report on Ward were already known to MI5 in broad outline. Their principal interest is, of course, the Russian diplomat, whose identity is known to them and in whose activities they are taking an interest. Officially they are not concerned with the Profumo aspect, but they do know that Profumo is aware of the position and that such action as is possible is being taken by his solicitors with the newspaper. They believe it to be true that Profumo has told the Prime Minister of the matter but they do not know that for certain.
>
> I think it wise for us to stay out of this business and MI5 agree.

The result of the Branch's reluctance to get involved and the local CID's misreading of their stand meant that no one from the police visited Christine Keeler until 4 April.

In the meantime, on 22 March, Profumo had made a statement to the House of Commons in which he stated that there had been "no impropriety whatsoever" in his acquaintanceship with Keeler and the Home Secretary had become increasingly anxious about Ward's role in the affair. Remarkably, no one had thought to inform the Prime Minister of the background. When, on 27 March, the Home Secretary, Henry Brooke, had convened a meeting with Hollis and the Commissioner, Sir Joseph Simpson, the Branch had not been represented. Neither Evan Jones nor the Assistant Commissioner (Crime), Sir Ranulph Bacon, had been invited to attend.

At the conclusion of this meeting the Commissioner agreed to reopen the CID's investigation of Stephen Ward and the following week the police visited Christine Keeler and obtained a formal statement from her. They also spoke to several other girls, and on the basis of their evidence Ward was prosecuted for living off their immoral earnings. He was subequently convicted and he committed suicide early in August 1963.

The *Denning Report,* which was published in September 1963, is a historic document because it detailed, for the first time, the relationship between MI5 and the Branch. Lord Denning also outlined the Special Branch's function, but was a little inaccurate when he described the Branch as having been "formed in 1886 to deal with Irish Republican activity". He went on to describe the work of the Branch in these terms:

(1) It is concerned with subversive or terrorist organisations. So one of its duties is to collect and pass on information regarding them to the Security Service.

(2) It is also concerned with offences against the State, such as treason, espionage, offences against the Official Secrets Act and the Public Order Act. If the Security Service, for instance, detect a spy they collect the information and material about the case and then pass it to Special Branch. The Special Branch make any necessary searches or arrests and prepare the case for trial. Conversely, if Special Branch comes across material which points to a risk to national security, they pass it to the Security Service for their information.

(3) It keeps watch on seaports and airports for criminals and other dangerous persons: makes inquiries into aliens: and so forth.

Lord Denning summed up the Branch's role by observing "there is very close co-operation between the Special Branch and the Security Service. They work together in harmony and each has the fullest confidence in the other."

Denning came to this conclusion after taking evidence from a number of MI5 witnesses and hearing the Branch's version of events from Jones and Grant. The Security Service was cleared of any blame in the Profumo affair but the Branch was not so lucky. Denning's main concern was Jones's reluctance to let the Branch get involved with Keeler's allegations. He stated: "the Criminal Investigation Department and the Special Branch did, I think, make an error in not following up these reports by seeing Christine Keeler, or making sure she was seen, or by seeing Stephen Ward.

This error was due to an error in co-ordination, for which no one individual can be blamed."

This was a remarkably mild rebuke for an error that was to have considerable consequences. If, for example, Evan Jones had immediately reported Keeler's story to the Commissioner or the Home Secretary, or even confronted Profumo, the Minister might not have made a patently untrue statement to the House of Commons and been obliged to resign.

According to the chronology of events presented by Jones, the Branch were informed of the Burrows report on 26 January 1963. An interview with Keeler was confirmed for the afternoon of 1 February but the Head of the Branch only learned of the arrangement on that morning. It had apparently taken six days for news to filter up through the Branch to Jones. It is worth repeating here a part of the Burrows report: Keeler

said that on one occasion when she was going to meet Mr Profumo, Ward had asked her to discover from him the date on which certain atomic secrets were to be handed to West Germany by the Americans, and that this was at the time of the Cuban crisis. She also said that she had been introduced to the Naval Attaché of the Soviet Embassy and had met him on a number of occasions.

This was, at the very least, a serious allegation of espionage against Ward, yet according to Jones and Grant the Branch sat on the information for six days and then ordered DI Morgan not to pursue the matter for fear of press interest. It was never suggested that the police disbelieved her story.

There are two points about Jones' account that are hard to swallow. Firstly, the Marylebone CID had taken the trouble to ask a third officer to attend the interview with Keeler. He was a sergeant from the Drugs Squad who had been called in because Keeler had alleged that Ward might try to silence her by having her arrested for possession of drugs. In all, there were going to be three plain clothes police officers in the room with Keeler. There was never any necessity for them to formally introduce Morgan as a Branch officer. He could have attended as either a Drugs Squad officer or a local CID officer. If one accepts that press interest really was Jones' concern, why did he not send Morgan in under cover? Such harmless deception had been employed often enough in the past.

The second point is the delay itself. In essence Keeler was accusing Ward of being a spy, or at least being in the pay of the Soviets. When he first heard of the Burrows report DI Morgan regarded it as being of "considerable security importance", yet the Head of the Branch had decided, apparently on his own initiative, not to pursue the matter in case the press found out. Did he really only discuss the matter with Douglas Grant?

If Jones' account is true then he escaped very lightly. A more probable explanation is that Jones sought advice from MI5. No doubt he would have followed this procedure even if Ward had been unknown to the Branch, which was not the case. Ward, as we know, was already on file in the Branch's Registry and had been the subject of two Security Service referrals. It seems odd that the Branch would have passed on details (in December 1962) of a shooting incident at Ward's home (in which he was not directly involved) as well as inconsequential reports to the effect that he was "sympathetic to Communism" (in April 1963) but neglected to mention an allegation of Soviet espionage. The evidence points to the Branch taking the blame for some sort of an MI5 cover-up. Yet this is not supported by Jones' account of his first meeting with an MI5 officer to discuss the Marylebone CID's report of Stephen Ward's theft allegation. When Jones had asked if there was a "security intelligence aspect" to the inquiries the MI5 man had simply said "No."

The Branch's reluctance to involve itself in an affair that was to prove a major political scandal is understandable but it is also inconsistent, judging by the Branch's history. The Branch exists to delve into exactly those sensitive areas of state that cannot be left to regular CID officers. It seems unlikely, however, that the questions raised in this case will be resolved for many years.

At the very time that Lord Denning was researching this unsavoury affair and taking evidence from witnesses in secret, the Branch were concentrating on a further matter of suspected espionage.

On 22 April 1963 MI5 had passed to the Branch what they believed was an important case of Soviet espionage. The case centred on Dr Giuseppe Martelli, a distinguished atomic physicist then working for the Atomic Energy Research Authority at Culham, in Berkshire. According to MI5 the scientist was a Soviet spy and was presently abroad on holiday. All the Port Units were alerted to detain him on his return. This order was executed four days later by the Essex Police's Port Unit at Southend Airport, and Detective Chief Inspector David Stratton took charge of the case. Martelli was charged with nine separate breaches of the Official Secrets Act and in July 1963 appeared at the Old Bailey in what many believed would be a prosecution similar to those of two other atomic scientists, Nunn May and Fuchs.

As the case developed it became clear that it bore no resemblance to either. Martelli had an explanation for every piece of evidence the Attorney-General produced and he was acquitted of all nine charges. Somewhat unusually, his defence had been aided by a former Branch officer, George Smith, who had retired the previous year. He confirmed that the defendant was quite unlike any Soviet spy he had met, and told the court that he believed the scientist to be innocent of the offences.

The Martelli case was unquestionably something of an embarrassment for MI5, and focused attention on the extraordinary relationship between the Branch and the Security Service. As David Stratton admitted in court, he had never heard of the scientist until four days before his arrest. There were to be further examples of MI5 suddenly springing espionage cases on the Branch during Evan Jones's tenure. In one such case, in March 1965, Detective Superintendent James Wise (later Deputy Head of the Branch) arrested Frank Bossard for stealing Air Ministry secrets and selling them to the Russians. On 10 May 1965 Bossard was sentenced to twenty-one years' imprisonment by the Lord Chief Justice, Lord Parker.

The day after Bossard's arrest, the Branch intercepted yet another spy. The second, in an unconnected MI5 case, was Staff Sergeant Percy Allen, a War Office employee who had offered British secrets to various representatives of countries in the Middle East. He too was convicted and sentenced at the Old Bailey to ten years' imprisonment.

CHAPTER XI

A Weapon Of Terror

The intelligence agencies of the state, including the Branch, have their own theory of the "international communist (or anarchist) conspiracy" which seeks the overthrow of civilised societies and the democratic way of life. Such a simplistic notion leads some on the Left to dismiss the activities of the Branch on the basis of their supposed general lack of understanding of ideological questions. Again this is to misunderstand their function.

Tony Bunyon in *The Political Police in Britain* (Friedmann, 1976)

Evan Jones retired in October 1966 and Detective Chief Superintendent Ferguson Smith succeeded him as Head of the Branch. This mild-mannered Scot was not, strictly speaking, the next senior Branch officer, but he had more than five years to serve before he was scheduled to retire. Harold Suttling had been the next in line, but he had only a matter of two years left before he reached retirement age. In the event Suttling took early retirement and Arthur Cunningham and James Wise were appointed the two Chief Superintendents of the Branch.

Smith had joined the Branch in 1936, and was quickly in demand for his knowledge of German. Except for wartime duty in the RAF (and eighteen months as a uniformed Constable in the West End) he had spent all his working life in the Branch.

Smith's promotion took him to the top of an organisation that had undergone tremendous changes over the previous decade. The provincial forces in England had been completely restructured, and their total number reduced from over two hundred to forty-one amalgamated forces. All had begun to establish small but permanent Special Branch units. The Branch in London had itself grown considerably, to a strength of some three hundred officers. This expansion was partly due to the extra surveillance duties required by the ever increasing number of political demonstrations, and partly by the lengthening of the Home Secretary's list of people requiring Personal Protection Officers. In 1967 the Branch moved into its present home, the eighteenth floor of the modern New Scotland Yard building in Victoria Street.

Even in the first weeks of his new job Smith was given little peace. George Blake made a daring escape from Wormwood Scrubs on Saturday 22 October and got clean away, despite one of the most intensive nationwide police manhunts ever. The recently released prisoner who made his escape possible, Sean Bourke, also escaped arrest. Detective Chief Inspector Stephen Cunningham travelled to Bourke's home in Southern Ireland to interview his mother, but to no avail.

In May the following year, in the middle of the Prime Minister's delicate negotiations with the illegal Smith regime in Salisbury, a Rhodesian spy, Norman Blackburn, was arrested in London by Victor Gilbert. Also arrested was his contact inside 10 Downing Street, Helen Keenan. Both subsequently pleaded guilty to Official Secrets Act charges and were sentenced to five years and six months respectively.

The first major Branch case of 1970 began on 14 January when Jock Wilson drove to Woodstock Road, Carshalton, and interviewed the Labour Member of Parliament for Morpeth, Mr Will Owen.

According to his MI5 dossier Owen had been in the pay of the Czech intelligence service for a decade. The file did not include vague allegations but consisted of a series of detailed charges; they came from the very Czech intelligence officers who had, over the years, paid Owen for information that he had been privy to until October 1968, when he came off the Defence Estimates Committee. The Czechs involved had recently defected to the west. When confronted with the contents of the file Owen simply lied, thus confirming his guilt. He later told an Old Bailey jury that he answered Wilson's questions "as they arose, some were truthful and some were untruthful".

Owen was arrested and charged with eight offences under the Official Secrets Act. He was taken to Scotland Yard where he made what the police interpreted as a confession. At his trial he retracted it, saying:

If I had understood as I do this day the full implication of what was involved, I would have done as you have done and looked at the words and sought interpretation in terms of modern English and in terms of legal English.

Owen was remanded to Brixton prison to await his appearance

at the Old Bailey, and it was while he was being visited there in February by Denis Hayes, a former Labour MP, that a warder overheard a remarkable conversation. Apparently Hayes had asked Owen how he had landed up in gaol. Owen replied, "I got into their hands. They squeezed and squeezed until I finally defected. This has been going on since 1964-65."

Owen resigned his seat in April 1970 and the following month appeared at the Old Bailey and gave an account of his relationship with two Czech diplomats who, he accepted, were really spies. Detective Inspector Peter Radford told of his investigation into Owen's finances and how he had concluded that the defendant had probably had a secret source of income. Owen admitted receiving money from the Czechs but denied he had ever passed them any secret information. The jury believed him and he was acquitted on all charges.

The Owen case was the only espionage prosecution of 1970 but it was to be followed early the next year by an arrest in Yorkshire of a former RAF Sergeant. Once again MI5 provided the necessary evidence, this time from a different Czech defector, and Nicholas Prager was convicted and sentenced to twelve years' imprisonment.

Later in 1970 an internal reorganisation at the Yard under the Commissioner, Sir John Waldron, had the Head of the Special Branch promoted to the rank of Deputy Assistant Commissioner. The heads of the three main Branch sections, Operations, Ports and Administration, were redesignated Commander.

At the end of August 1970 Sir John Waldron's home in Putney was attacked with a bomb, and responsibility was claimed by a previously unknown group of revolutionary Anarchists, the self-styled "Angry Brigade". This was the first of nineteen explosions, two machine gun attacks, and six attempted bombings carried out by members of the same group. Little was known of its organisation, but the Branch suspected its members were part of a revolutionary Anarchist movement which, according to the French authorities, had been active in France during the 1968 Paris riots.

In January 1971 there were further internal changes at the Yard. A home-made explosive device went off outside the Barnet home of the Employment Secretary, Robert Carr, on 12 January and a Bomb Squad was created to trace those responsible. The initial investigation into the Barnet bomb had been conducted by the recently appointed CID chief in Barnet, Detective Chief Superintendent Roy Habershon. Habershon had previously served in the Yard's Fraud Squad, and was named head of the new Bomb Squad. By June the squad had been enlarged to twenty officers and Ernest Bond was appointed its permanent Commander. On 22

May a bomb was actually left outside a computer room at Tintagel House, the Bomb Squad's headquarters on the south bank of the Thames.

The Bomb Squad's big break came when a drug addict already in custody for a cheque fraud was reported by a fellow prisoner to have boasted about his connections with the Angry Brigade. Both men shared cell C334 in Brixton, and both were awaiting trial for different offences. As soon as this news reached the Squad, on 11 February, Roy Habershon interviewed the addict, Jack Prescott.

Prescott was a twenty-seven year old Scot who had been in trouble most of his life. His list of convictions dated back to when he was eleven. When interviewed he was on parole from Albany prison in the Isle of Wight, where he was serving a five and a half year sentence for resisting arrest with a firearm and possession of drugs. The fraud charges were due to be considered shortly but the detectives were satisified he had been involved in at least some of the bombings. Although he denied having had the conversation with his cell-mate his handwriting was found to match an Angry Brigade press communiqué sent to the *Daily Mirror*. It was later established that in 1970 he had shared a cell at Albany with a known Anarchist named Ian Purdie. On 6 March Purdie was arrested at his home in Wandsworth. He and Prescott were jointly charged with conspiracy to cause explosions and sent for trial at the Old Bailey.

By August the Bomb Squad had accumulated enough evidence to launch a raid on 359 Amhurst Road, Stoke Newington, where four people, Anna Mendleson, John Barker, James Greenfield and Hilary Creek, were arrested and various bomb-making equipment recovered. The following day two further suspects, Stuart Christie and Christopher Bott were arrested when they visited the flat. The Bomb Squad were sufficently confident of the evidence against their suspects to reduce its permanent establishment, two months later, to fifteen officers.

Christie was no stranger to the Branch. In 1964 he had been arrested in Spain for possession of explosives and had been sentenced to twenty years' imprisonment. He had been repatriated after serving just three years, and, within a few months of his return, bombs had gone off outside various Spanish diplomatic buildings. Christie's flat had been raided by the Branch on an Explosive Substances warrant in February 1968, but there was no evidence of any connection between him and the Spanish bombs. Instead they found a quantity of counterfeit dollar bills, and Christie was subsequently given a two-year suspended sentence for their possession.

Christie had not in fact been involved in the Spanish bombings. Police later arrested two men, Carver and Barlow, after an explosion and a chase outside the Bank of Bilbao in London.

Altogether twelve people had been arrested and charged with offences relating to the Angry Brigade, and in December 1971 the first to be arrested, Jack Prescott, was convicted and sentenced to fifteen years' imprisonment. Ian Purdie was acquitted but remanded in custody to face fraud charges. A year later, in December 1972, the remaining eight accused of being members of the Angry Brigade went on trial at the Old Bailey.

The trial, which lasted 111 days, was the longest on record and the all-male jury returned a majority verdict of ten to two after deliberating for more than two days. Eventually they convicted four of the defendants, Mendleson, Greenfield, Creek and Barker, and acquitted the remaining four. The jury also asked the judge, Mr Justice James, to treat the four with leniency and clemency. They were sentenced to ten years' imprisonment; the following June Prescott had his fifteen-year sentence reduced to ten years by the Court of Appeal.

1972 became one of most successful years ever for the Branch when MI5 passed over the personal files of three Soviet agents who had all been named by a defector. Detective Chief Inspector Fryer arrested all three (Constantinos Martianon, Kyricos Costi and Sirioj Abdoolcader) and when they appeared in court to answer Official Secrets Act offences they all pleaded guilty and were sentenced to long terms of imprisonment.

It was during the course of 1972 that Sir Robert Mark was appointed by the Home Secretary, Robert Carr, to succeed Sir John Waldron as Commissioner of Police. Mark was the first Commissioner of the Metropolis to have had first-hand experience of the Special Branch, having undertaken such duties in Manchester during the war and, of course, during his brief tenure as Deputy Commissioner at the Yard in 1968. One of his first jobs on taking office was to deal with the disclosure, during a trial of IRA suspects, that the Branch routinely "vetted" members of the jury in sensitive trials. This jury-vetting took the form of checking the names and addresses of potential jurors against Branch records, and supplying the prosecution with relevant information. This practice had been going on for twenty-five years, according to the Attorney-General, Sam Silkin, when the matter was eventually raised in Parliament two years later.

Mark's main task on moving into the Yard was to cope with a wave of IRA bombings in central London, so he authorised an expansion of the Bomb Squad to a strength of two hundred detectives, mainly drawn from the Branch. He also initiated a number of other changes. When Ferguson Smith retired in October 1972, he was succeeded as Head of the Branch by DAC Victor Gilbert, the former Branch detective who, five years earlier, had handled the Keenan case, the spy in Number Ten.

The Assistant Commissioner (Crime), Peter Brodie, was replaced by the AC (Traffic), Colin Woods. Three years later, in 1975, Woods was promoted to Deputy Commissioner and the DAC (CID), Jock Wilson, took over. Wilson, who had dealt with the Will Owen case, had joined the Metropolitan Police in 1946 and three years later had transferred to the Branch. In 1969 he had been chosen to co-ordinate the security arrangements for the Investiture of the Prince of Wales at Caernarvon. This operation had proved hugely successful, with only one incident on the day itself: a Welsh extremist blew himself to pieces at home some hours before the ceremony. Evidently he had been preparing a time bomb without the necessary skill.

The Branch was now to experience a major controversy. For some years the Branch had been running an informant named John Parker. Parker was a well-known figure in Irish circles in London's East End, and in November 1969 he had introduced an undercover Branch officer, "Dave Lee", to a group of Irish nationalist supporters from Belfast. They were Edmund Petticrew and his wife Marjorie, Patrick O'Sullivan, Donald de Faoit and Lawrence McGrandles. They had apparently planned to open a clothes shop in the East End and send the profits to a Northern Ireland relief fund. The Branch suspected that the group, of whom two had criminal records, were members of the IRA and were establishing a suitable cover from which to run operations in England. All were listed as members of Sinn Fein or Saor Eire (Free Ireland) movements. In any event the group had been provided with a float of £500 to pay three months' rent on their premises and to buy some stock.

The shop site chosen was a disused draper's shop located at 257 Wick Road, Hackney. The Branch set up an observation post nearby and monitored the activity of the Irishmen which, in the main, seemed to consist of visiting pubs. They also applied for and obtained a warrant to tap the shop's telephone.

Early in the morning of Monday 15 November 1971, a building in Sidcup used by the Kent Sea Cadets as an armoury and store was broken into and eleven .303 rifles and eight bayonets were stolen. The rifles were useless as weapons because the firing pins had been removed and the barrels had been drilled. They were clearly marked "for drill use only". It has never been established who exactly participated in the raid but on that Monday Lawrence McGrandles flew home to Belfast with Martin Crawford.

Later that same afternoon Crawford was detained by an army unit in Belfast and questioned by RUC Special Branch officers at Girdwood Barracks. Crawford, who later alleged that he had been beaten by his interrogators, signed a confession in which he admitted his part in the raid. He named Edward Parker as having also been present.

Two days later, on Wednesday 17 November, O'Sullivan and de Faoit announced that they too were returning to Ireland, but before they left they arranged to meet Parker at their shop to sign some business documents. When they arrived they were surrounded by twenty armed detectives. O'Sullivan, de Faoit, McGrandles, Petticrew and his wife Marjorie were all arrested and charged with possession of stolen weapons. Branch detectives found the eleven stolen .303 rifles in the flat above the shop, together with three automatics. All five insisted that the weapons had been dumped in the flat by Parker.

The five were joined in the dock at the Old Bailey on 12 June by Martin Crawford who had been escorted to England by Branch detectives. On the first day of the trial the judge, Mr Justice Bean, ruled Crawford's "confession" inadmissible and directed the jury to acquit Crawford. The trial of the remaining defendants continued for a few days but then, without warning, the Attorney-General, Sir Peter Rawlinson, announced that the Crown was abandoning the prosecution forthwith. He explained that the judge's ruling on Crawford's confession "necessarily affected the course of the case" and said that "the full facts could not be put before the jury".

The new Commissioner, Sir Robert Mark, announced that the circumstances of the "discontinuance of the prosecution" would be investigated, but in the meantime there was an extraordinary sequel to the affair.

Not long after the Branch's raid on Wick Road, they learned that the Official wing of the IRA had dispatched an Active Service Unit to England to mount a retaliatory operation for the "Bloody Sunday" incident in Londonderry. The attack took the form of a car bomb which exploded at midday on 22 February outside the officers' mess of the Parachute Regiment in Aldershot. Five waitresses, a civilian gardener and a Roman Catholic padre were killed when the 200 pounds of gelignite exploded. Eighteen others were badly injured.

The following day two uniformed police officers in Merton, South London, did a routine "stop-in-the-street" and questioned a suspicious-looking Irishman who was carrying a plastic holdall. Sergeant Laidlaw and Constable Pitches demanded to know what was inside the holdall, an item much favoured by burglars. The man replied (truthfully) that he was on his way to the river to throw it away! Inside was a gun, 280 rounds of ammunition and an assortment of IRA literature.

The police promptly arrested their suspect and he was later identified as Michael Duignan, a twenty-nine year old carpenter. A Branch officer, Detective Sergeant John Barnett, was then sent to Duignan's flat in Amity Grove, Raynes Park, where he found several books on guerrilla warfare, but nothing incriminating. Meanwhile the Hampshire CID had discovered an important clue in the smoking wreckage of the car bomb. A small part of the cylinder block had been found intact. The car had been a Ford Cortina and a number on the block, LC 08732, was identified by Ford as a 1971 model made by their factory at Dagenham. Once the engine number had been found the Branch checked with the Greater London Council's vehicle registration records to trace the owner. The Cortina's log book showed that it had last been sold to a car rental firm in North London. Their records showed the hirer to be Francis Kissane of Victoria Road, Finsbury Park. Duignan confirmed that he did indeed know such a person, and Kissane was then arrested.

More questioning, some eight thousand separate interviews and two thousand individual statements finally led the police to the organiser of the Active Service Unit: Noel Jenkinson, a forty-two year old traffic supervisor.

On 3 March Noel Jenkinson was visited at his flat in St James's Lane, Muswell Hill, by Detective Chief Inspector Edwin Smith and Detective Inspector Derek Bryce. Jenkinson denied knowing anything about the Aldershot bomb and at first there seemed nothing in the flat to link him to the IRA. Then one of the Branch officers present noticed a rate demand from the local authority. According to the demand Jenkinson was the tenant of a lock-up garage nearby. Jenkinson hesitated and then agreed to show it to the police. However, when the garage door was opened by Smith, Jenkinson warned him to call for an explosives officer. Inside were two large gelignite bombs, fortunately without detonators, and several sets of paratroop uniforms.

Jenkinson, Duignan and Kissane were sent for trial at Winchester Assizes in October 1972. The Branch regarded the case as a tremendous success for one of the three defendants had named two further Irishmen who had been involved in the plot. But when Jenkinson came to give evidence he demonstrated that he had read of the recent Old Bailey prosecution that had been abandoned. He alleged that the person responsible for the Aldershot bomb was someone he knew as Pat Egan. He claimed that he had subsequently recognised Egan as Edward Parker, the Branch informant who had been involved in the Saor Eire case. The defendant insisted that Parker had driven the Cortina to Aldershot and claimed to have seen him in the Yard on 3 March.

The allegation of a Branch *agent provocateur* at work was little more than mischief-making but the defence ploy was taken seriously. In a surprise move the Crown called John Parker as a prosecution witness and he confirmed that he had never seen Jenkinson before, at the Yard or elsewhere. Jenkinson's defence collapsed and he was found guilty on seven charges of murder. Mr Justice Shaw sentenced him to life imprisonment with a recommendation that he serve at least thirty years. Kissane was cleared of the murder charges but sentenced to two years for conspiracy to pervert the course of justice. Duignan was found guilty of the same charge and one of possessing a gun and received three and a half years.

The conviction of Jenkinson was particularly important to the Branch for he was regarded as an important IRA explosives expert. The only regret was that he was an "Official" and not a member of the Provisional wing of the IRA, which was generally considered to be more dangerous and more sophisticated. In any event it was a good result.

In the following year, 1973, the Home Secretary authorised the creation of two more specialist intelligence bodies to reduce the Branch's burden: the Illegal Immigrants Intelligence Unit and the Drugs Intelligence Unit, both based at Tintagel House with the Bomb Squad. The former took over many of the Branch's immigration responsibilities and had been designed to liaise closely with the Home Office's own Immigration Service Intelligence Unit, based at West Drayton, near Heathrow Airport.

In the twelve months leading up to September 1973 there were more than sixty IRA-related incidents involving incendiary devices posted through the mails. On 8 March 1973 the campaign was stepped up with a series of car bombs in London.

The first the police heard of this new development was when two members of the Special Patrol Group, PCs Stanley Conley and George Burrows noticed something odd about a vehicle registration number. It was on a Ford Corsair parked in Broadway, near Scotland Yard, and it appeared not to match the year of the vehicle's manufacture. A radio check with the police national computer confirmed that the index number was false.

As soon as the driver's door was opened detectives recognised the unmistakably pungent smell of explosives. Altogether 170 pounds of gelignite were removed from under the rear seats.

The Bomb Squad were called in, although its head, Roy Habershon, was in Spain on holiday. His deputy, Detective Chief Inspector George Mould took charge and Detective Chief Superintendent Gordon Seage of the Branch was alerted.

News of the alert reached the Port Unit at Heathrow shortly before the scheduled 10.45 departure of a Dublin-bound BEA jet. The travel documents of all the passengers were scrutinised with extra care by Branch officers. Under normal circumstances Branch detectives sit alongside immigration officers at the departure gates to check for fugitives and monitor the movements of suspects. This routine surveillance had been stepped up on the Irish flights because of the IRA's forced reliance on mobile teams based in Ireland. The Branch had been so successful over the years in documenting known IRA sympathisers that the Provisionals had been obliged to use specially selected teams to undertake their operations on the English mainland. Although this freed the IRA from the notoriously insecure IRA units in England it did have the disadvantage of requiring the returning Active Service Units to pass through one of the Branch's Port Units. On this occasion the IRA had tried to reduce the risk by using time bombs with a suffcent delay to enable the team to escape. The detonators were set for 2.50 pm, but the SPG unit had managed to spot the Ford Corsair soon after 9 am.

The first to be stopped at Heathrow's departure gate four were two Irish sisters, who gave their name as Devlin, and their companion, Hugh Feeney, who was carrying a large roll of five pound notes. Detective Sergeant Nigel Somers questioned them and became suspicious. He quickly established that all three had consecutively numbered airline tickets, and when the other passengers on the Dublin flight were asked to produce their counterfoils a further three people, Roisin McNearney, Martin Brady and Gerald Kelly, were discovered by Detective Sergeant Denis Welch to be holding similar tickets. Brady gave his name as Baker and claimed that he was using an alias because he was married to someone else. Altogether seven people were detained at Heathrow but this did not prevent two car-bombs exploding in the centre of London later in the day, one in Great Scotland Yard, the other outside the Old Bailey. More than two hundred people were injured in the blasts. A fourth car-bomb in Dean Stanley Street was successfully defused.

Of the group arrested at Heathrow only Roisin McNearney

agreed to help the police, and eight months later her co-operation won her an acquittal at Winchester Assizes. Nine of her companions, who all came from Belfast, were sentenced to life imprisonment by Mr Justice Shaw. The trial was held in Winchester so that special security measures could be taken.

The convictions were a tremendous success for the Port Unit at Heathrow which had anyway acquired an impressive record for spotting criminals on their way out of the country. In this instance the detectives on duty at the departure gates had contributed to the elimination of several important IRA activists, including the notorious Price sisters, Dolours and Marion. George Mould later stated that Marion, the younger of the two, was refusing to answer his questions at the very moment that the two remaining car bombs went off in London. She had said nothing, but had theatrically lifted her arm off the table in the interview room and looked at her watch. She had then smiled.

The reoganisation of local government in 1973 gave the Branch responsibility for investigating electoral offences, a job previously carried out by the local CIDs.

In November 1974 there was a further development to reduce the burden of responsibilities on the Branch. With the agreement of the Commander (Operations), Matthew Rodger, a new specialist "Diplomatic Protection Group" (DPG) was created to guard embassies and other diplomatic premises in London. The Branch's Personal Protection Squad continued to perform bodyguard duties for those on the Home Secretary's list but the creation of the DPG provided a pool of armed volunteers from the London divisions. They operated from four independent bases (which happened to house traffic wardens), each conveniently close to concentrations of foreign missions. Soon after the Iranian Embassy Siege in 1980 the DPG was designated a permanent unit and it lost its "volunteer" status.

The Saor Eire case, which was reported fully by the national press, had created a certain unease about the use of informants. The Branch in particular have always been dependent on their various sources, but clear rules existed to prevent an informant from becoming an *agent provocateur*. On 13 April 1974 the body of a man was discovered in a lane in Banstead, Surrey. It was to spark off an important episode in the Branch's history, and a public debate about the use of informants.

The man had been shot twice in the back of the head, in a classic gangland-style execution. It was only when his identity was announced that the Branch realised the full implications of the murder. The victim was Kenneth Joseph Lennon, a Branch source who had, the previous year, tipped off the Branch to the location of three IRA suspects in Luton. All three had been arrested and sentenced to ten years' imprisonment. He had also been a defendant in a trial at which another Irishman, Patrick O'Brien, had been sentenced to three years for conspiring to help the original three escape from Winson Green Prison. Lennon himself had been acquitted, but evidently the IRA had not been fooled.

In all probability there would have been a minimum of press coverage of such an event, even in the light of the Saor Eire case. But three days after the murder the National Council for Civil Liberties disclosed that they possessed a long statement from Lennon, in which he claimed to have supplied the Branch with information about the IRA. Most damagingly of all, Lennon claimed that he had only done so under duress. The next day Sir Robert Mark and the Head of the Branch, Victor Gilbert, were called to the Home Office to discuss with Merlyn Rees the growing public concern about the Lennon murder. It was agreed that the Commissioner would submit a detailed report of the Branch's involvement with Lennon, and the Deputy Commissioner, James Starritt, was instructed to prepare it. Starritt had spent his career in the uniform branch of the police and had a reputation as a tough disciplinarian. There was no possibility of a cover-up, and his report was to prove a remarkable document.

According to the National Council for Civil Liberties, Lennon had walked into their offices in King's Cross on the morning of 10 April 1974 and had volunteered a long account to the NCCL's Senior Legal Officer, Lawrence Grant. Grant had taken notes at the meeting and had arranged for Lennon to call back a few days later to sign a typed statement. He was murdered before he could return.

The statement released by the NCCL made a series of charges against the Branch. It alleged that Lennon had been coerced into becoming an *agent provocateur* and had then been left without protection to the mercy of the IRA. The allegations struck right to the heart of the Branch because Branch detectives have always had to rely on information received from informants. If it were indeed true that the Branch merely discarded their sources once their usefulness was over, every other informant would quickly lose confidence.

The first charge was that Lennon had been pressured into becoming an agent under the threat of being prosecuted for his involvement in a riot in Northern Ireland in 1969. Lennon had also stated that he had been told his sister, Bernadette, would also be locked up by the police if he failed to co-operate. These threats had

apparently been made by two Branch officers who had intercepted
Lennon just as he had finished visiting his wife in hospital. As it
turned out, neither claim was true. Records kept by the Information Room at Scotland Yard showed that on 27 July 1973 Lennon
had telephoned the Yard and asked to meet a Branch detective.
Detective Constables Dwyer and Turner were assigned to meet the
anonymous caller at St Pancras Station, and when they got there
they met Lennon and his eight year old daughter. According to
notes kept by the two officers, Lennon offered to sell them
information about an IRA cell in Luton.

Lennon told the Branch officers that three IRA men, Philip
Sheridan, Gerry Meely and Sean Campbell, were planning a
robbery to finance a major kidnapping or assassination. It was
believed that the target was to be Brigadier Frank Kitson, a former
commander of an infantry brigade in Northern Ireland. The
Branch alerted the local police in Luton and No. 5 Regional Crime
Squad to the IRA's plan, and an elaborate surveillance operation
was mounted on the three suspects. On 9 August 1973 Sheridan,
Meely and Campbell, all armed to the teeth, were arrested in a
stolen car. Evidently they were on their way to rob a payroll
delivery. Four months later the trio were convicted of conspiracy to
rob and were sentenced to ten years' imprisonment.

In the intervening period Lennon continued to meet Branch
detectives, principally DI Ronald Wickens, and give them information about other Irish extremists. He was considered a generally
reliable source, and on one occasion in October 1973 he identified
the location of an IRA arms cache to Detective Inspectors Wickens
and Cawthorne. In order to protect Lennon the Branch leaked a
story to the press suggesting that some building workers had
discovered the buried arms by accident.

Lennon's relationship with the Branch continued well until early
in the New Year of 1974 when Lennon was arrested in
Birmingham. Apparently he and his companion, Patrick O'Brien,
had been spotted behaving suspiciously near the perimeter wall of
Winson Green prison. By the time the Branch had been told of
their informant's misfortune he had already been charged with
conspiring to help "persons unknown" escape from Winson Green
prison. This put the Branch in a terrible dilemma. If they arranged
for the charge to be dropped (which was quite within their power)
O'Brien would realise that his companion was a police spy. To
release them both would simply place them both in jeopardy.
Accordingly it was decided to let the prosecution proceed, and hope
that the evidence against Lennon was sufficiently weak to secure his
acquittal. This is indeed what happened. On 8 April Lennon was

found not guilty by the jury, but O'Brien was convicted and sentenced to three years' imprisonment.*

Lennon came up to London on the day following his release and attended a meeting with Detective Sergeant Harper and Detective Inspector Wickens at Euston Station. It was the last time that a police officer saw him alive.

The Deputy Commissioner's report established that Lennon had volunteered his services and had never been blackmailed, as alleged. Indeed, at the time of his first meeting with Branch officers at St Pancras his name had not even appeared in the Branch's records. The Criminal Records Office noted one minor conviction for him, but neither he nor his sister were wanted for participating in a riot or anything else. The meticulous diaries kept by the detectives concerned in the case confirmed that Lennon's account of being "picked up" by the police was untrue, but no doubt he had been reluctant to tell the NCCL about his offer to sell information to the Branch. His stories about acting as an *agent provocateur* were also proved to be untrue. He had been warned by DI Wickens not to participate in any robberies, so the allegation of being an *agent provocateur* who had egged on the "Luton Three" failed to hold water.

The question of protecting Lennon was, from the Branch's point of view, the most serious. In fact the report demonstrated that they had gone to considerable lengths to keep their source a secret. For example, during the trial of the Luton Three it was acknowledged that the suspects had been kept under observation prior to the planned date of their robbery. During this period they had been spotted with Lennon so on the day of the arrest his house in Francis Street, Luton, was raided so as to preserve his cover.

The Starritt Report† examined every allegation made against the Branch and investigated the case thoroughly. In the end it concluded, in convincing detail, that each of the NCCL's charges was baseless. The Report was published in July 1974 and remains a unique analysis of the Branch's conduct in a particular case.

* A conviction that was subsequently quashed on Appeal.
† HMSO, 1974

CHAPTER XII

A Hundred Years Of Bombs

Having gathered dossiers, by secret means, the
Special Branch may again, officially or unofficially,
secretly distribute the information.

David Leigh in *The Frontiers of Secrecy* (Junction Books,
1980)

By 1975 the total of Branch detectives at the Yard had grown to
550, a development that reflected the increasing threat from the
Provisional IRA of assassinations and attacks on prominent figures.
To meet this challenge the Yard formed yet another specialist
squad, a paramilitary intervention squad, D11, to cope with
terrorist sieges. Their first major incident was the Balcombe Street
siege, in which four gunmen were trapped after a car chase through
central London. The IRA "Active Service Unit" machine-gunned
Scott's Restaurant in Mount Street in December 1975 and were
then pursued by two detectives in a commandeered taxi.

During the previous twelve months there had been considerable
evidence of an IRA unit operating in London, including seven
bombings and eight murders. The violence had been on an
unprecedented scale. In August 1975 a civilian Bomb Squad
expert, Roger Goad, was killed while trying to defuse a device in
Kensington Church Street. The targets included top class restau-
rants like Walton's in Walton Street and Lockets in Marcham
Street. Bombs were left in army towns such as Caterham and
Aldershot, and senior politicians were singled out for assassination.
Edward Heath, the former Prime Minister, had two lucky escapes.
On the first occasion, on 22 December 1974, a bomb was tossed
onto the first floor balcony of his house in Wilton Street. In the
second attempt, eleven months later, a sophisticated time-bomb
was left in a duffle-bag attached to the underside of Mr Heath's
official Rover, which was parked outside his house. It detached
itself as the car pulled away from the kerb and was spotted later the
same night by the owner of a second vehicle parking in the same
space. A similar device intended for Sir Hugh Fraser went off under
his car in Camden Hill Square and killed a neighbour, an eminent

162

cancer specialist, Professor Gordon Hamilton-Fairley, who happened to be out walking his dog.

The attacks had taken place in two waves. The first was between December 1974 and January the following year; the second began at the end of August 1975 and included the IRA's first attack on Scott's Restaurant on 12 November 1975. A bomb was thrown into the Oyster Bar, killing two customers and injuring eighteen others.

The IRA had concentrated their attention on the West End, and in particular Mayfair. A bomb in the Hilton Hotel went off on 5 September, killing one man, and early the next month another man was killed outside the Ritz Hotel. Then a bomb was thrown through the window of an Italian restaurant on the corner of Mount Street and South Audley Street. It so happened that the Security Service maintained a field office directly above the restaurant, and there was speculation that other MI5 premises in Mayfair might have been targeted.

On 27 November 1975 the IRA carried out their most daring attack to date. Ross McWhirter, a popular broadcaster and journalist, was shot dead by two gunmen at his home in Enfield, North London. McWhirter had previously offered a £50,000 reward for anyone offering information that would lead to the arrest of those responsible for the bombings in London.

Nine days after McWhirter's cold-blooded murder the IRA unit returned to Mayfair in a stolen Ford Cortina. The West End was now saturated with detectives in plain clothes, and two officers on patrol spotted a gun on the lap of a passenger in the back seat. Moments later a rifle was fired out of the front window into Scott's Restaurant. The policemen instantly radioed details of the Cortina to the Yard and within minutes every officer in the West End was on the alert for the car. It was spotted again, heading North in Portman Street where two policemen, Detective Inspector Purnell and Sergeant Murtagh McVeigh, commandeered a taxi and chased the gunmen towards Regents Park.

The men in the stolen car were evidently unfamiliar with the area for they turned into Alfa Close, a cul-de-sac. They then ran into neighbouring Rossmore Road with the police hot on their heels. A Special Patrol Group van arrived on the scene and the gunmen opened fire. Unarmed officers continued to close in and one, Detective Inspector Henry Dowswell, was fired on from a range of just five yards. The shot missed. The pursuit continued into Balcombe Street, where the gunmen burst into a small block of council flats and barricaded themselves into 22A, the home of Mr and Mrs John Matthews. The siege continued for five days, at the end of which the gunmen gave up their two hostages and surrendered to the police.

In subsequent interrogations the police established that the four men were part of a six-man team, led by Harry Duggan, a well-known IRA activist from Feakle, County Clare. In fact Duggan, then aged twenty-three, had been reported dead so his name had not appeared on the Branch's wanted list. His three Irish companions were identified as Hugh Doherty, Edward Butler and Martin O'Connell.

Duggan, who had used the alias Michael Wilson, and O'Connell had shared a flat together in Milton Grove, North London, while the other two members of the Active Service Unit had made their base at Fairholme Road, West Kensington. O'Connell developed something of a rapport with the police during the prolonged telephone negotiations during the siege and he revealed that prior to the departure to Ireland of the missing two members of the Active Service Unit they had planned more than sixty killings. Their arrest had come after their seventh.

All four men were tried at the Old Bailey in February 1977 and were convicted on twenty separate charges. They each received twelve life sentences with the recommendation that none be released until they had served a minimum of thirty years' imprisonment. The four convictions also helped improve the Yard's statistics. In the previous four years 130 IRA terrorists had been arrested. They had been responsible for nearly fifty incidents in London involving the deaths of eighteen people. Altogether 68% of the terrorist crimes had been solved or "cleaned up" to the Yard's satisfaction.

Soon after this success Jim Neville was appointed Head of the Bomb Squad on the retirement of Robert Huntley. The following year the Bomb Squad was absorbed into a new body, the Anti-Terrorist Squad (C13).

In February 1977 the Branch embarked on one of the most controversial cases for many years, the arrest and prosecution of two radical journalists. Crispin Aubrey and Duncan Campbell had written articles on the subject of signals intelligence for *Time Out* magazine. One of their colleagues, Mark Hosenball, was fighting a deportation order served on him, as was a renegade CIA officer, Philip Agee, who was also due for deportation. Campbell had been active in a campaign to have the deportation orders rescinded, and had thus come to the Branch's attention. One of his sources for his articles on signals intelligence, Winslow Peck, had been refused entry to the UK at Heathrow the previous June.

As a result of a *Time Out* article entitled "The Eavesdroppers" in May 1976, a former Intelligence Corps corporal, John Berry, contacted the magazine and offered to tell Aubrey of his own experience in the 9th Signals Regiment at an interception base in

Eastern Cyprus. Campbell also attended the interview, which took place in Berry's flat at 232 Alexandra Park Road, in North London. When the two journalists left the flat they were arrested by Branch detectives. Aubrey had tape-recorded their conversations, and it was the evidence on his recordings which led to their conviction of offences under the Official Secrets Act.

The case became a *cause célèbre* for a number of reasons. One of the prosecution witnesses, Colonel Hugh Johnstone, was initially only referred to as "Colonel B", until his name was mentioned in Parliament. The effect of this was to give the signals intelligence expert more publicity than if the prosecution had used his real name from the beginning. The trial coincided with a growing public debate about the scope of the Act and, since it was conceded that two of the three defendants were *bona-fide* journalists and not spies, the Crown gradually reduced the number of charges against them until only three remained out of the original nine.

All three men were convicted in November 1978 but discharged by the judge after a trial and a retrial. During the course of the two trials the defendants proved that much of the "secret" information accumulated by Campbell was, in fact, freely available to the public. The Branch had recovered more than fifteen thousand documents from his flat in Brighton, most of which related to military establishments in the UK. He had obtained all of it from perfectly legal sources.

In March 1977 the Home Secretary, Merlyn Rees, appointed the Chief Constable of Strathclyde, Sir David McNee, to replace Sir Robert Mark on the latter's retirement. In June McNee's Deputy Commissioner, Colin Woods, was appointed HM Chief Inspector of Constabulary, and Patrick Kavanagh, the AC (Traffic), was promoted in his place. The AC (Crime), Jock Wilson, was switched to the Traffic and Technical Support Division and replaced by Assistant Commissioner Gilbert Kelland.

In October 1977 the Head of the Branch, DAC Victor Gilbert, was appointed Chief Constable of Cambridge and DAC Robert Bryan selected to replace him. Bryan boasted more than twenty-two years' service in the the Branch, having first been transferred to it in 1952. His experience also included a stint as the senior uniformed officer in the Wembley (Q) Division and then as the Commander (Community Relations), a job increasingly regarded as a stepping-stone to senior police appointments.

Bryan was one of the four Deputy Assistant Commissioners in C Department. Beneath him were three senior officers in charge of the Branch's main roles: Rollo Watts (Operations), Kenneth Pendered

(Ports) and Philip Saunders (Administration). A further change was made in the composition of the Anti-Terrorist Squad which, with the reduction in IRA activity on the mainland, had its permanent establishment cut to thirty officers. Some of its personnel were transferred back to the Branch's Irish Squad, which grew to about eighty-strong.

Bryan's arrival marked the completion of an ambitious plan to computerise the Branch's records. The Yard had purchased a suitable machine from the British firm International Computers Limited at a reported cost of £935,000, a sum provided by a Home Office grant. Based at Jubilee House, at the southern end of Putney Bridge, the giant data processor, known as the C Department computer, was programmed with information from most of the specialist squads, including the Criminial Intelligence Unit and the Drugs Intelligence Unit (C11). Special visual display units in the Branch's offices at the Yard allowed instant retrieval of the accumulated information and, of course, an up-dating facility. Other VDUs were located at the Branch's Port Unit at Heathrow and a restricted access terminal at the Police National Computer's fortress-like home in Hendon.

In May the following year Merlyn Rees gave the House of Commons details of the Branch's strength, the second time ever that such information had been disclosed publicly. He confirmed the current number of Metropolitan Police officers in the Branch as 409 at Scotland Yard, and a further 850 in the other forty-one provincial forces. Of this total, some three hundred were based at ports and airports. When the figures for the Royal Ulster Constabulary (279) and the eight Scottish forces (70) were taken into account the number of detectives employed by the various Special Branches nationwide grew to 1,608.

In November 1981 Robert Bryan was transferred to the Foreign Office as Overseas Police Adviser, and his place was taken by Colin Hewett, formerly the DAC for A Department at the Yard.

To read the newspaper headlines of the 1980s is not so very different from reading those of the 1880s. The summer of 1982 witnessed a renewed IRA bomb campaign in central London and the announcement that the Queen's detective, Commander Michael Trestrail, had resigned following his involvement with a male prostitute. The scandal surrounding Trestrail's departure from the police indirectly touched the Branch, but not because Trestrail had ever been a member of the Branch. As we have seen, the Branch had long since transferred their royal duties to A Department, the Metropolitan Police's uniform branch. During the course of a statement on the case made by Home Secretary William Whitelaw, it was admitted that Trestrail had only recently undergone a routine Positive Vetting. Positive Vetting is a series of background inquiries to ascertain an individual's loyalty, and is usually conducted when a person is promoted into a position where he or she is given regular access to secrets. Each government department has a civilian security department to carry out the procedure, but police vettings are generally conducted by the Branch. In Trestrail's case the vetting had failed to register the fact that he was a homosexual, and when news of this broke Buckingham Palace was considerably embarrassed.

Even before this unhappy summer the Commissioner, Sir David McNee, had told the Home Secretary that he would be retiring from the Yard at the end of September. He was replaced by Sir Kenneth Newman, only the second Commissioner to have experienced Branch work first-hand.

Sir Kenneth had first joined the police in 1946, when he was recruited into the British Palestine Police and posted to Jerusalem. After only eight months as a constable he was transferred to the local Special Branch to fight the Irgun. In 1948 he returned to London and joined the Metropolitan Police. Twenty-five years later, with the rank of Commander, he transferred to the Royal Ulster Constabulary, where he was appointed the Chief Constable in 1976. His tenure in Northern Ireland was marked by a determination to isolate the IRA from the rest of the Catholic community, and to this end he created three Regional Crime Squads to "target" IRA suspects and keep them under close surveillance until enough evidence could be obtained to convict them.

Within a month of Sir Kenneth taking office the Branch were involved in two important Official Secrets cases, those of Rhona Ritchie, a Foreign Service diplomat who had passed information to her Egyptian lover, and Professor Hugh Hambleton, a Canadian academic who had been recruited by the KGB in 1947.

Rhona Ritchie, who had been serving at the British Embassy in Tel Aviv since September 1981, was arrested at Heathrow Airport in March 1982 after her love affair with an Egyptian diplomat, Refaat El-Ansary, had become known. She was questioned by Branch detectives at Rochester Row police station and admitted communicating five Foreign Office telegrams to El-Ansary. She pleaded guilty to one charge under the Official Secrets Act and was given a nine month suspended prison sentence.

Hambleton's case began in June 1982 after the Royal Canadian Mounted Police had alerted the Branch to his impending arrival in London. The sixty year-old professor of economics had already been the subject of an intensive investigation in Ottawa and had been granted an immunity from prosecution in exchange for details of his work for the Soviets. The immunity, however, had not extended to the United Kingdom and Hambleton had been advised not to risk visiting England. He had ignored that advice and had been interviewed as soon as he had arrived by Detective Superintendent Peter Westcott. Hambleton volunteered a lengthy statement running to some 260 pages and was then charged with two offences under the Official Secrets Act. When Hambleton's trial began at the Old Bailey in November he pleaded not guilty, but later changed his plea after making several damaging admissions whilst under cross-examination by the Attorney-General. Hambleton was sentenced to ten years' imprisonment.

The Branch of 1983 may well undergo some changes at Sir Kenneth's hands, and there will, no doubt, be a continuing tendency to create specialist units to deal with particular threats. It is equally certain that the new Commissioner, who fully understands and appreciates the value of accurate intelligence, will defend the Special Branch from external political pressures, particularly from the extreme left. In one of his first public pronouncements in October 1982 he extolled the virtues of good intelligence, and stated his intention to concentrate the intelligence effort in the inner-city trouble spots like Brixton, that had been the scene of serious riots in the summer of 1980.

In the hundred years of its existence the Branch has grown from a handful of detectives with Irish backgrounds to a sophisticated intelligence-gathering organisation using the very latest surveillance techniques and data storage technology. What has not changed is its controversial image.

The concept of a secret police is anathema to the British public although the world-wide increase in urban terrorism has awakened many to the dangers of not taking adequate precautions. Continued unrest in such trouble-spots as Iran, Israel and Libya is reflected in the metropolis, where diplomats and exiled politicians provide relatively easy targets. The key to prevention is good intelligence, but as electronic data storage facilities multiply, so the public's desire for privacy becomes more vocal.

There is not, in Britain, a national system of identity cards, nor is it mandatory to carry a form of identity. There is, however, a useful basis already in existence which the Branch utilises with great effect: the National Insurance system. Virtually every adult member of the population has a National Insurance code number. By accessing the information relating to a person's contributions it is possible to learn his place of work, if he or she has one, or the area in which the individual lives. This information can be cross-referred with details from the Criminal Records Office and the C

Department computer to obtain up-to-date information on a large percentage of the population.

The fear commonly expressed is two-fold: the misuse of the information already on file and the potential dangers of such a sophisticated system being used against society. To date there have been only occasional examples of unlawful access to the Police National Computer. One such case involved a corrupt police officer tracing the vehicle index numbers of high-spending punters as they visited a West End casino so that a competitor could identify them and persuade them to patronise his premises. Such cases, few as they are, result in criminal proceedings.

The question of unlawful access to the C Department computer is more difficult to judge. Sir Robert Mark always specifically excluded the Branch when he commented on the corruption he uncovered in London's CID. The difficulty in assessing the misuse of the Branch's information lies in the very nature of the material. On one well-publicised occasion an employee of a television company nearly lost her job because her husband had been mistakenly identified as a Baader-Meinhof terrorist suspect while on a motoring holiday on the Continent. The information, un-checked, had been entered on a Special Branch file. Fortunately the situation was rectified by the intervention of the suspect's father-in-law, who happened to be a retired Scotland Yard man himself.

What makes the Branch different from the popular idea of a secret police is a measure of accountability. One former Head of the Branch told me that he stresses to newcomers to the Branch that they hold the same warrant cards as the rest of the Metropolitan Police and are, through the Commissioner, accountable to the public. This is certainly not the case with officers of the Security Service. Indeed, MI5 traditionally "request" the Branch's co-operation and have no power to demand it. Apparently there have been occasions when such requests have been declined.

The fact that the Branch have been associated with unpopular causes is inevitable. Government is a process of perpetual change and the Branch is on the front line of those changes. Before the First World War women's suffrage was a key issue; in the early Sixties it was the Campaign for Nuclear Disarmament. In both cases the Branch has been under an obligation to report on developments and identify those supporters with sinister motives.

Whatever the technology of the next hundred years some aspects of the Branch's work will not change: there will always be a necessity to gather information about terrorists and potentially subversive groups; VIPs will always require personal protection. There will, in effect, be a continuing demand for the specialist services of the Branch.

SPECIAL BRANCH
Roll of Honour

Officers of the Special Branch who lost their lives during the Second World War

Royal Navy

A/Sub Lieutenant   Douglas Gordon FERRIER

Royal Air Force

Flying Officer	Ronald Charles ARTHUR
Flying Officer	Leonard Douglas CLAY
Leading Aircraftman	Peter Ernest COLES
Pilot Officer	Peter Newman DIX
Sergeant	Edward James GRAY
Pilot Officer	Walter James HAVIES
Flying Officer	Arthur Gwyn JONES
Aircraftman	William George M MANN
Flight Lieutenant	Conal B T McSWEENEY DFC
Flight Lieutenant	Harold F MORRISH DFC
Flying Officer	William Arthur C MORRIS
Flight Lieutenant	F D J THOMPSON DFC & Bar
Flying Officer	Alan Owen WHAPHAM

On Police Service

Detective Sergeant	Harvey BALL
Detective Sergeant	Harry BATTLEY
Detective Constable	Bernard McLAUGHLIN

INDEX